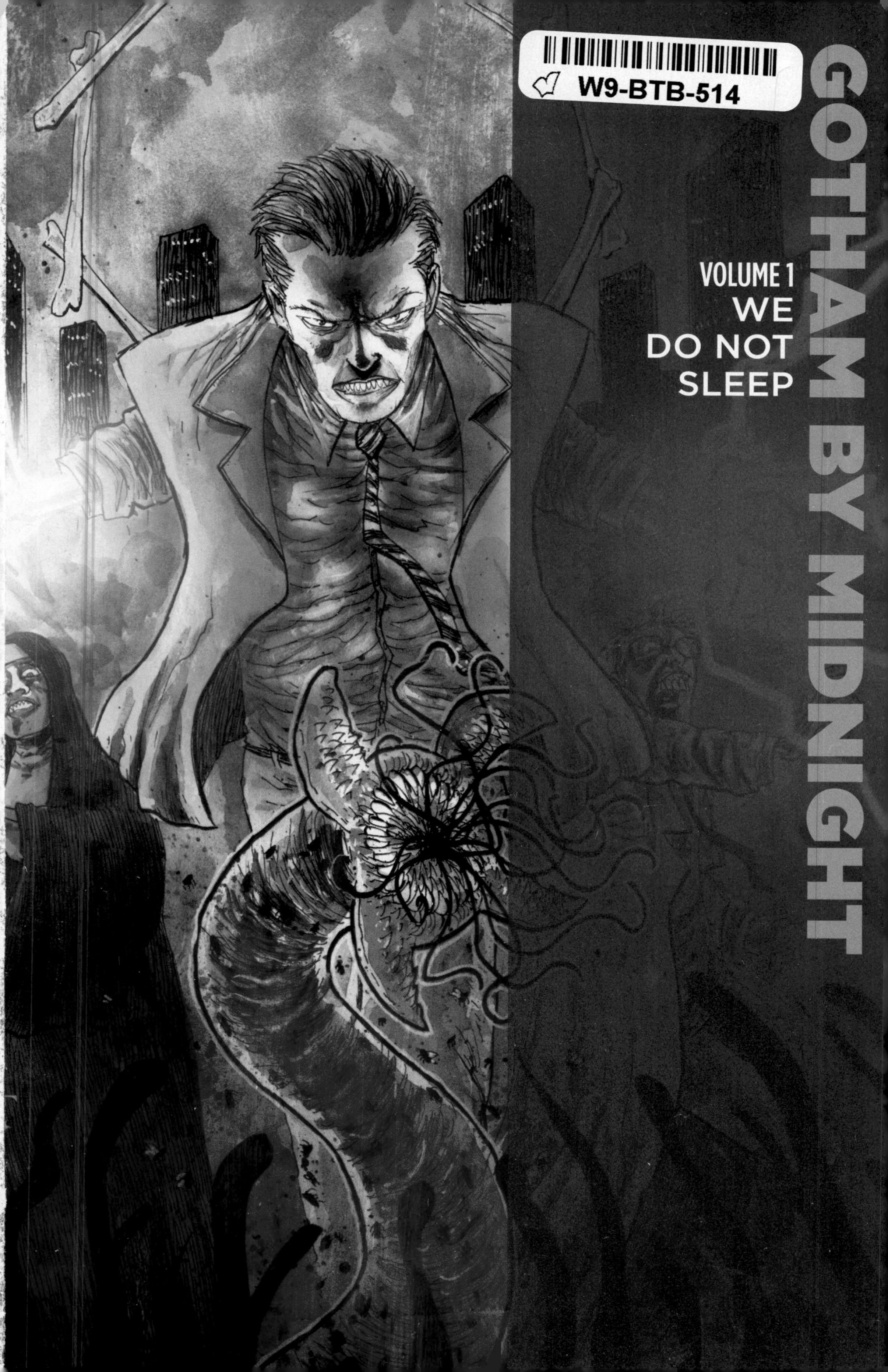
GOTHAM BY MIDNIGHT
VOLUME 1
WE
DO NOT
SLEEP

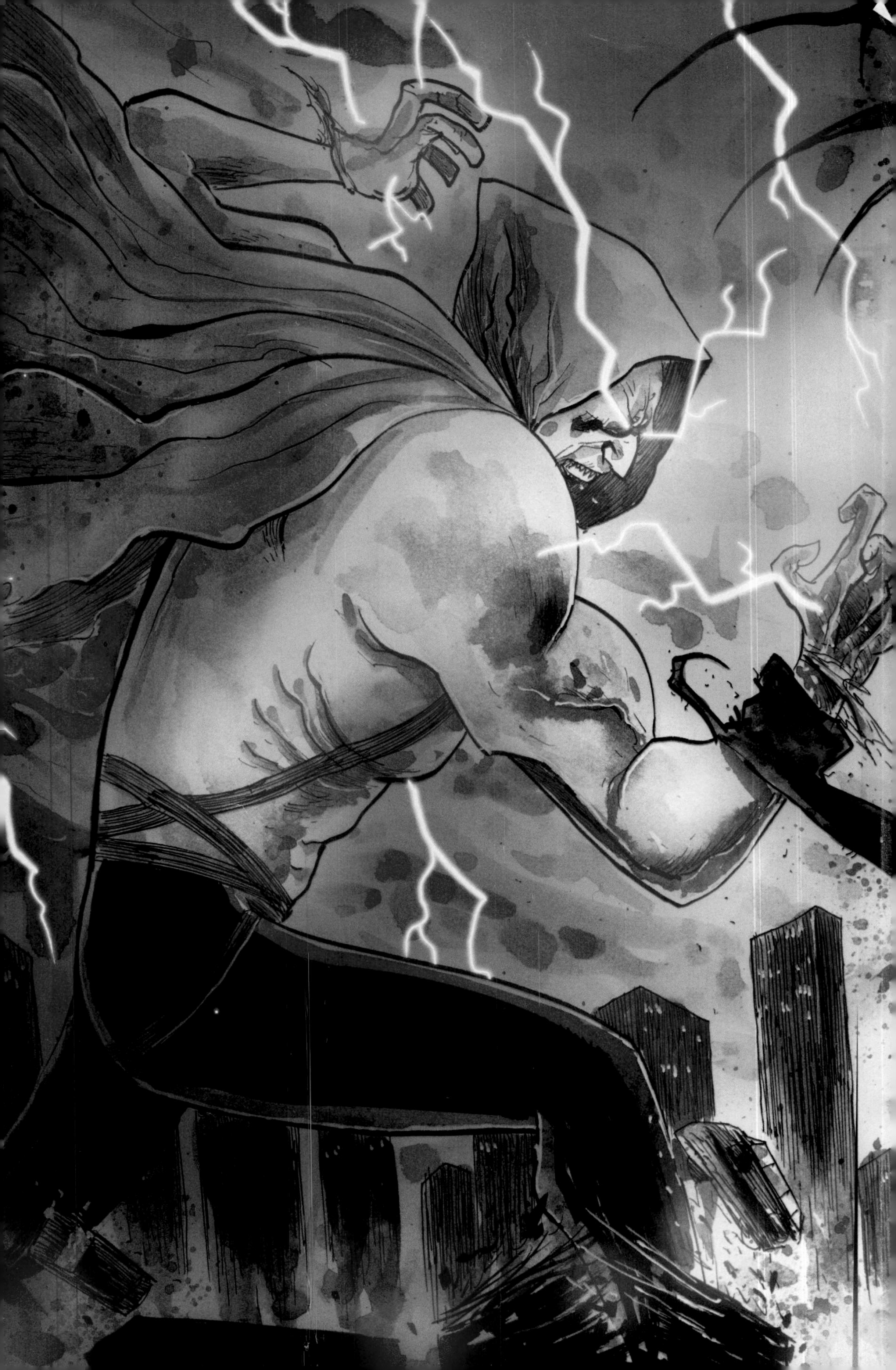

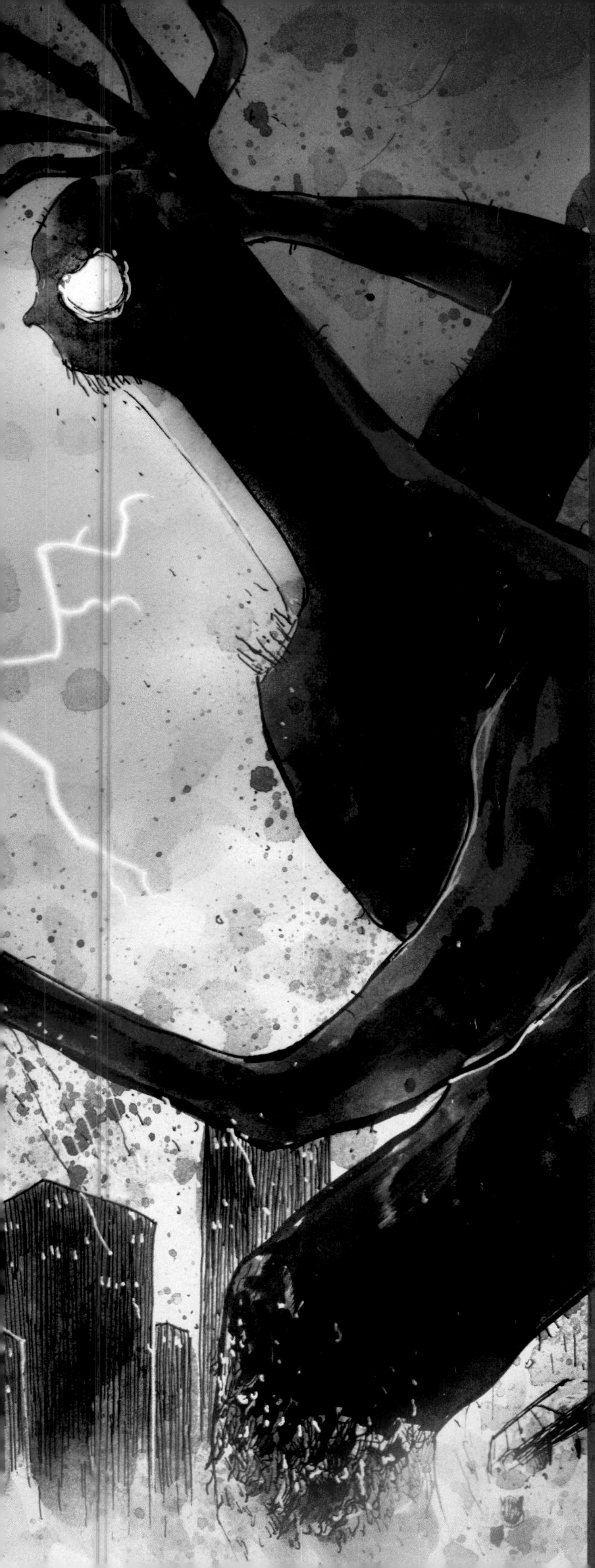

GOTHAM BY MIDNIGHT

VOLUME 1
WE DO NOT SLEEP

WRITTEN BY
RAY FAWKES

ART BY
BEN TEMPLESMITH

LETTERS BY
DEZI SIENTY
SAIDA TEMOFONTE

COVER ART BY
BEN TEMPLESMITH

BATMAN CREATED BY
BOB KANE

RACHEL GLUCKSTERN Editor – Original Series
DAVE WIELGOSZ Assistant Editor – Original Series
JEB WOODARD Group Editor – Collected Editions
PAUL SANTOS Editor
DAMIAN RYLAND Publication Design

BOB HARRAS Senior VP – Editor-in-Chief, DC Comics

DIANE NELSON President
DAN DIDIO and JIM LEE Co-Publishers
GEOFF JOHNS Chief Creative Officer
AMIT DESAI Senior VP – Marketing & Global Franchise Management
NAIRI GARDINER Senior VP – Finance
SAM ADES VP – Digital Marketing
BOBBIE CHASE VP – Talent Development
MARK CHIARELLO Senior VP – Art, Design & Collected Editions
JOHN CUNNINGHAM VP – Content Strategy
ANNE DePIES VP – Strategy Planning & Reporting
DON FALLETTI VP – Manufacturing Operations
LAWRENCE GANEM VP – Editorial Administration & Talent Relations
ALISON GILL Senior VP – Manufacturing & Operations
HANK KANALZ Senior VP – Editorial Strategy & Administration
JAY KOGAN VP – Legal Affairs
DEREK MADDALENA Senior VP – Sales & Business Development
DAN MIRON VP – Sales Planning & Trade Development
NICK NAPOLITANO VP – Manufacturing Administration
CAROL ROEDER VP – Marketing
EDDIE SCANNELL VP – Mass Account & Digital Sales
SUSAN SHEPPARD VP – Business Affairs
COURTNEY SIMMONS Senior VP – Publicity & Communications
JIM (SKI) SOKOLOWSKI VP – Comic Book Specialty & Newsstand Sales

GOTHAM BY MIDNIGHT VOLUME 1: WE DO NOT SLEEP
Published by DC Comics. Compilation Copyright © 2015 DC Comics. All Rights Reserved.
Originally published in single magazine form in GOTHAM BY MIDNIGHT 1-5 © 2014, 2015 DC Comics.
All Rights Reserved. All characters, their distinctive likenesses and related elements featured in this publication
are trademarks of DC Comics. The stories, characters and incidents featured in this publication are entirely fictional.
DC Comics does not read or accept unsolicited ideas, stories or artwork.

DC Comics, 4000 Warner Blvd., Burbank, CA 91522
A Warner Bros. Entertainment Company
Printed by RR Donnelley, Owensville, MO, USA. 7/17/15.
ISBN: 978-1-4012-5473-5
First Printing.

Library of Congress Cataloging-in-Publication Data

Fawkes, Ray, author.
Gotham by Midnight. Volume 1 / Ray Fawkes ; Andrea Sorrentino.
pages cm
ISBN 978-1-4012-5473-5 (paperback)
1. Graphic novels. I. Sorrentino, Andrea, illustrator. II. Title.
PN6728.G646F39 2015
741.5'973—dc23
2015008034

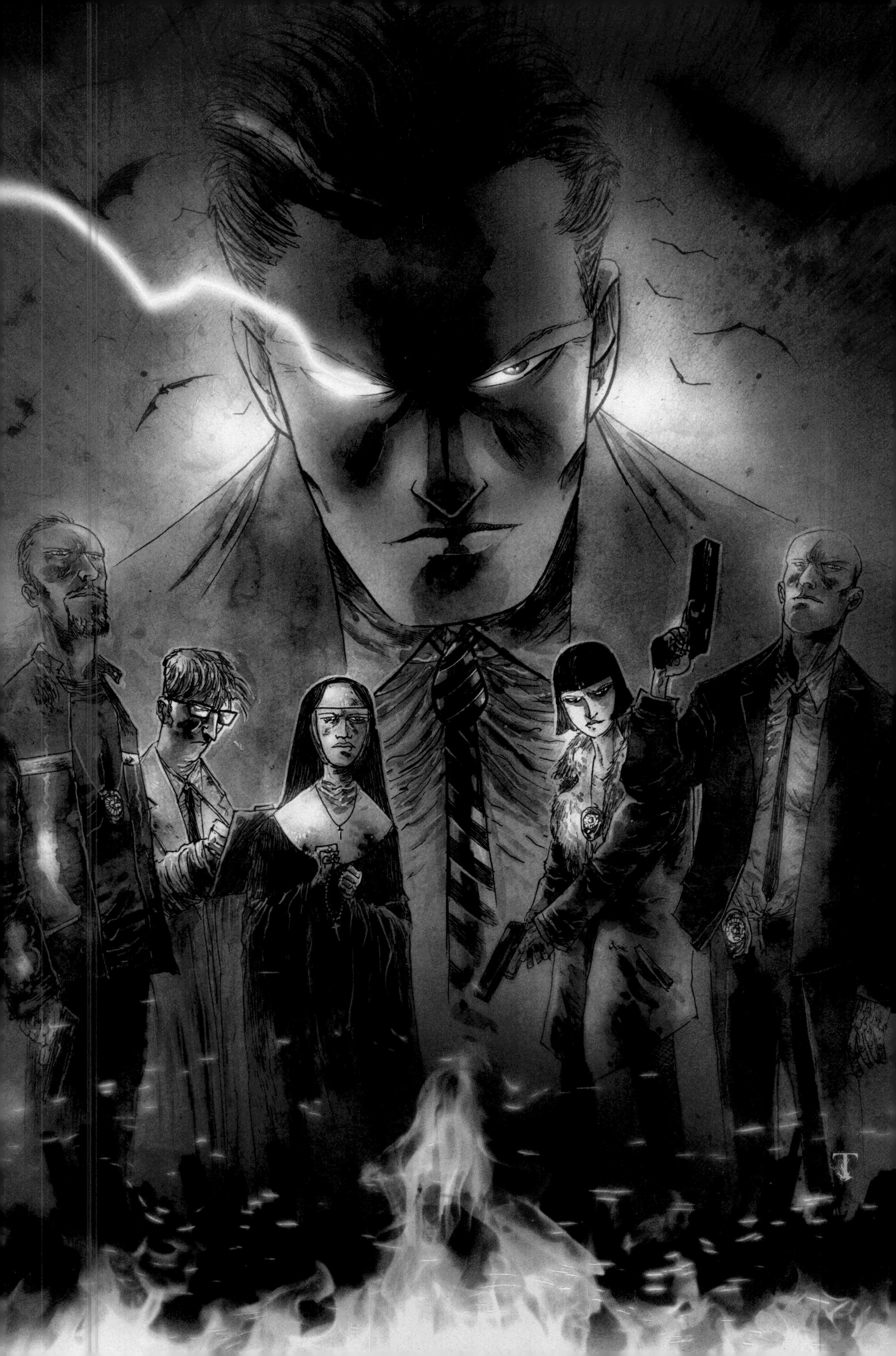

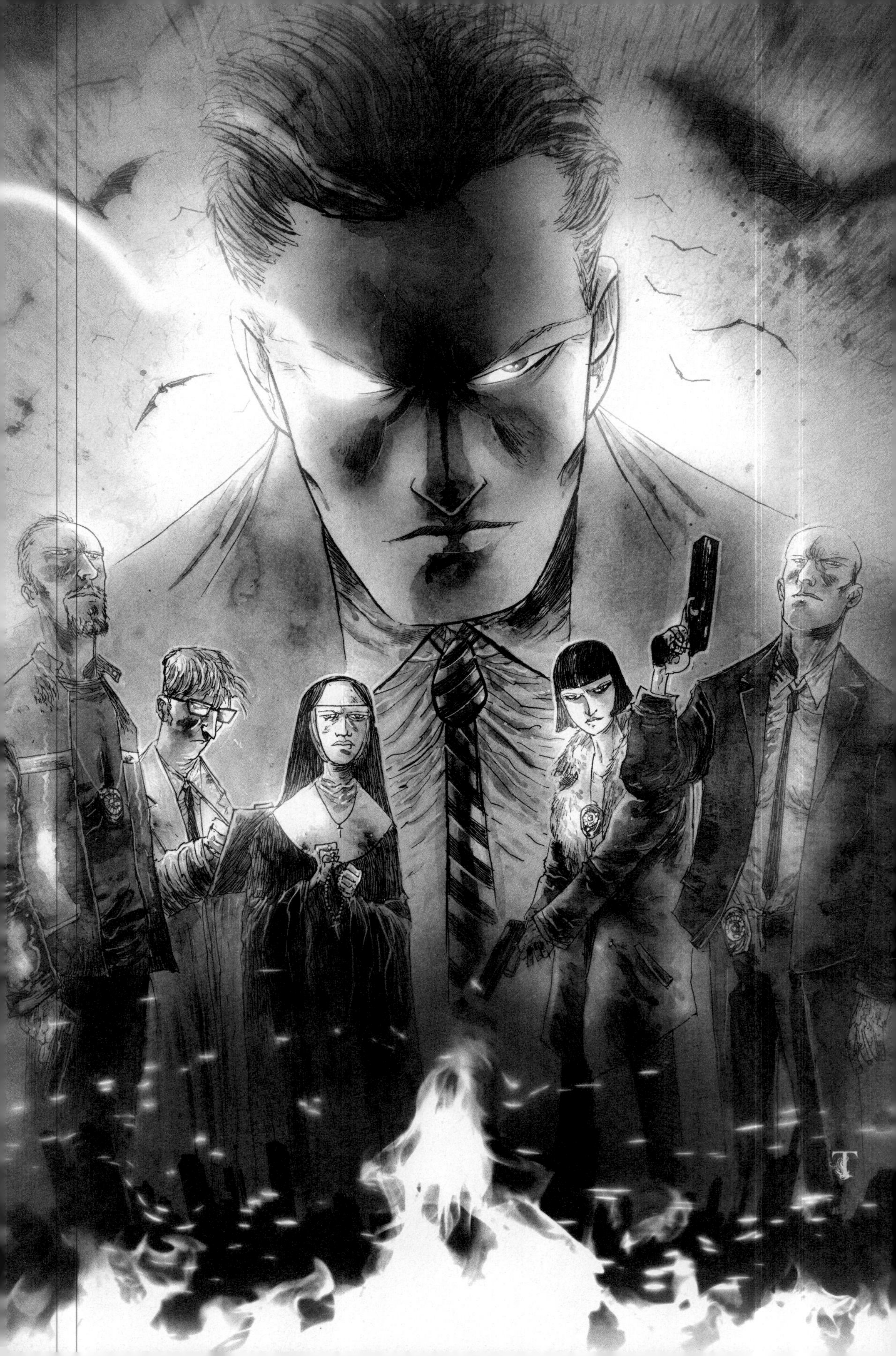

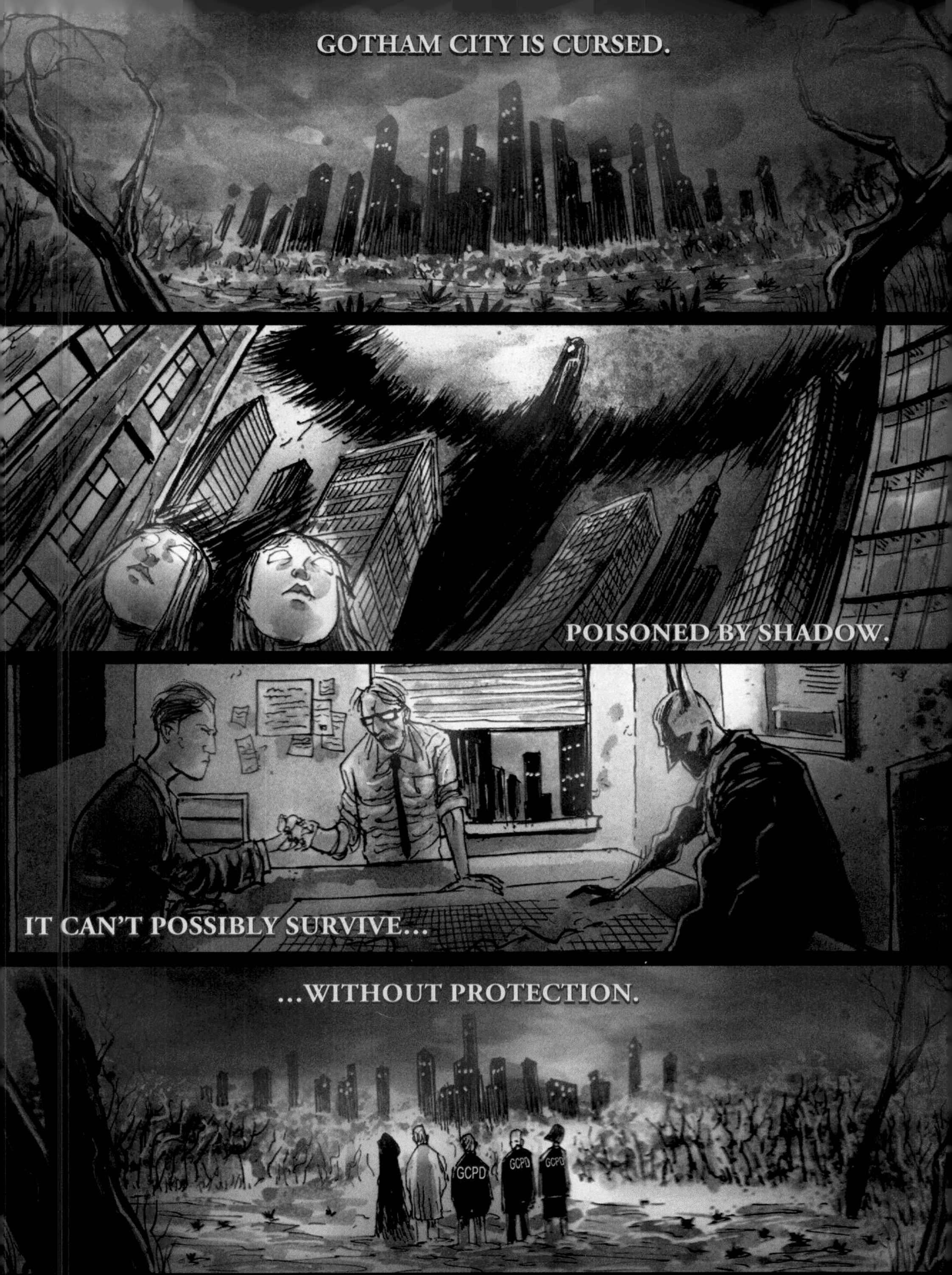
GOTHAM CITY IS CURSED.
POISONED BY SHADOW.
IT CAN'T POSSIBLY SURVIVE...
...WITHOUT PROTECTION.
GCPD
GCPD
GCPD

HAPTER ONE:

WE DO NOT SLEEP

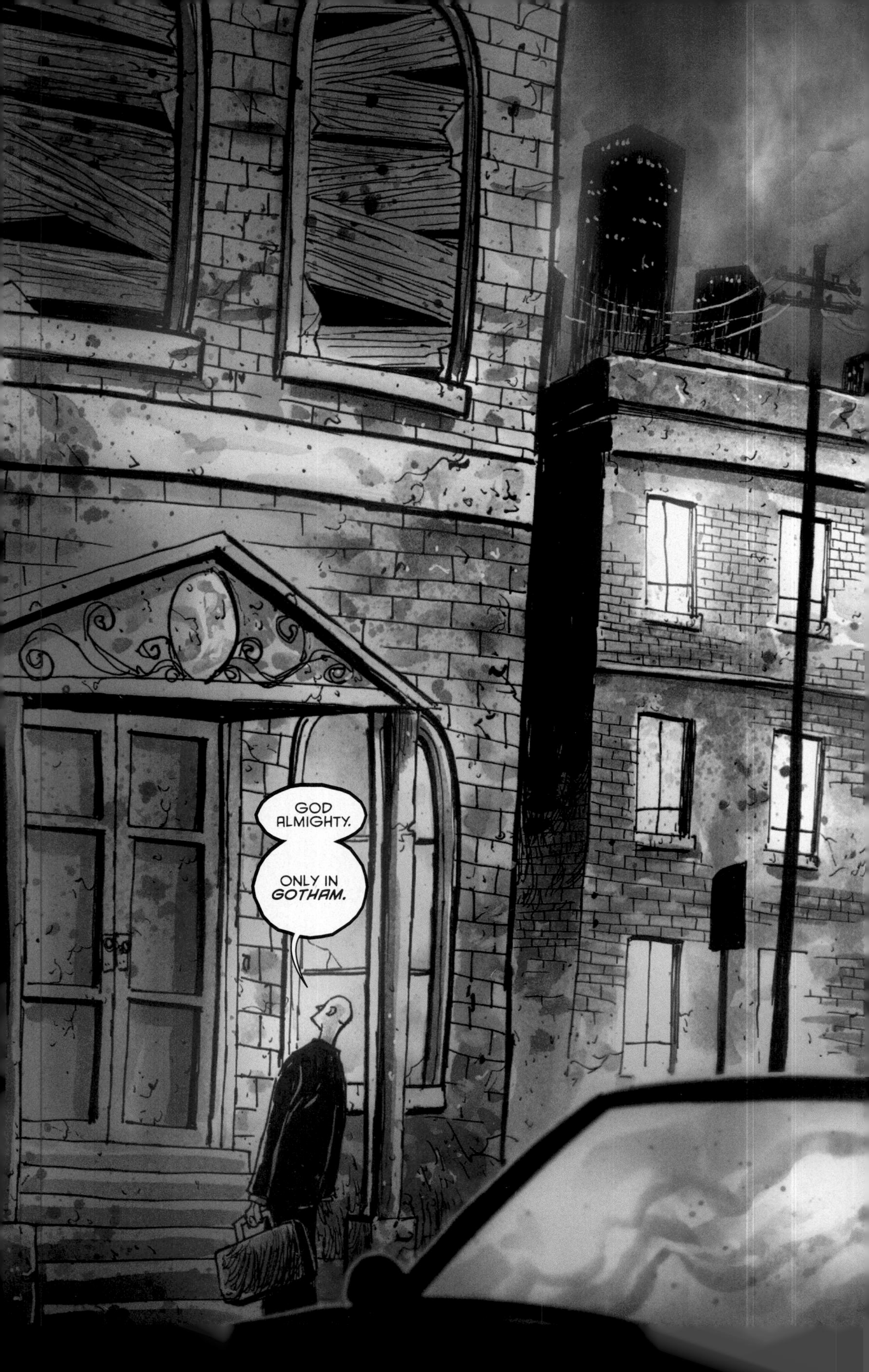
GOD ALMIGHTY.
ONLY IN *GOTHAM.*

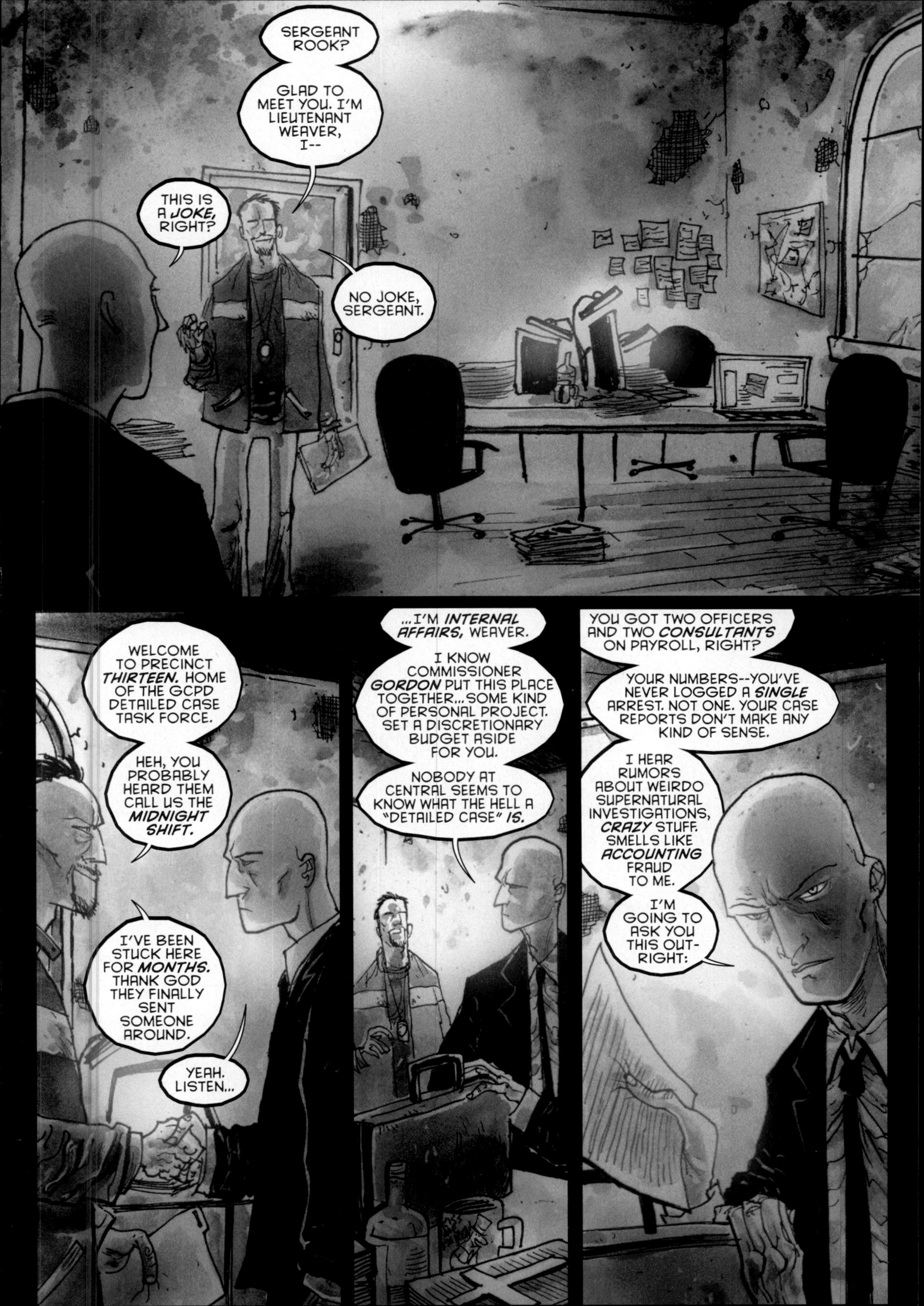
SERGEANT ROOK?
GLAD TO MEET YOU. I'M LIEUTENANT WEAVER, I--
THIS IS A *JOKE,* RIGHT?
NO JOKE, SERGEANT.
WELCOME TO PRECINCT *THIRTEEN.* HOME OF THE GCPD DETAILED CASE TASK FORCE.
HEH, YOU PROBABLY HEARD THEM CALL US THE *MIDNIGHT SHIFT.*
I'VE BEEN STUCK HERE FOR *MONTHS.* THANK GOD THEY FINALLY SENT SOMEONE AROUND.
YEAH. LISTEN...
...I'M *INTERNAL AFFAIRS,* WEAVER.
I KNOW COMMISSIONER *GORDON* PUT THIS PLACE TOGETHER... SOME KIND OF PERSONAL PROJECT. SET A DISCRETIONARY BUDGET ASIDE FOR YOU.
NOBODY AT CENTRAL SEEMS TO KNOW WHAT THE HELL A "DETAILED CASE" *IS.*
YOU GOT TWO OFFICERS AND TWO *CONSULTANTS* ON PAYROLL, RIGHT?
YOUR NUMBERS--YOU'VE NEVER LOGGED A *SINGLE* ARREST. NOT ONE. YOUR CASE REPORTS DON'T MAKE ANY KIND OF SENSE.
I HEAR RUMORS ABOUT WEIRDO SUPERNATURAL INVESTIGATIONS, *CRAZY* STUFF. SMELLS LIKE *ACCOUNTING* FRAUD TO ME.
I'M GOING TO ASK YOU THIS OUT-RIGHT:

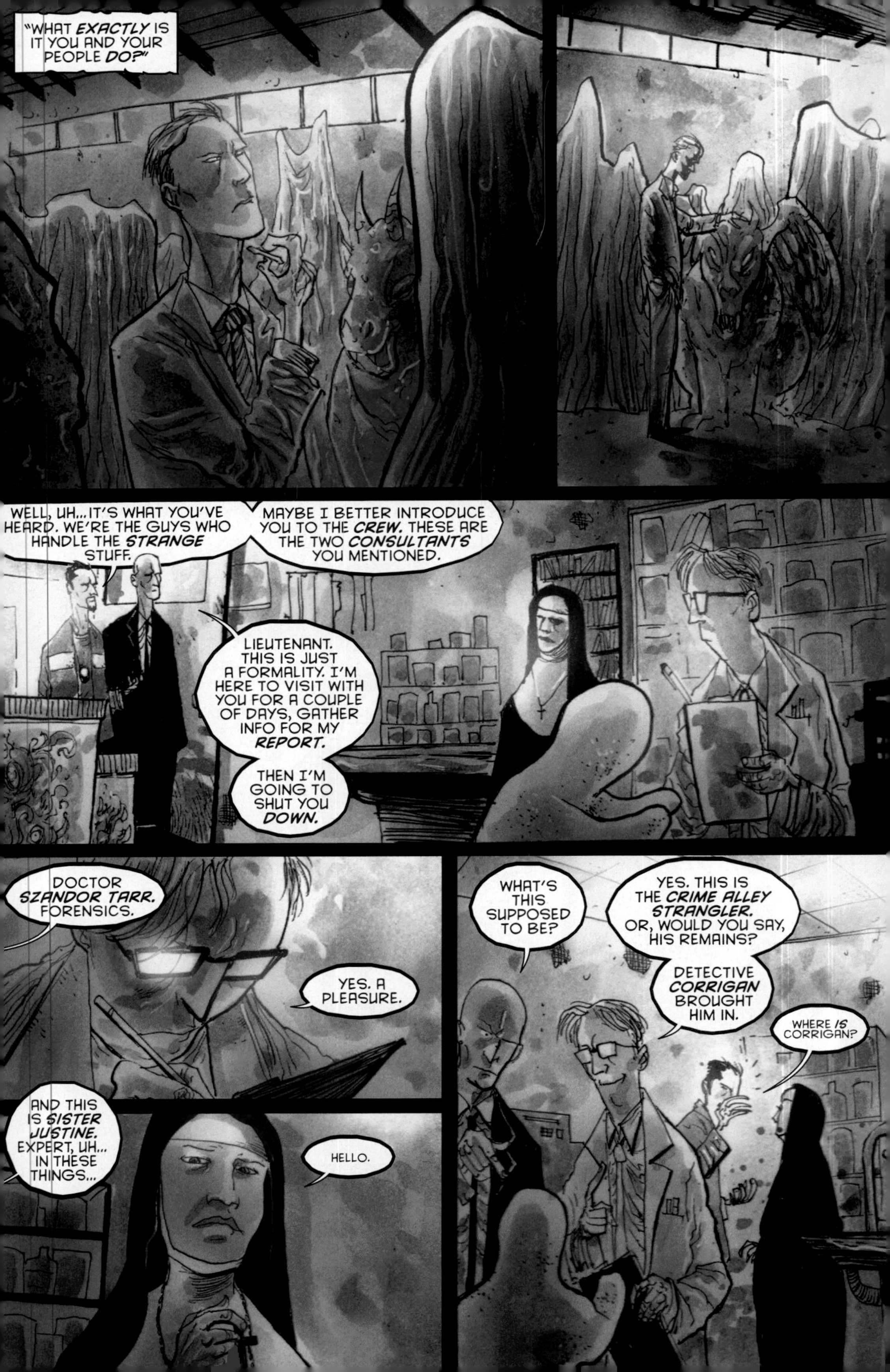
"WHAT EXACTLY IS IT YOU AND YOUR PEOPLE DO?"
WELL, UH... IT'S WHAT YOU'VE HEARD. WE'RE THE GUYS WHO HANDLE THE STRANGE STUFF.
MAYBE I BETTER INTRODUCE YOU TO THE CREW. THESE ARE THE TWO CONSULTANTS YOU MENTIONED.
LIEUTENANT. THIS IS JUST A FORMALITY. I'M HERE TO VISIT WITH YOU FOR A COUPLE OF DAYS, GATHER INFO FOR MY REPORT.
THEN I'M GOING TO SHUT YOU DOWN.
DOCTOR SZANDOR TARR. FORENSICS.
YES. A PLEASURE.
AND THIS IS SISTER JUSTINE. EXPERT, UH... IN THESE THINGS...
HELLO.
WHAT'S THIS SUPPOSED TO BE?
YES. THIS IS THE CRIME ALLEY STRANGLER. OR, WOULD YOU SAY, HIS REMAINS?
DETECTIVE CORRIGAN BROUGHT HIM IN.
WHERE IS CORRIGAN?

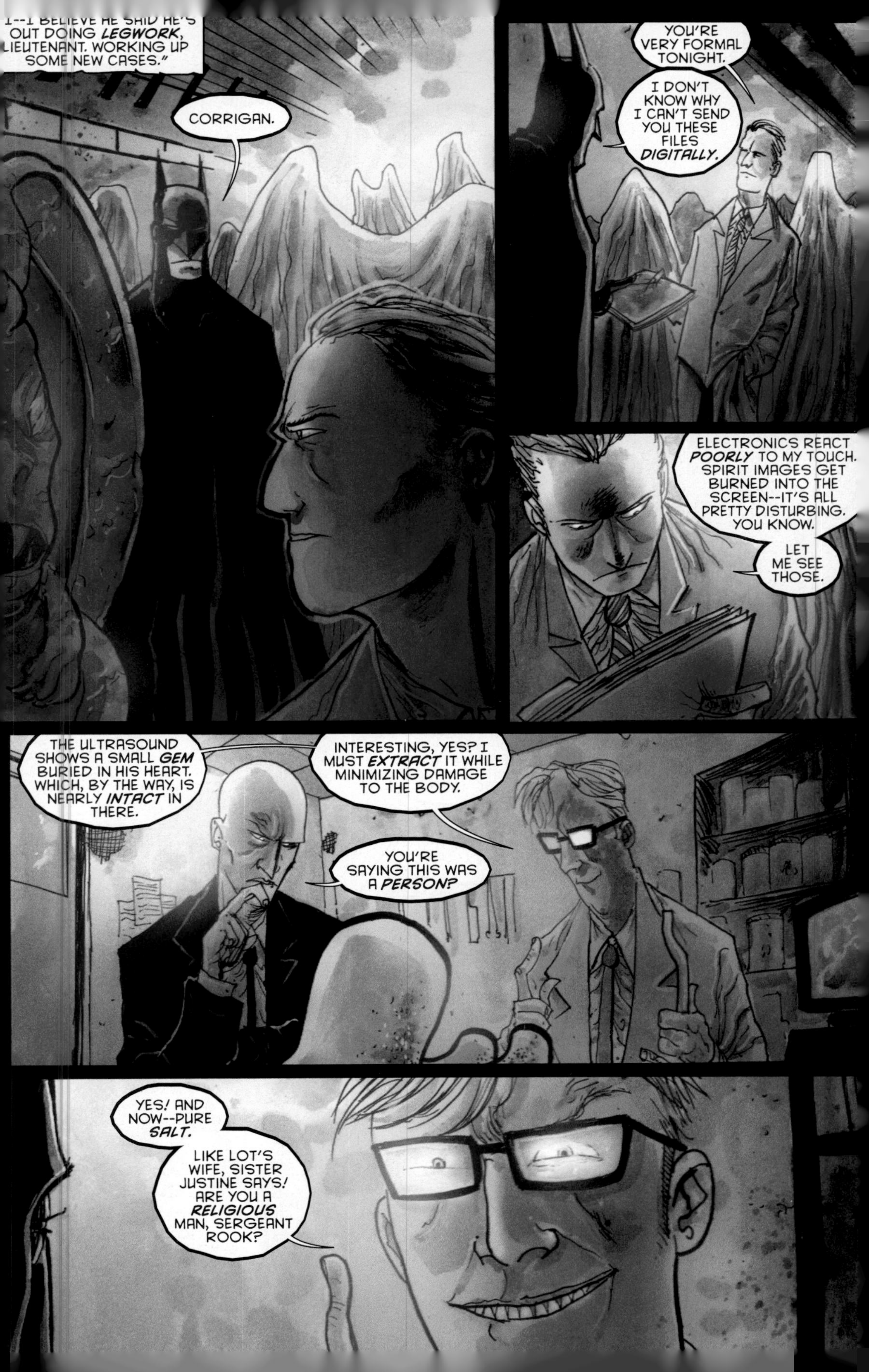

I--I BELIEVE HE SAID HE'S OUT DOING LEGWORK, LIEUTENANT. WORKING UP SOME NEW CASES."
CORRIGAN.
YOU'RE VERY FORMAL TONIGHT.
I DON'T KNOW WHY I CAN'T SEND YOU THESE FILES DIGITALLY.
ELECTRONICS REACT POORLY TO MY TOUCH. SPIRIT IMAGES GET BURNED INTO THE SCREEN--IT'S ALL PRETTY DISTURBING. YOU KNOW.
LET ME SEE THOSE.
THE ULTRASOUND SHOWS A SMALL GEM BURIED IN HIS HEART. WHICH, BY THE WAY, IS NEARLY INTACT IN THERE.
INTERESTING, YES? I MUST EXTRACT IT WHILE MINIMIZING DAMAGE TO THE BODY.
YOU'RE SAYING THIS WAS A PERSON?
YES! AND NOW--PURE SALT.
LIKE LOT'S WIFE, SISTER JUSTINE SAYS! ARE YOU A RELIGIOUS MAN, SERGEANT ROOK?

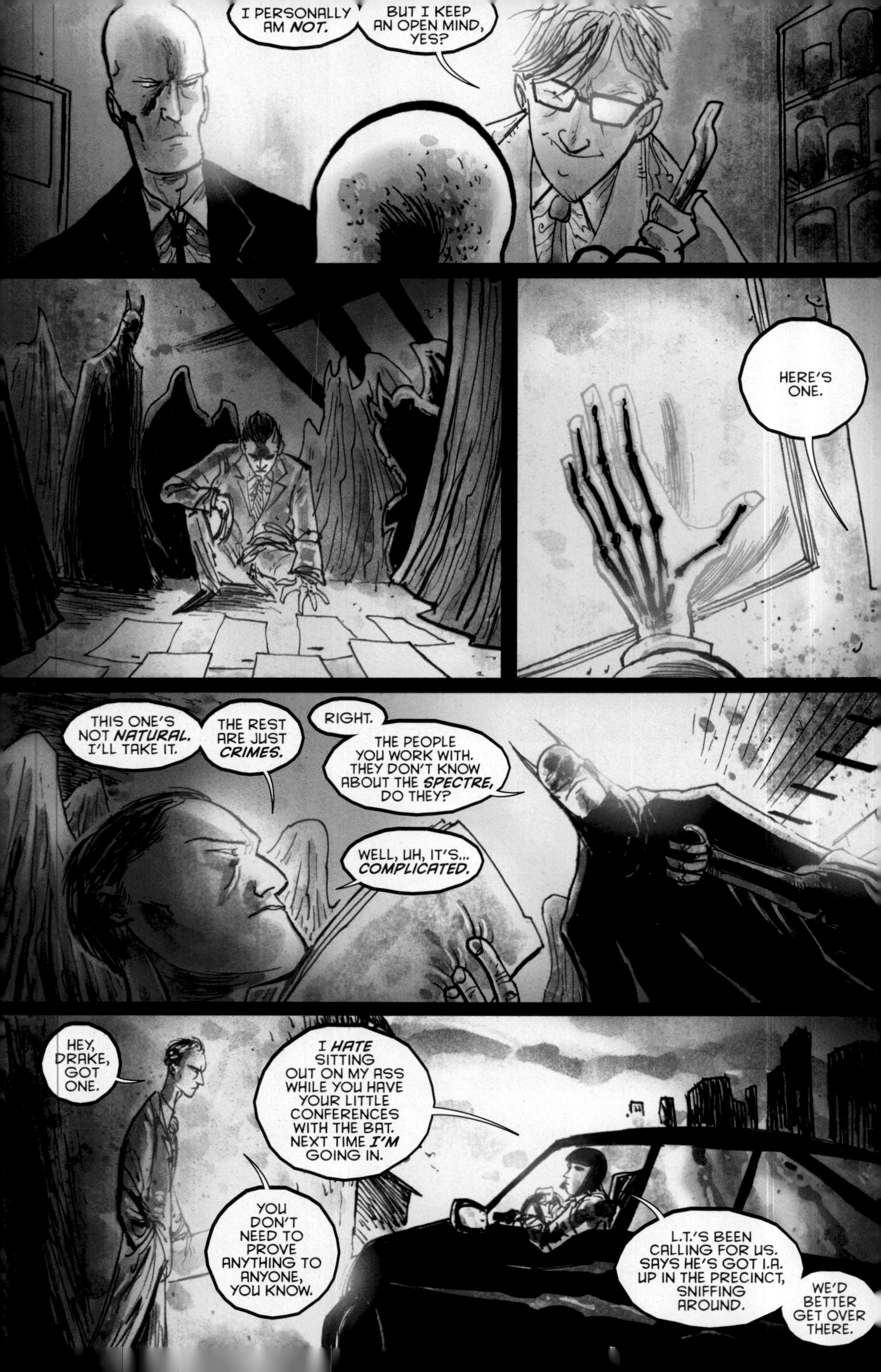

I PERSONALLY AM NOT.
BUT I KEEP AN OPEN MIND, YES?
HERE'S ONE.
THIS ONE'S NOT NATURAL. I'LL TAKE IT.
THE REST ARE JUST CRIMES.
RIGHT.
THE PEOPLE YOU WORK WITH. THEY DON'T KNOW ABOUT THE SPECTRE, DO THEY?
WELL, UH, IT'S... COMPLICATED.
HEY, DRAKE, GOT ONE.
I HATE SITTING OUT ON MY ASS WHILE YOU HAVE YOUR LITTLE CONFERENCES WITH THE BAT. NEXT TIME I'M GOING IN.
YOU DON'T NEED TO PROVE ANYTHING TO ANYONE, YOU KNOW.
L.T.'S BEEN CALLING FOR US. SAYS HE'S GOT I.A. UP IN THE PRECINCT, SNIFFING AROUND.
WE'D BETTER GET OVER THERE.

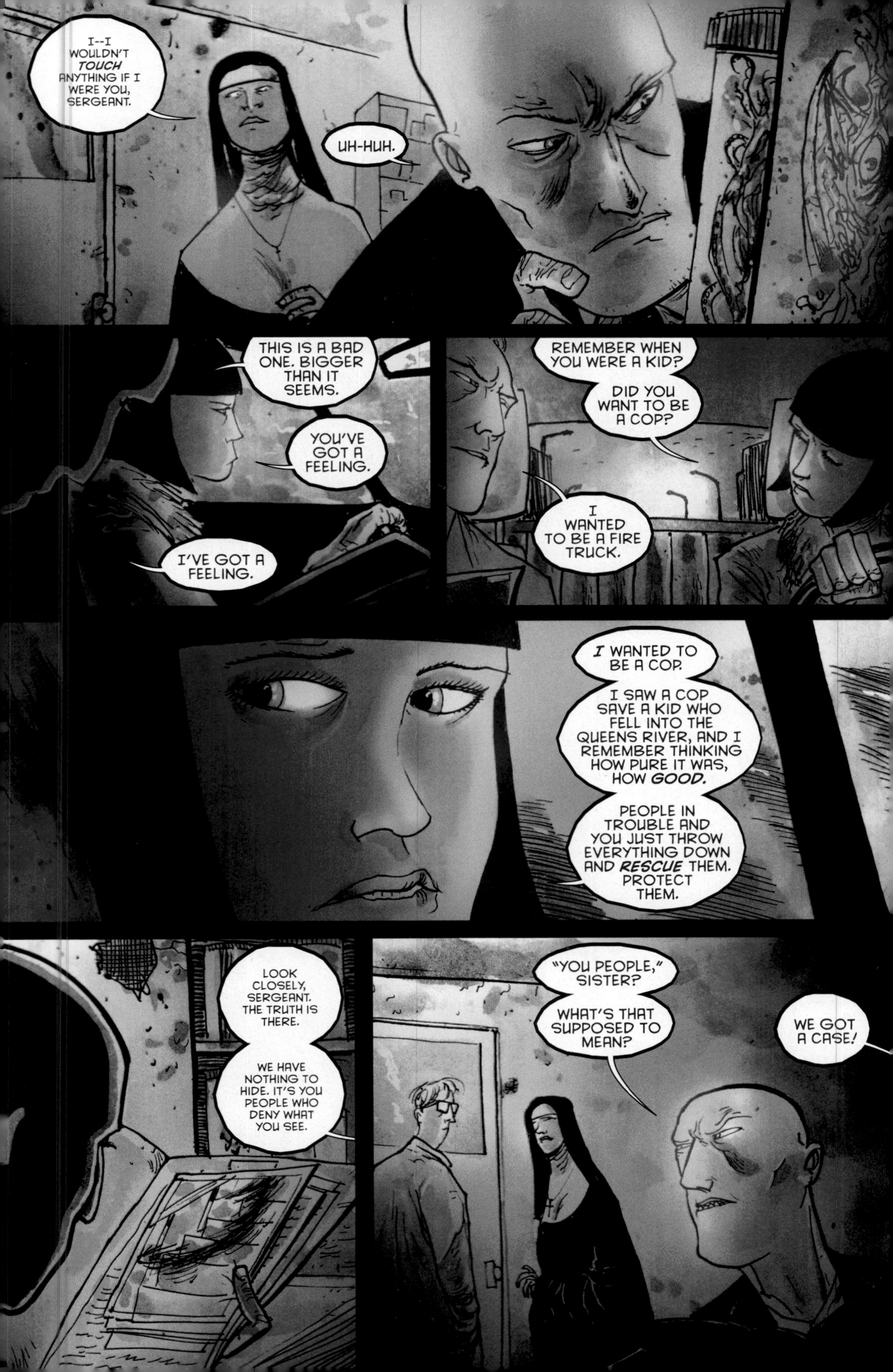
I--I WOULDN'T *TOUCH* ANYTHING IF I WERE YOU, SERGEANT.
UH-HUH.
THIS IS A BAD ONE. BIGGER THAN IT SEEMS.
YOU'VE GOT A FEELING.
I'VE GOT A FEELING.
REMEMBER WHEN YOU WERE A KID?
DID YOU WANT TO BE A COP?
I WANTED TO BE A FIRE TRUCK.
I WANTED TO BE A COP.
I SAW A COP SAVE A KID WHO FELL INTO THE QUEENS RIVER, AND I REMEMBER THINKING HOW PURE IT WAS, HOW *GOOD.*
PEOPLE IN TROUBLE AND YOU JUST THROW EVERYTHING DOWN AND *RESCUE* THEM. PROTECT THEM.
LOOK CLOSELY, SERGEANT. THE TRUTH IS THERE.
WE HAVE NOTHING TO HIDE. IT'S YOU PEOPLE WHO DENY WHAT YOU SEE.
"YOU PEOPLE," SISTER?
WHAT'S THAT SUPPOSED TO MEAN?
WE GOT A CASE!

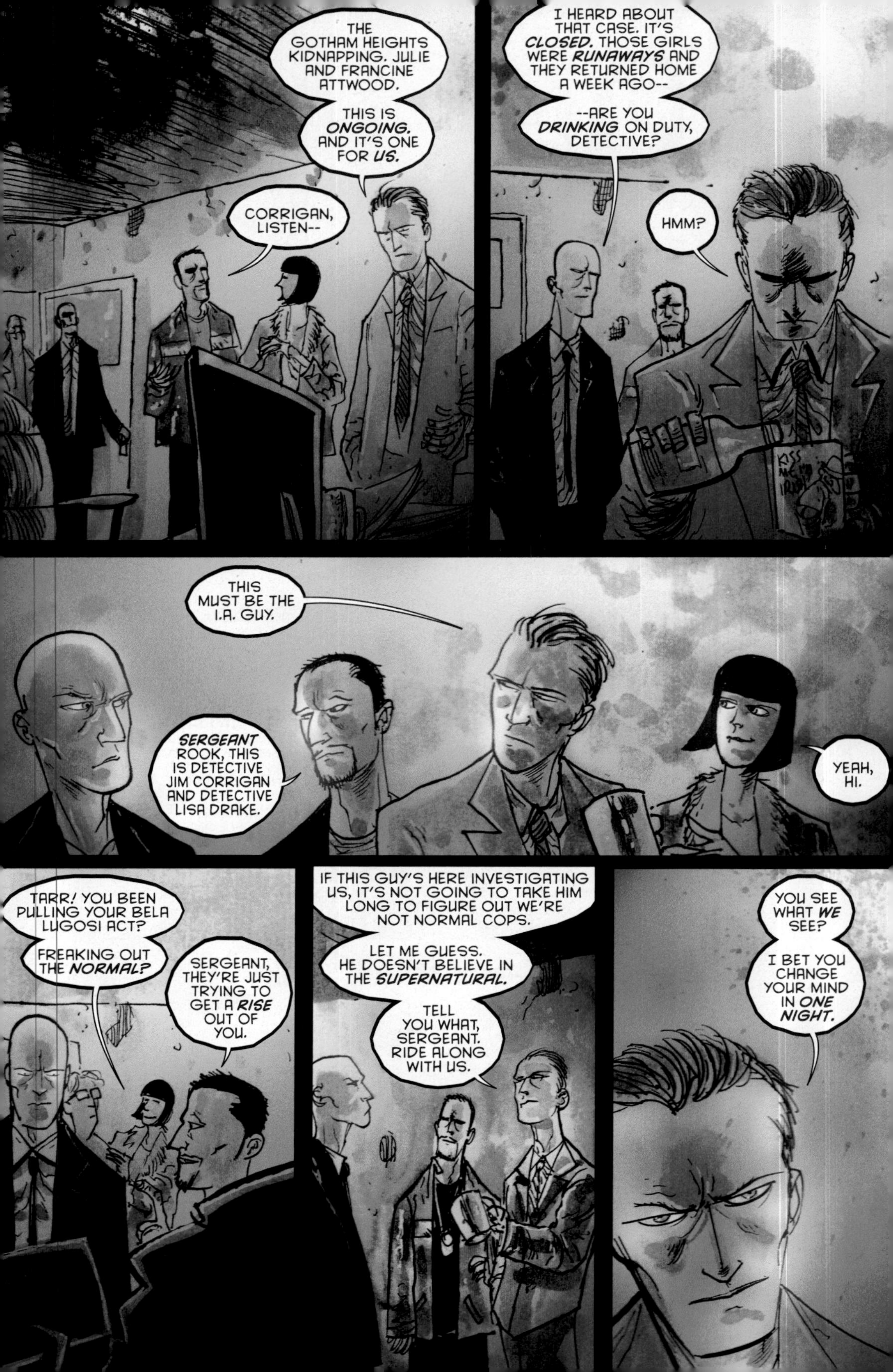
THE GOTHAM HEIGHTS KIDNAPPING. JULIE AND FRANCINE ATTWOOD.
THIS IS ONGOING. AND IT'S ONE FOR US.
CORRIGAN, LISTEN--
I HEARD ABOUT THAT CASE. IT'S CLOSED. THOSE GIRLS WERE RUNAWAYS AND THEY RETURNED HOME A WEEK AGO--
--ARE YOU DRINKING ON DUTY, DETECTIVE?
HMM?
KISS ME I'M IRISH
THIS MUST BE THE I.A. GUY.
SERGEANT ROOK, THIS IS DETECTIVE JIM CORRIGAN AND DETECTIVE LISA DRAKE.
YEAH, HI.
TARR! YOU BEEN PULLING YOUR BELA LUGOSI ACT?
FREAKING OUT THE NORMAL?
SERGEANT, THEY'RE JUST TRYING TO GET A RISE OUT OF YOU.
IF THIS GUY'S HERE INVESTIGATING US, IT'S NOT GOING TO TAKE HIM LONG TO FIGURE OUT WE'RE NOT NORMAL COPS.
LET ME GUESS. HE DOESN'T BELIEVE IN THE SUPERNATURAL.
TELL YOU WHAT, SERGEANT. RIDE ALONG WITH US.
YOU SEE WHAT WE SEE?
I BET YOU CHANGE YOUR MIND IN ONE NIGHT.

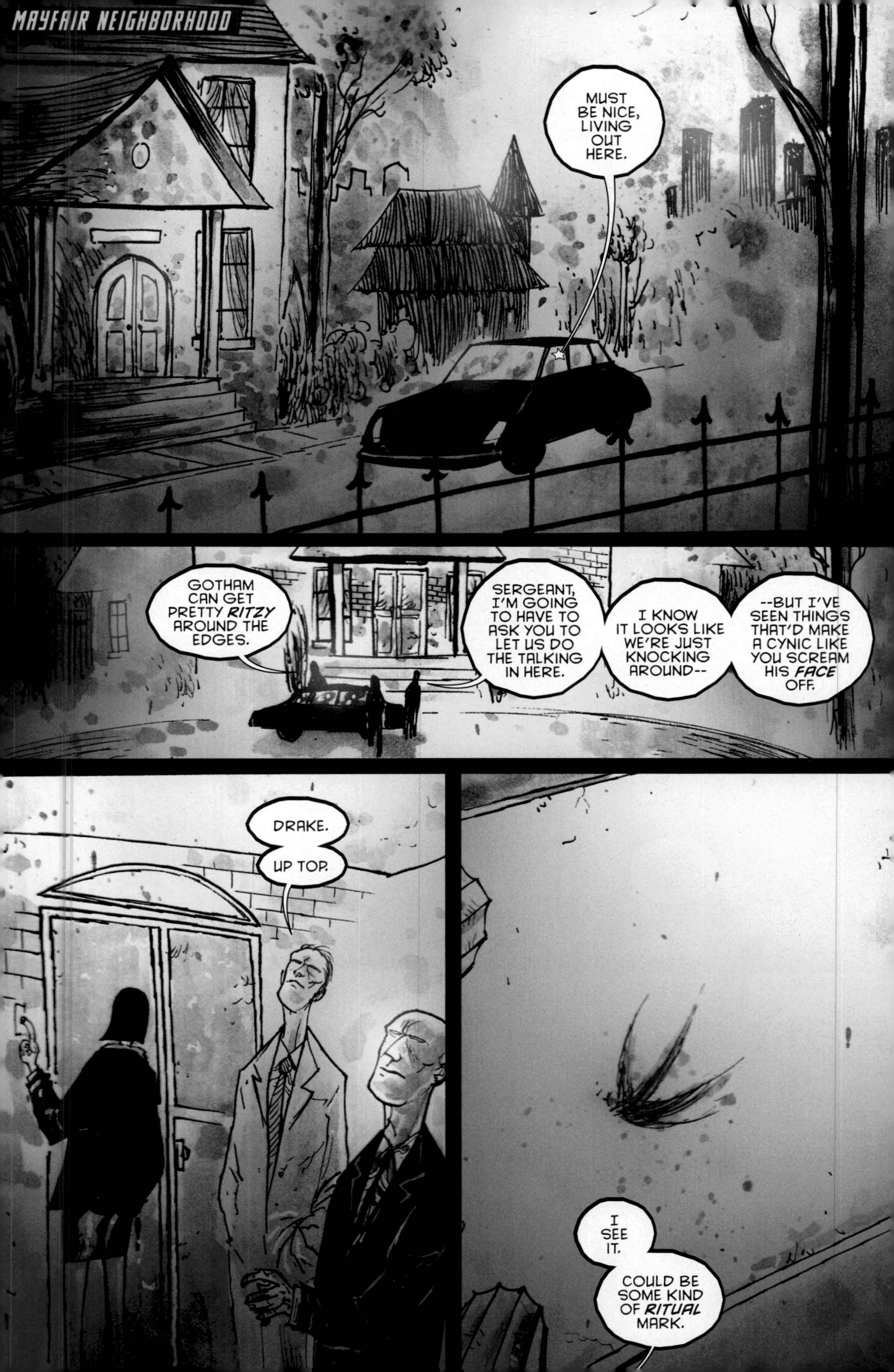
MAYFAIR NEIGHBORHOOD
MUST BE NICE, LIVING OUT HERE.
GOTHAM CAN GET PRETTY RITZY AROUND THE EDGES.
SERGEANT, I'M GOING TO HAVE TO ASK YOU TO LET US DO THE TALKING IN HERE.
I KNOW IT LOOKS LIKE WE'RE JUST KNOCKING AROUND--
--BUT I'VE SEEN THINGS THAT'D MAKE A CYNIC LIKE YOU SCREAM HIS FACE OFF.
DRAKE.
UP TOP.
I SEE IT.
COULD BE SOME KIND OF RITUAL MARK.

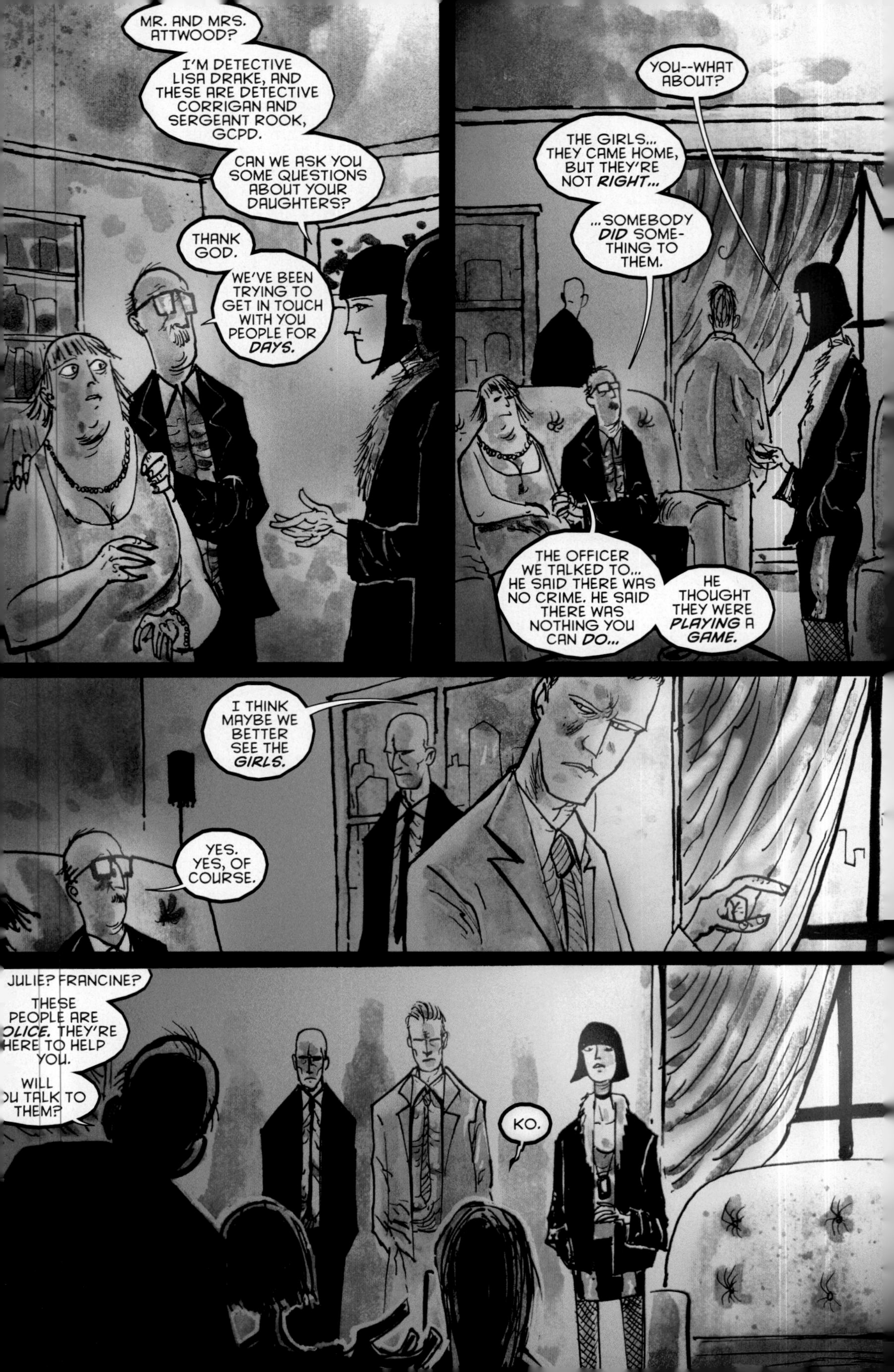

MR. AND MRS. ATTWOOD?
I'M DETECTIVE LISA DRAKE, AND THESE ARE DETECTIVE CORRIGAN AND SERGEANT ROOK, GCPD.
CAN WE ASK YOU SOME QUESTIONS ABOUT YOUR DAUGHTERS?
THANK GOD.
WE'VE BEEN TRYING TO GET IN TOUCH WITH YOU PEOPLE FOR *DAYS.*
YOU--WHAT ABOUT?
THE GIRLS... THEY CAME HOME, BUT THEY'RE NOT *RIGHT*...
...SOMEBODY *DID* SOMETHING TO THEM.
THE OFFICER WE TALKED TO... HE SAID THERE WAS NO CRIME. HE SAID THERE WAS NOTHING YOU CAN *DO*...
HE THOUGHT THEY WERE *PLAYING* A *GAME.*
I THINK MAYBE WE BETTER SEE THE *GIRLS.*
YES. YES, OF COURSE.
JULIE? FRANCINE?
THESE PEOPLE ARE *OLICE.* THEY'RE HERE TO HELP YOU.
WILL U TALK TO THEM?
KO.

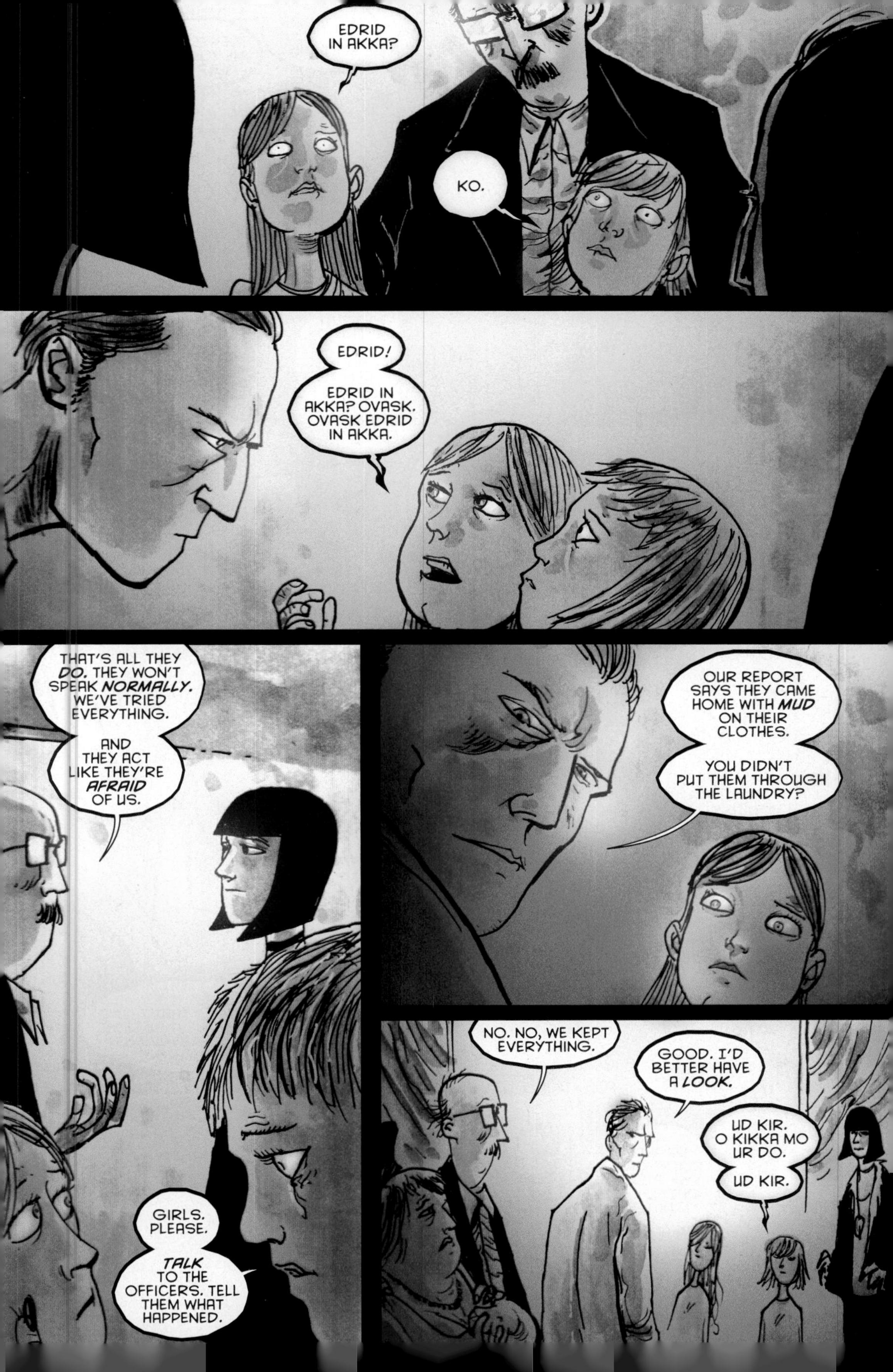
EDRID IN AKKA?
KO.
EDRID!
EDRID IN AKKA? OVASK. OVASK EDRID IN AKKA.
THAT'S ALL THEY *DO.* THEY WON'T SPEAK *NORMALLY.* WE'VE TRIED EVERYTHING.
AND THEY ACT LIKE THEY'RE *AFRAID* OF US.
GIRLS. PLEASE.
TALK TO THE OFFICERS. TELL THEM WHAT HAPPENED.
OUR REPORT SAYS THEY CAME HOME WITH *MUD* ON THEIR CLOTHES.
YOU DIDN'T PUT THEM THROUGH THE LAUNDRY?
NO. NO, WE KEPT EVERYTHING.
GOOD. I'D BETTER HAVE A *LOOK.*
UD KIR. O KIKKA MO UR DO.
UD KIR.

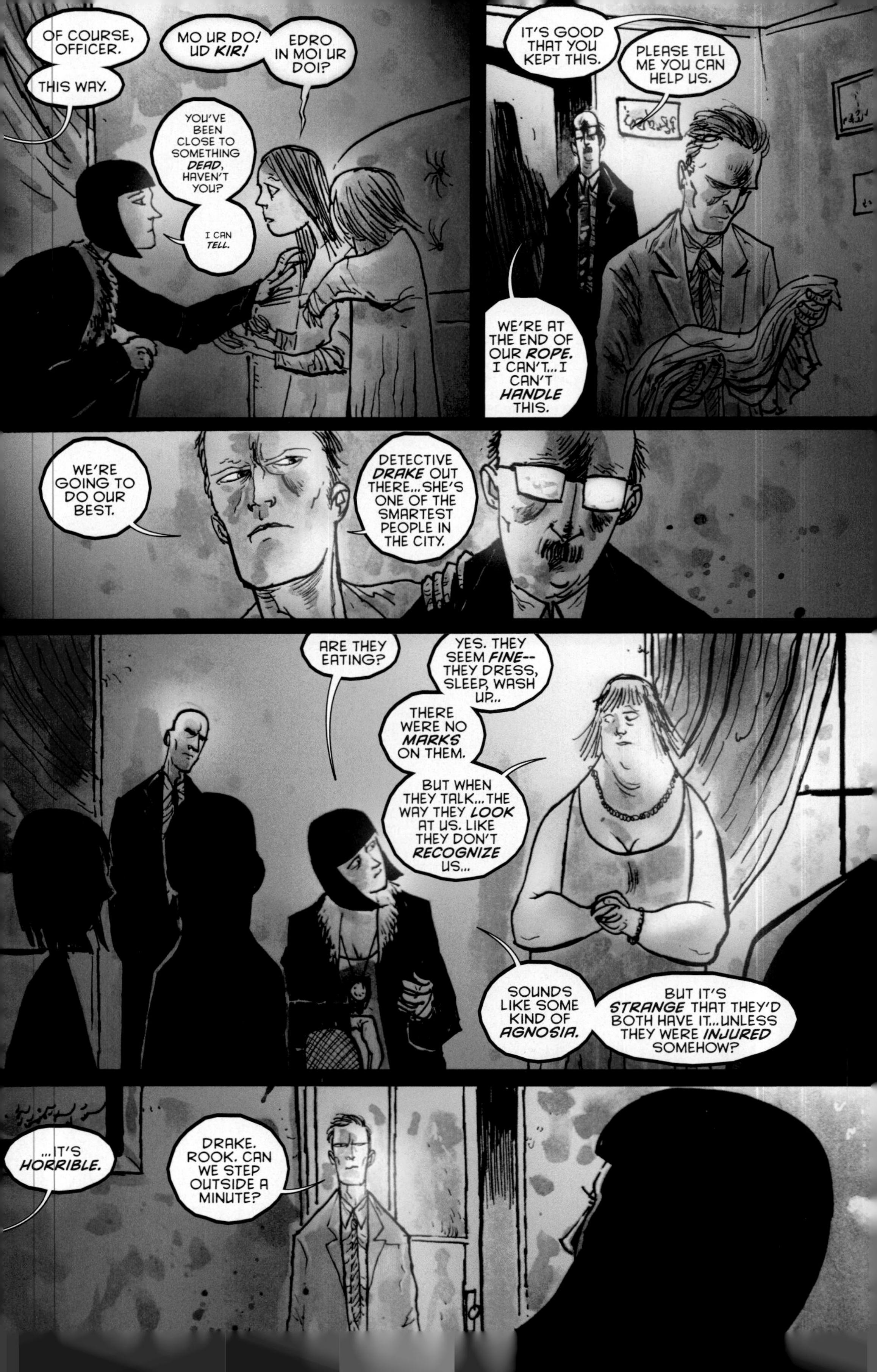

OF COURSE, OFFICER.
THIS WAY.
MO UR DO! UD KIR!
EDRO IN MOI UR DOI?
YOU'VE BEEN CLOSE TO SOMETHING DEAD, HAVEN'T YOU?
I CAN TELL.
IT'S GOOD THAT YOU KEPT THIS.
PLEASE TELL ME YOU CAN HELP US.
WE'RE AT THE END OF OUR ROPE. I CAN'T...I CAN'T HANDLE THIS.
WE'RE GOING TO DO OUR BEST.
DETECTIVE DRAKE OUT THERE...SHE'S ONE OF THE SMARTEST PEOPLE IN THE CITY.
ARE THEY EATING?
YES. THEY SEEM FINE-- THEY DRESS, SLEEP, WASH UP...
THERE WERE NO MARKS ON THEM.
BUT WHEN THEY TALK...THE WAY THEY LOOK AT US. LIKE THEY DON'T RECOGNIZE US...
SOUNDS LIKE SOME KIND OF AGNOSIA.
BUT IT'S STRANGE THAT THEY'D BOTH HAVE IT...UNLESS THEY WERE INJURED SOMEHOW?
...IT'S HORRIBLE.
DRAKE. ROOK. CAN WE STEP OUTSIDE A MINUTE?

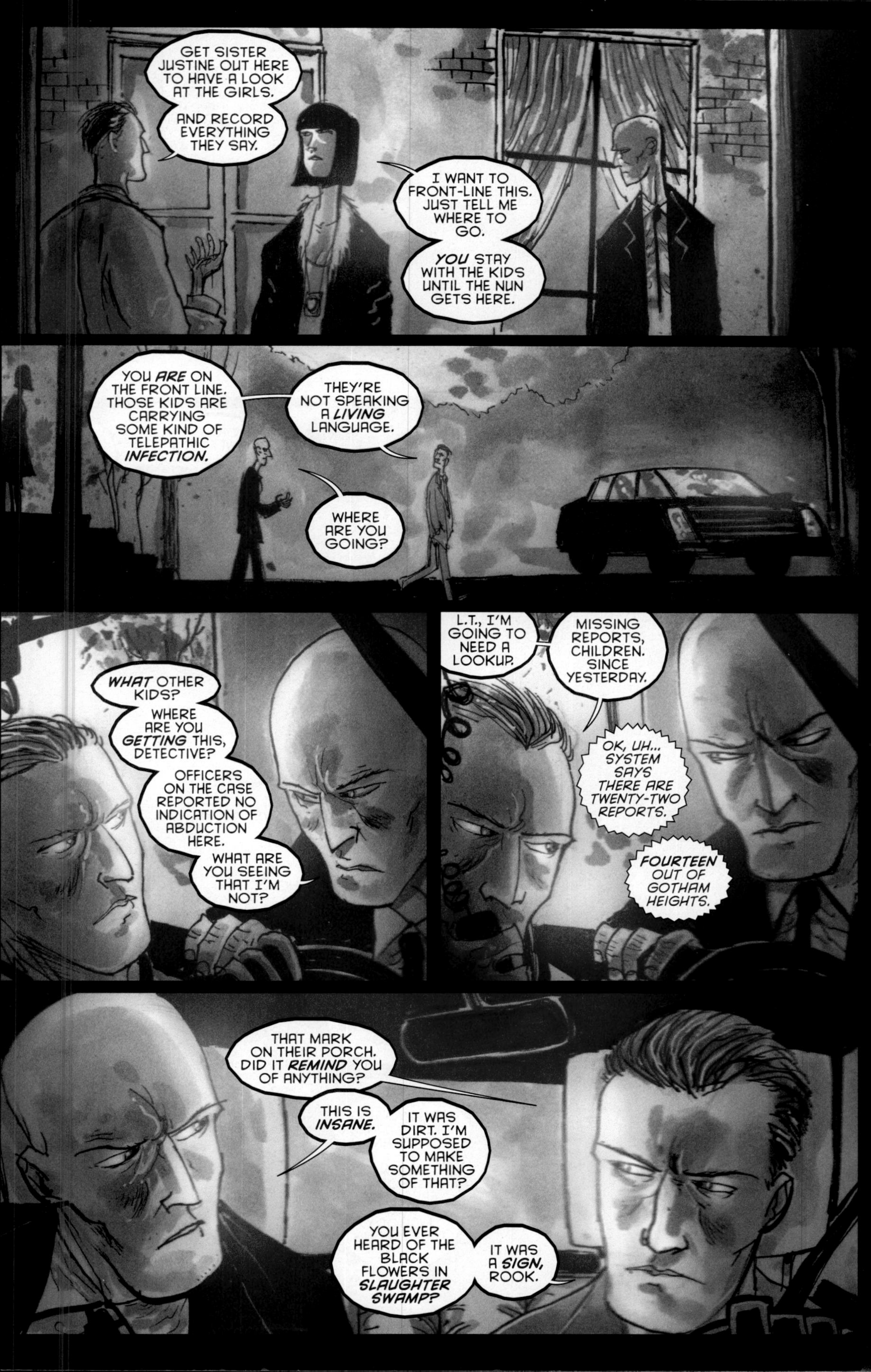

GET SISTER JUSTINE OUT HERE TO HAVE A LOOK AT THE GIRLS.
AND RECORD EVERYTHING THEY SAY.
I WANT TO FRONT-LINE THIS. JUST TELL ME WHERE TO GO.
YOU STAY WITH THE KIDS UNTIL THE NUN GETS HERE.
YOU ARE ON THE FRONT LINE. THOSE KIDS ARE CARRYING SOME KIND OF TELEPATHIC INFECTION.
THEY'RE NOT SPEAKING A LIVING LANGUAGE.
WHERE ARE YOU GOING?
WHAT OTHER KIDS?
WHERE ARE YOU GETTING THIS, DETECTIVE?
OFFICERS ON THE CASE REPORTED NO INDICATION OF ABDUCTION HERE.
WHAT ARE YOU SEEING THAT I'M NOT?
L.T., I'M GOING TO NEED A LOOKUP.
MISSING REPORTS, CHILDREN. SINCE YESTERDAY.
OK, UH... SYSTEM SAYS THERE ARE TWENTY-TWO REPORTS.
FOURTEEN OUT OF GOTHAM HEIGHTS.
THAT MARK ON THEIR PORCH. DID IT REMIND YOU OF ANYTHING?
THIS IS INSANE.
IT WAS DIRT. I'M SUPPOSED TO MAKE SOMETHING OF THAT?
YOU EVER HEARD OF THE BLACK FLOWERS IN SLAUGHTER SWAMP?
IT WAS A SIGN, ROOK.

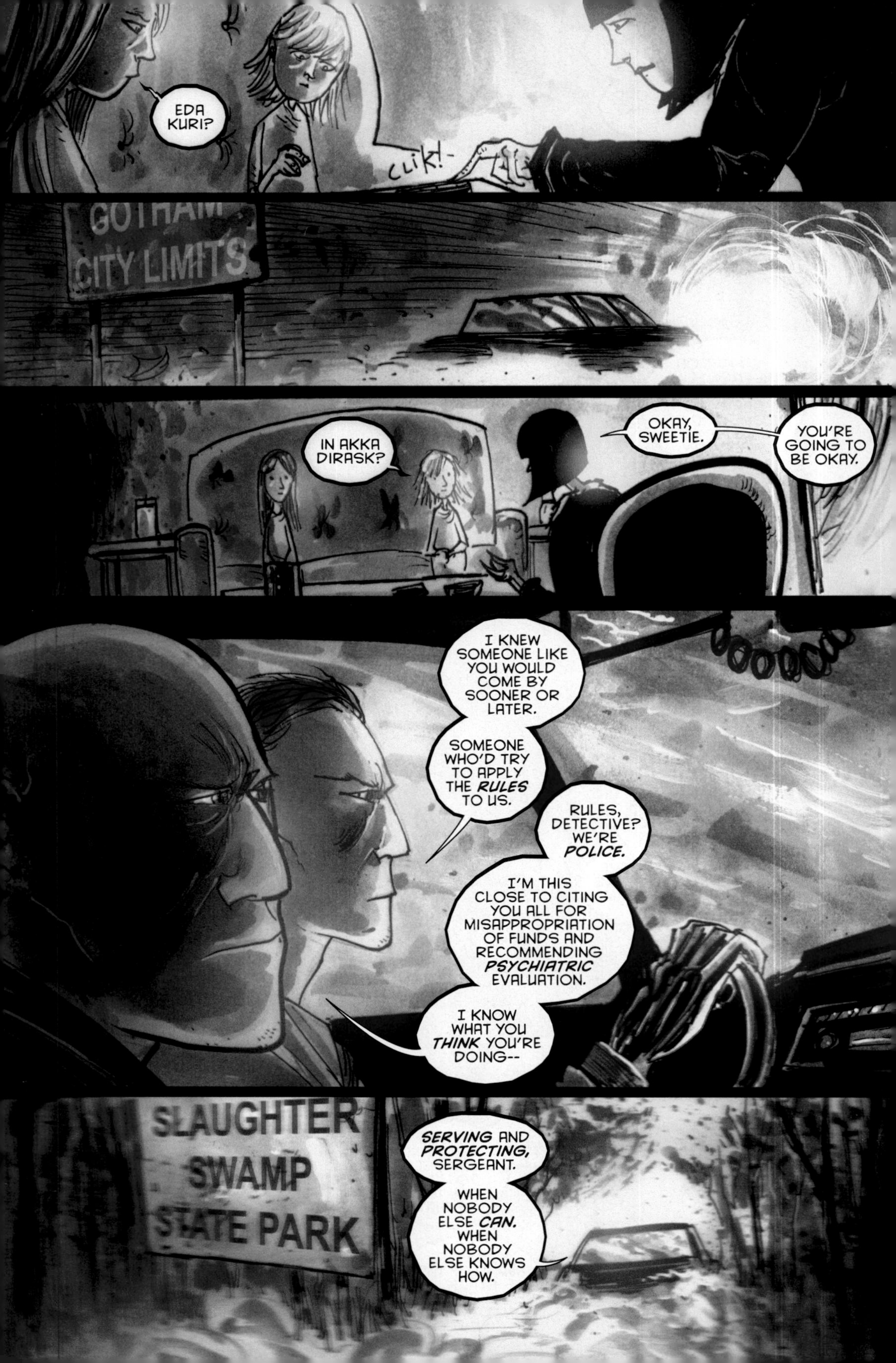
EDA KURI?
CLIK!-
GOTHAM CITY LIMITS
IN AKKA DIRASK?
OKAY, SWEETIE.
YOU'RE GOING TO BE OKAY.
I KNEW SOMEONE LIKE YOU WOULD COME BY SOONER OR LATER.
SOMEONE WHO'D TRY TO APPLY THE *RULES* TO US.
RULES, DETECTIVE? WE'RE *POLICE.*
I'M THIS CLOSE TO CITING YOU ALL FOR MISAPPROPRIATION OF FUNDS AND RECOMMENDING *PSYCHIATRIC* EVALUATION.
I KNOW WHAT YOU *THINK* YOU'RE DOING--
SLAUGHTER SWAMP STATE PARK
SERVING AND *PROTECTING,* SERGEANT.
WHEN NOBODY ELSE *CAN.* WHEN NOBODY ELSE KNOWS HOW.

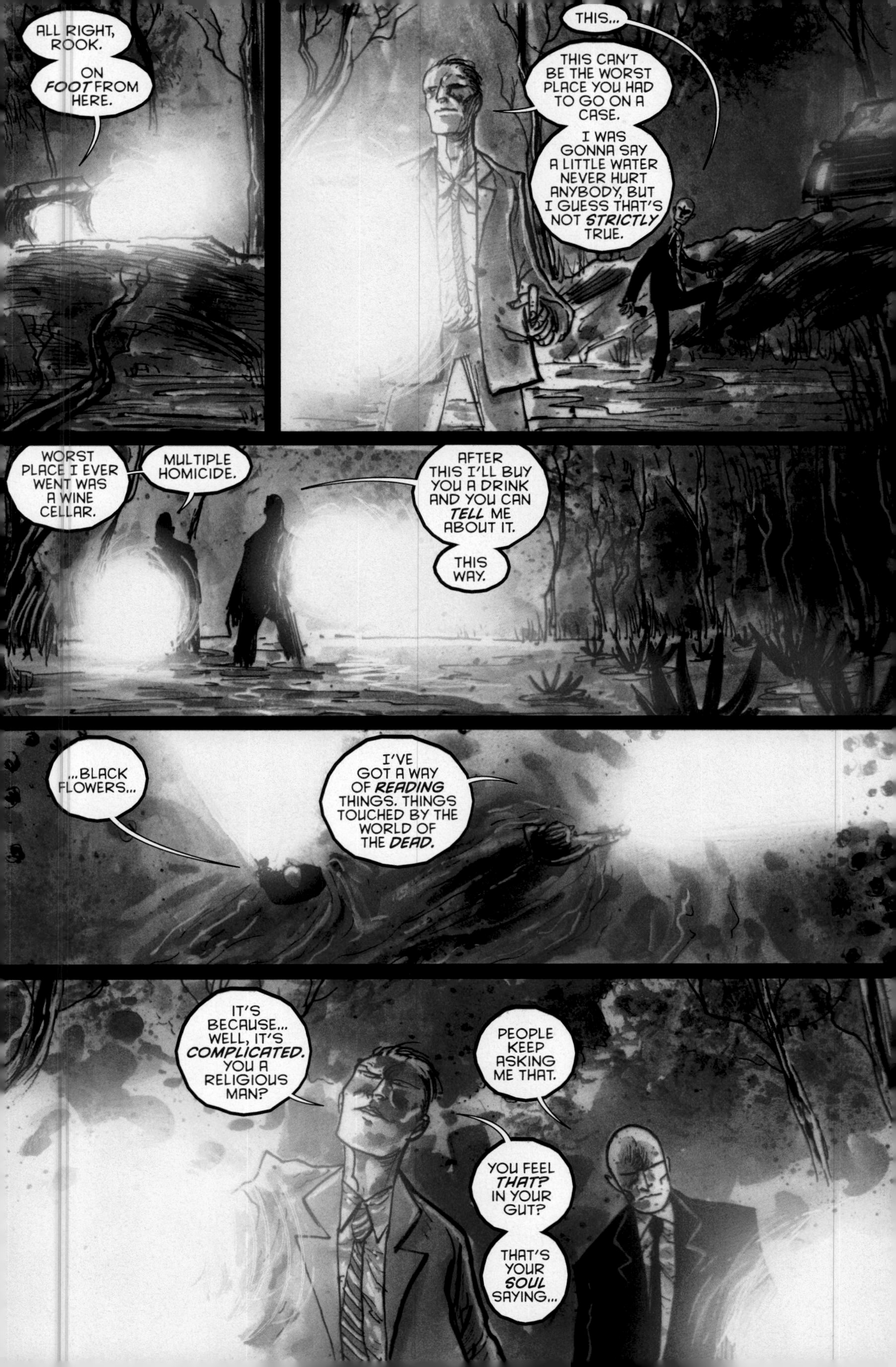
ALL RIGHT, ROOK.
ON *FOOT* FROM HERE.
THIS...
THIS CAN'T BE THE WORST PLACE YOU HAD TO GO ON A CASE.
I WAS GONNA SAY A LITTLE WATER NEVER HURT ANYBODY, BUT I GUESS THAT'S NOT *STRICTLY* TRUE.
WORST PLACE I EVER WENT WAS A WINE CELLAR.
MULTIPLE HOMICIDE.
AFTER THIS I'LL BUY YOU A DRINK AND YOU CAN *TELL* ME ABOUT IT.
THIS WAY.
...BLACK FLOWERS...
I'VE GOT A WAY OF *READING* THINGS. THINGS TOUCHED BY THE WORLD OF THE *DEAD.*
IT'S BECAUSE... WELL, IT'S *COMPLICATED.* YOU A RELIGIOUS MAN?
PEOPLE KEEP ASKING ME THAT.
YOU FEEL *THAT?* IN YOUR GUT?
THAT'S YOUR *SOUL* SAYING...

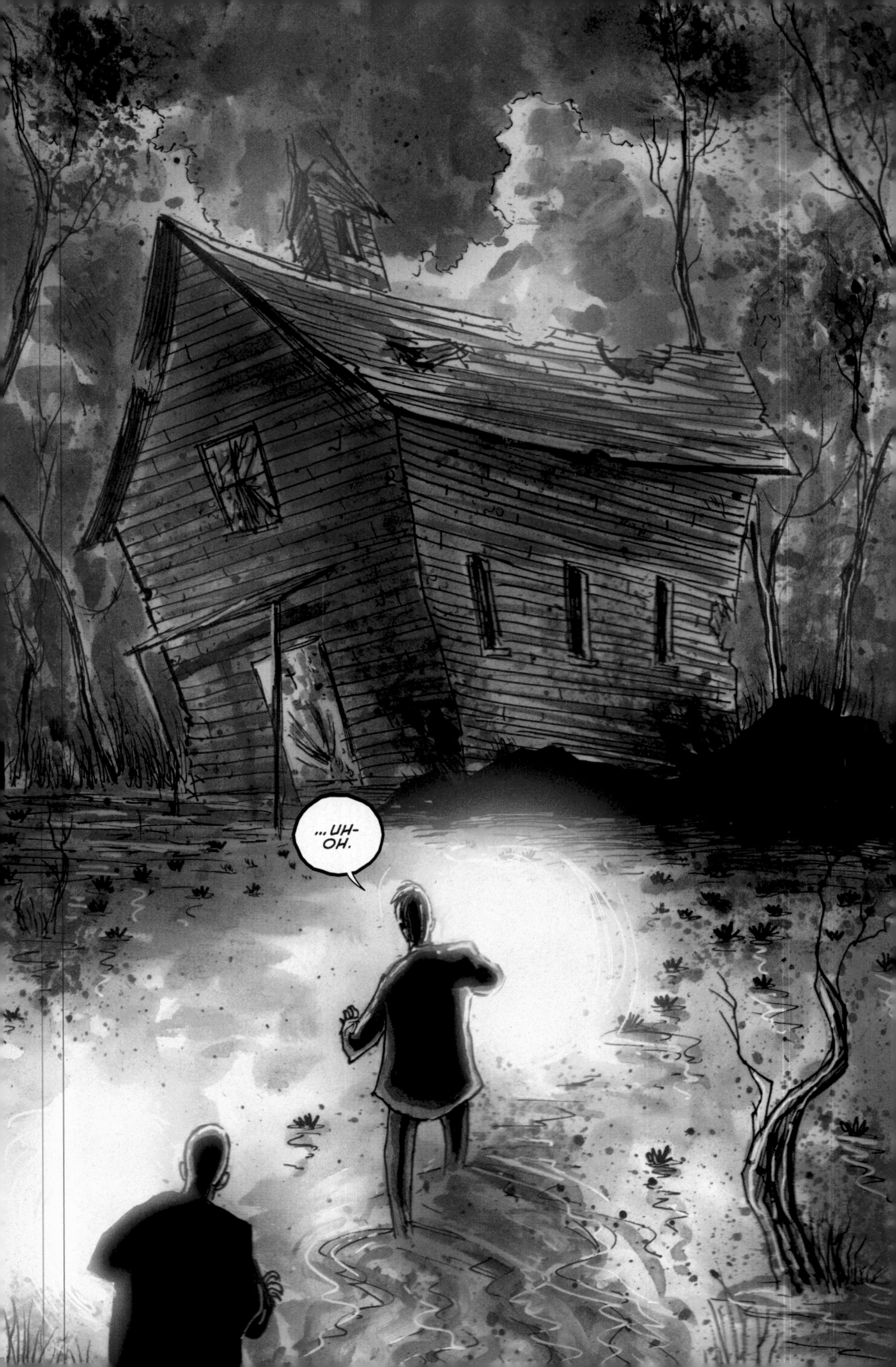
...UH-OH.

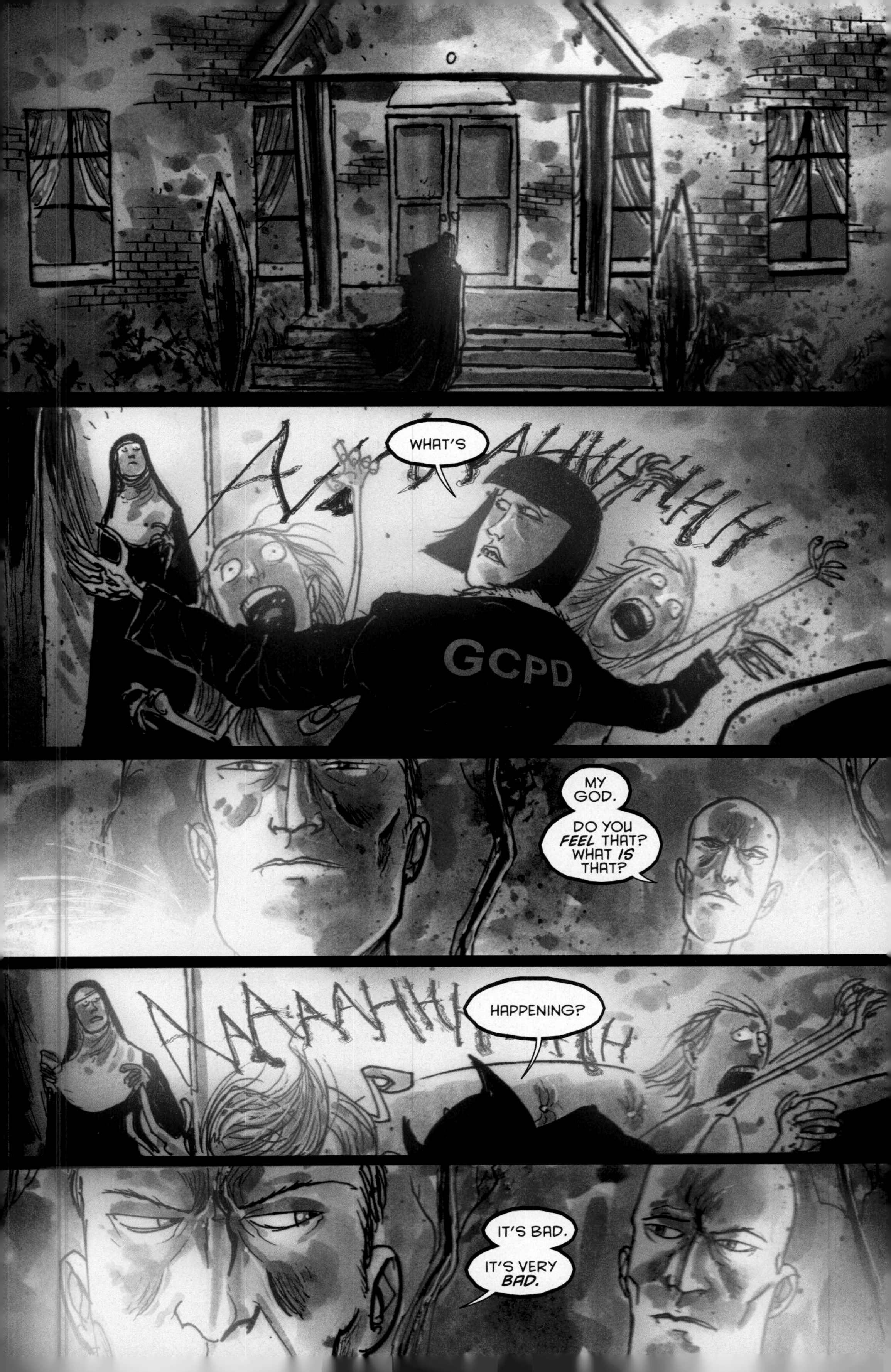
WHAT'S
GCPD
MY GOD.
DO YOU FEEL THAT? WHAT IS THAT?
HAPPENING?
IT'S BAD.
IT'S VERY BAD.

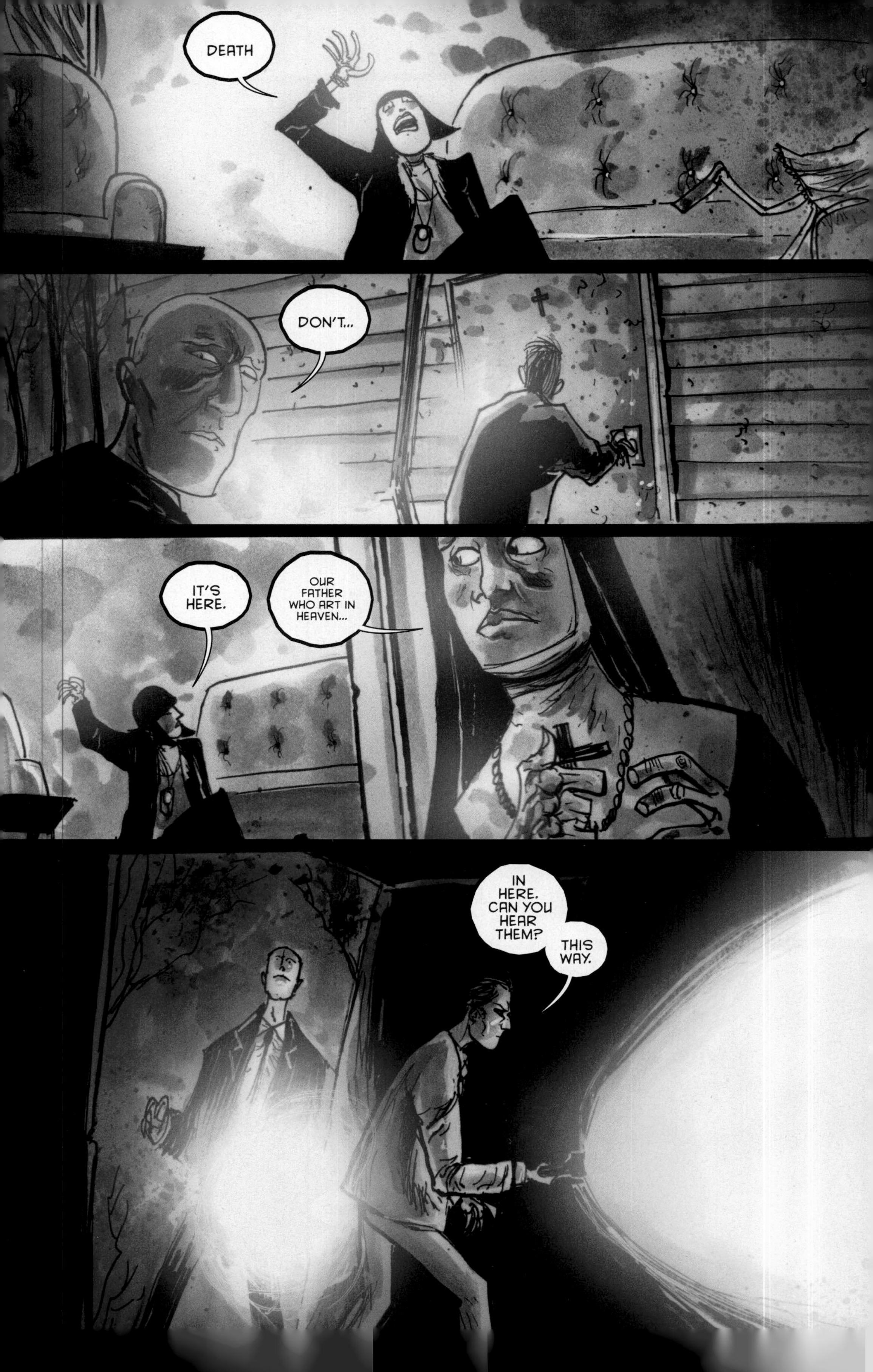
DEATH
DON'T...
IT'S HERE.
OUR FATHER WHO ART IN HEAVEN...
IN HERE. CAN YOU HEAR THEM?
THIS WAY.

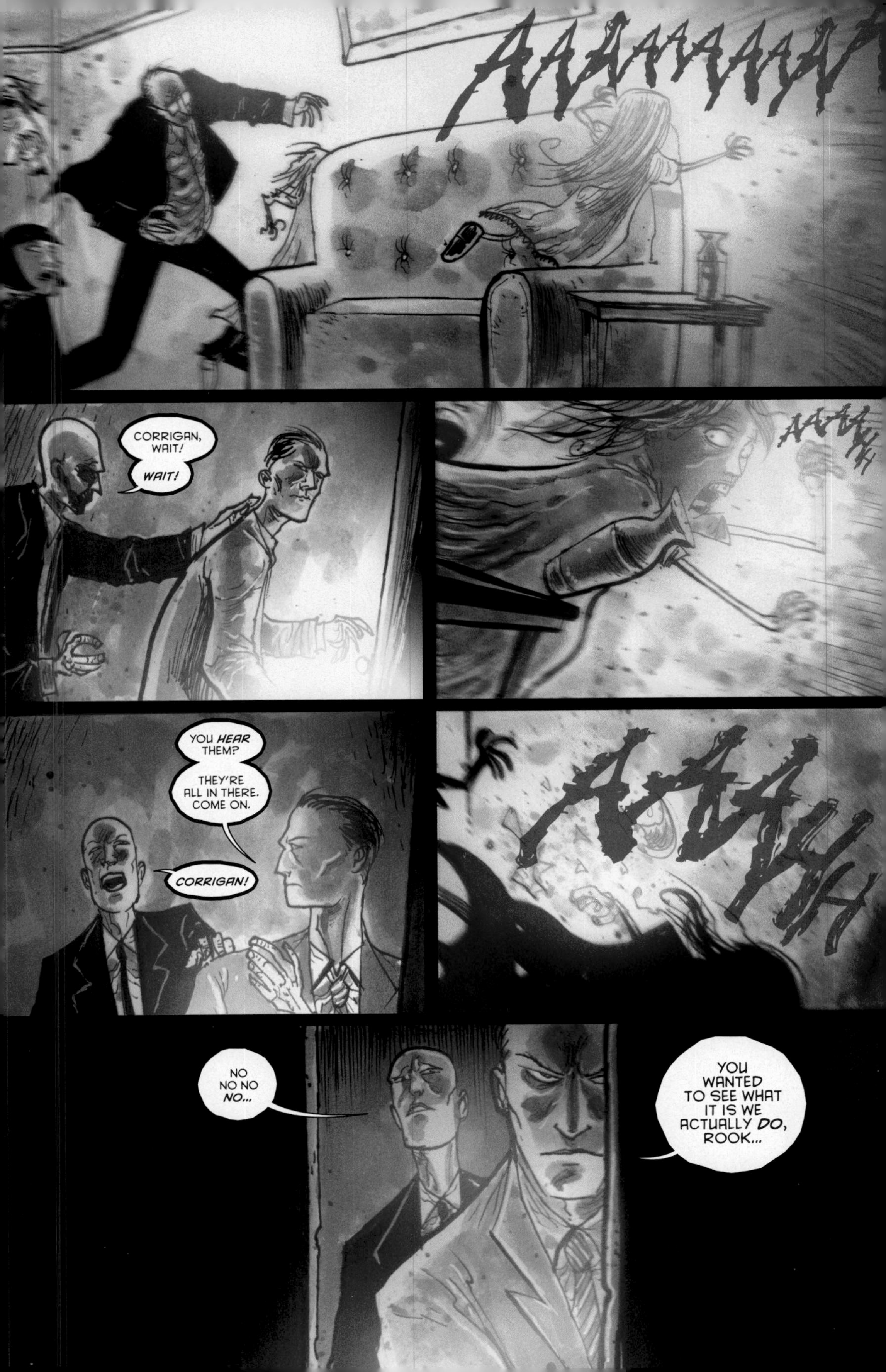
AAAAAAAAA
CORRIGAN, WAIT!
WAIT!
AAAAH
YOU HEAR THEM?
THEY'RE ALL IN THERE. COME ON.
CORRIGAN!
AAAH
NO NO NO NO...
YOU WANTED TO SEE WHAT IT IS WE ACTUALLY DO, ROOK...

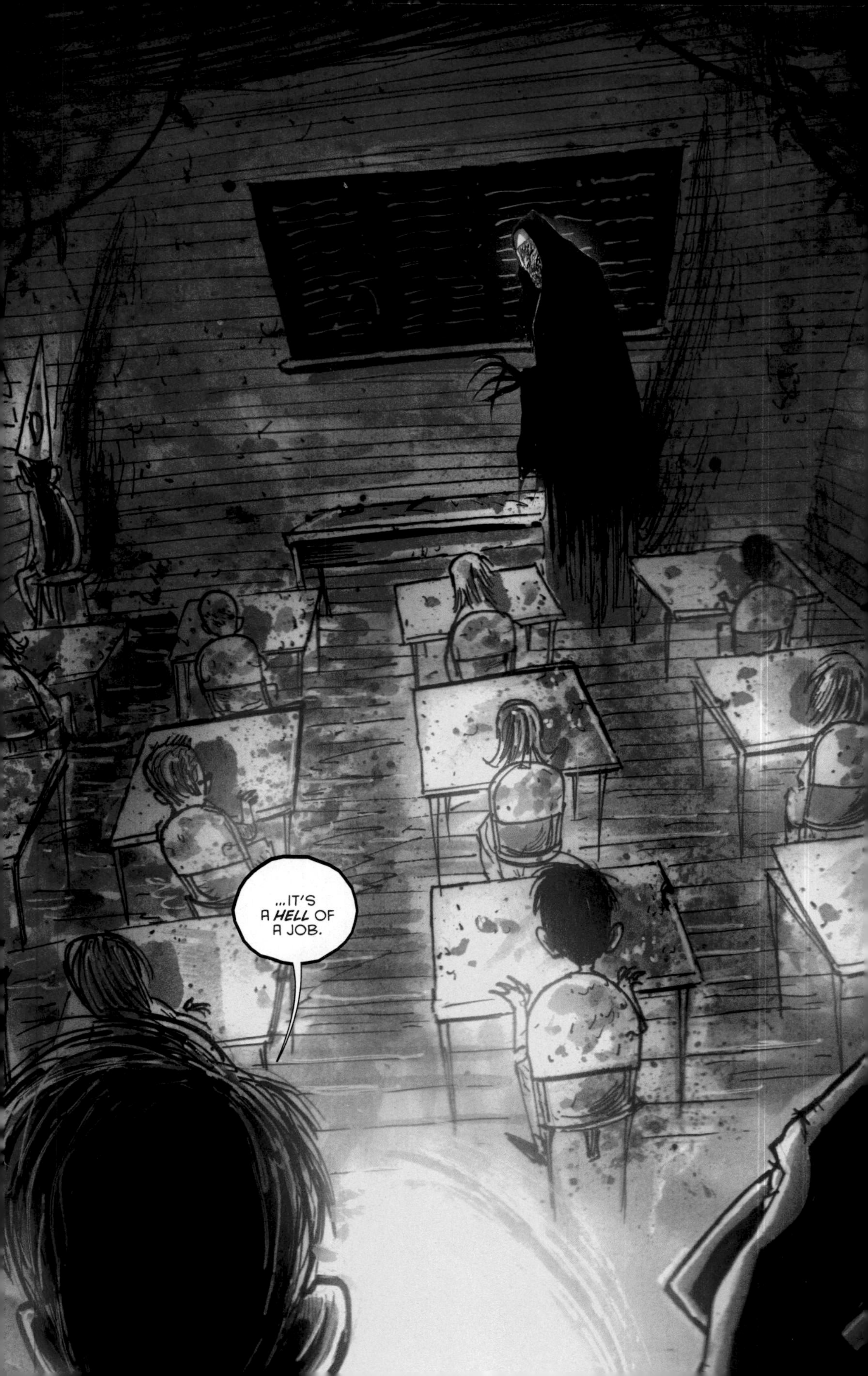
...IT'S A HELL OF A JOB.

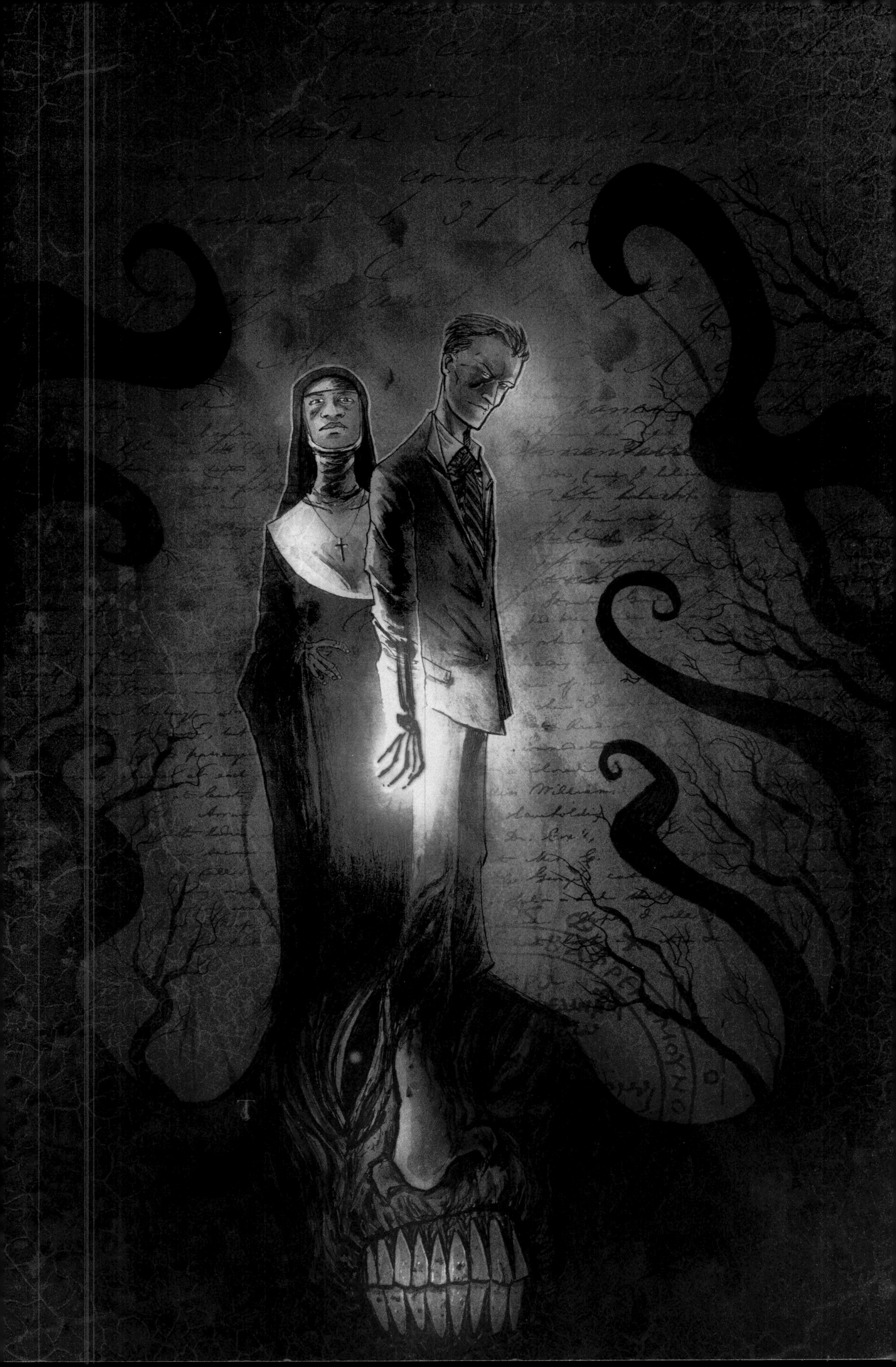

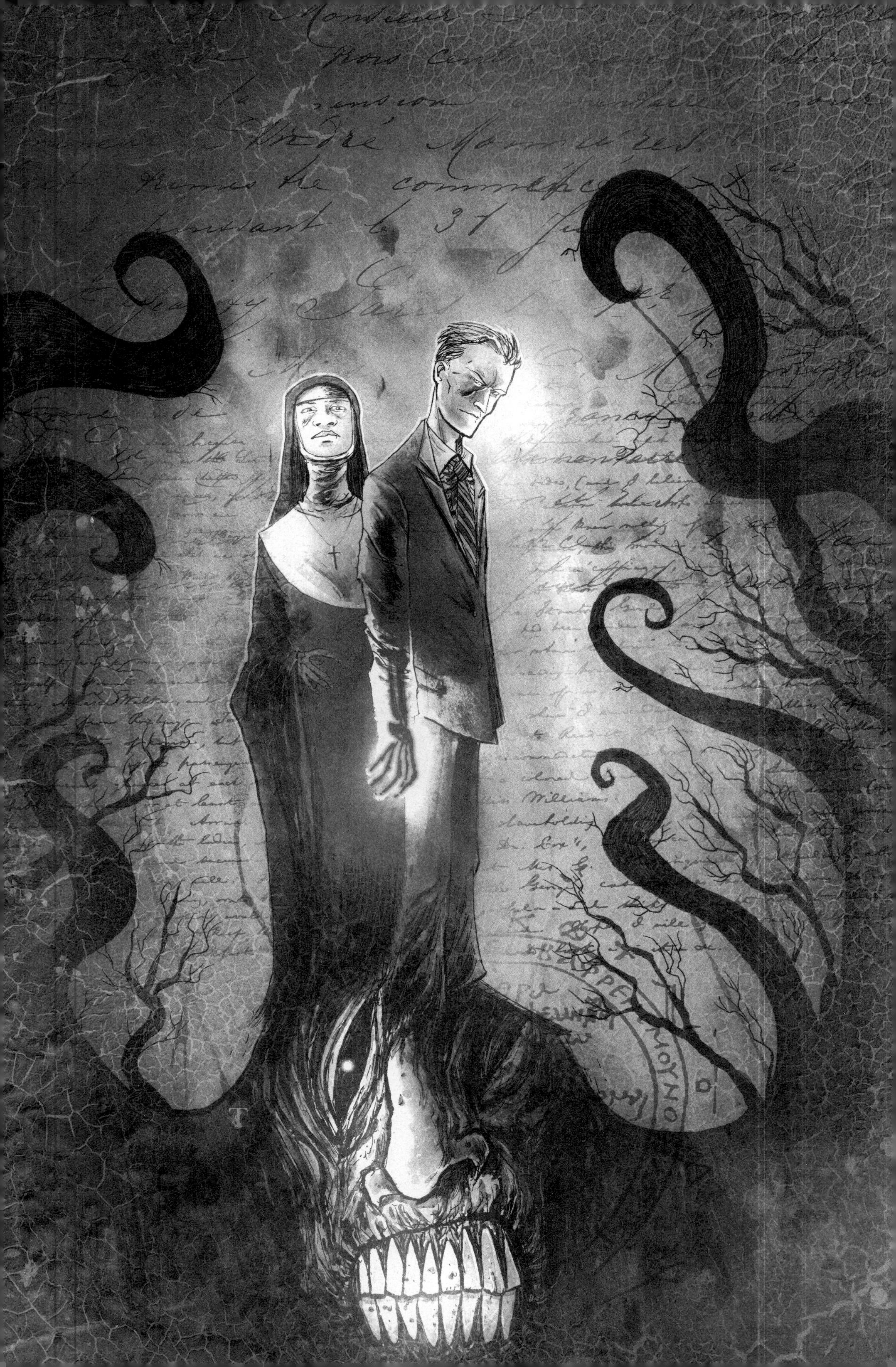

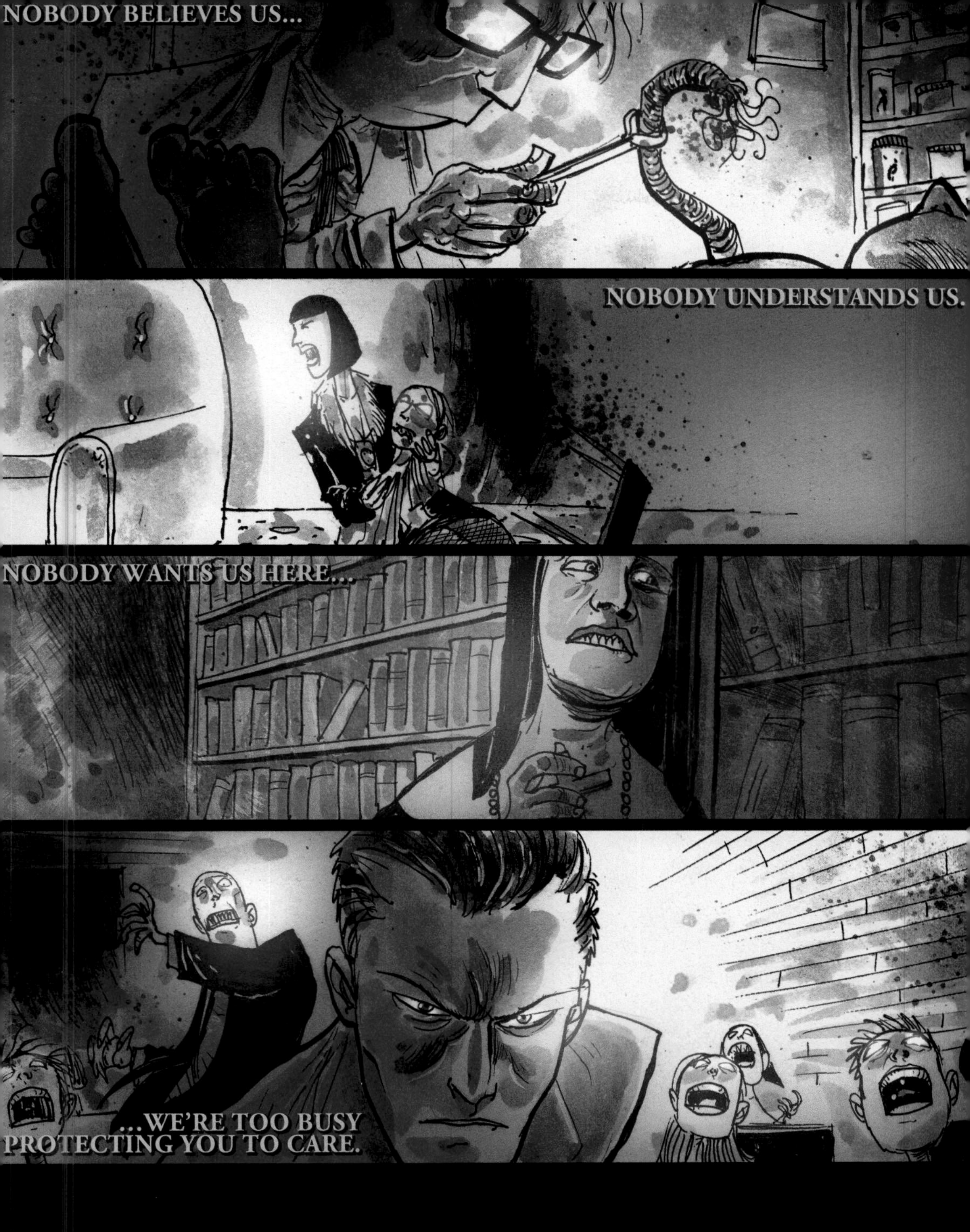
NOBODY BELIEVES US...
NOBODY UNDERSTANDS US.
NOBODY WANTS US HERE...
...WE'RE TOO BUSY PROTECTING YOU TO CARE.

CHAPTER TWO:

WE WILL NOT REST

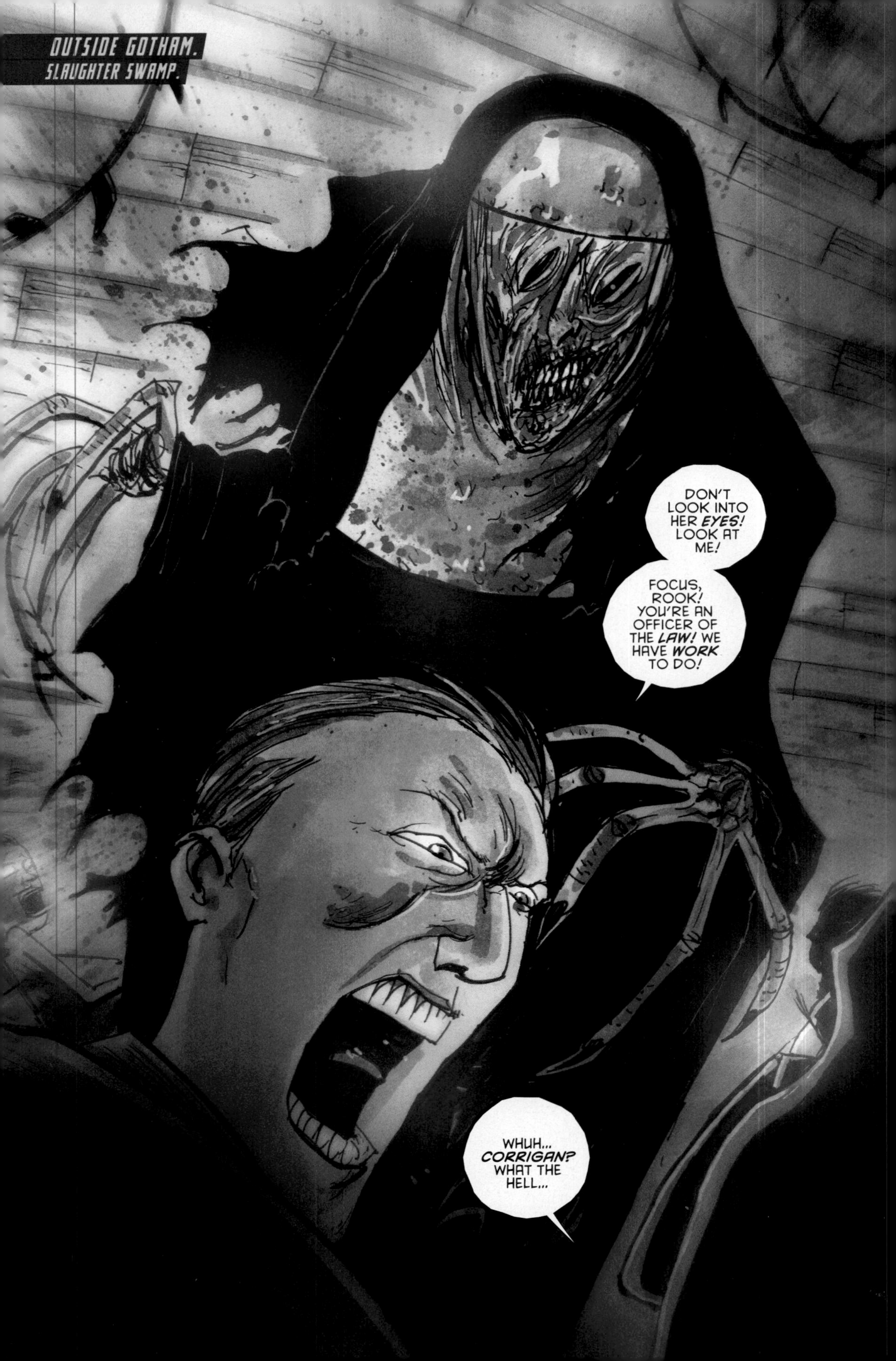
OUTSIDE GOTHAM.
SLAUGHTER SWAMP.
DON'T LOOK INTO HER *EYES!* LOOK AT ME!
FOCUS, ROOK! YOU'RE AN OFFICER OF THE *LAW!* WE HAVE *WORK* TO DO!
WHUH... *CORRIGAN?* WHAT THE HELL...

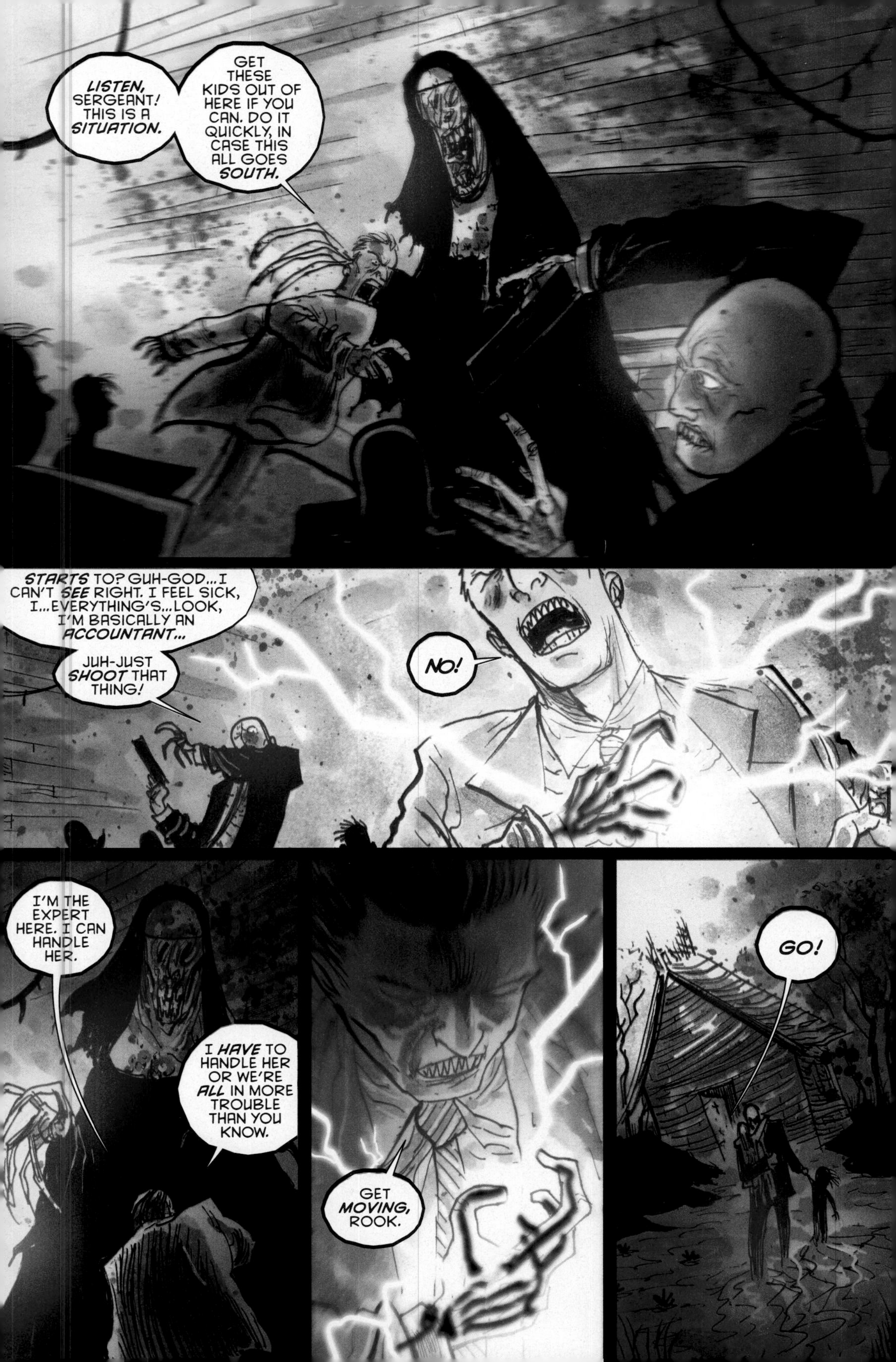
LISTEN, SERGEANT! THIS IS A SITUATION.
GET THESE KIDS OUT OF HERE IF YOU CAN. DO IT QUICKLY, IN CASE THIS ALL GOES SOUTH.
STARTS TO? GUH-GOD...I CAN'T SEE RIGHT. I FEEL SICK, I...EVERYTHING'S...LOOK, I'M BASICALLY AN ACCOUNTANT...
JUH-JUST SHOOT THAT THING!
NO!
I'M THE EXPERT HERE. I CAN HANDLE HER.
I HAVE TO HANDLE HER OR WE'RE ALL IN MORE TROUBLE THAN YOU KNOW.
GET MOVING, ROOK.
GO!

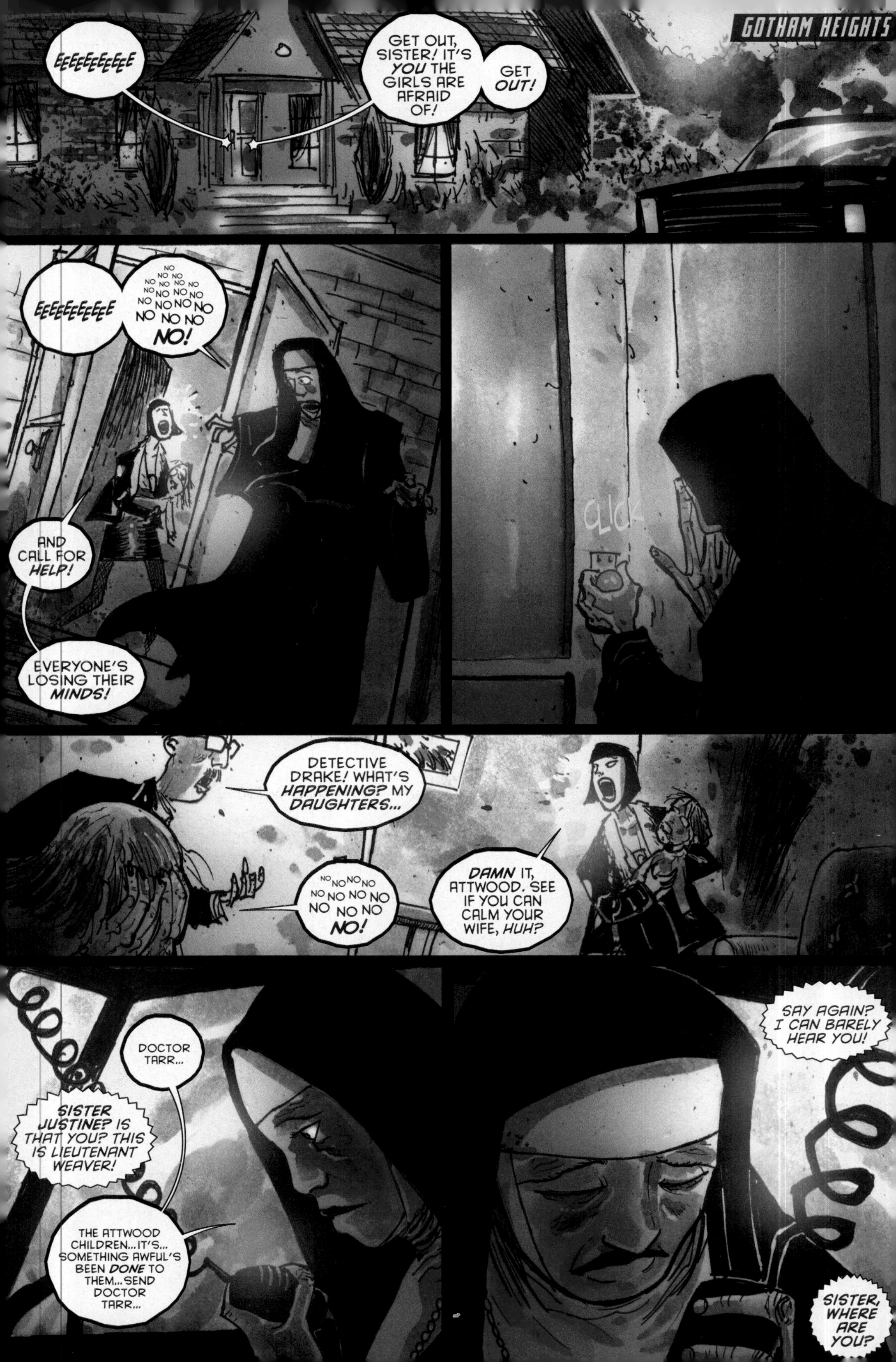
GOTHAM HEIGHTS
EEEEEEEEEEE
GET OUT, SISTER! IT'S YOU THE GIRLS ARE AFRAID OF!
GET OUT!
EEEEEEEEEEE
NO NO NO NO NO NO NO NO NO NO NO NO NO NO NO NO NO!
AND CALL FOR HELP!
EVERYONE'S LOSING THEIR MINDS!
CLICK
DETECTIVE DRAKE! WHAT'S HAPPENING? MY DAUGHTERS...
NO NO NO NO NO NO NO NO NO NO NO NO NO!
DAMN IT, ATTWOOD. SEE IF YOU CAN CALM YOUR WIFE, HUH?
DOCTOR TARR...
SISTER JUSTINE? IS THAT YOU? THIS IS LIEUTENANT WEAVER!
THE ATTWOOD CHILDREN...IT'S... SOMETHING AWFUL'S BEEN DONE TO THEM...SEND DOCTOR TARR...
SAY AGAIN? I CAN BARELY HEAR YOU!
SISTER, WHERE ARE YOU?

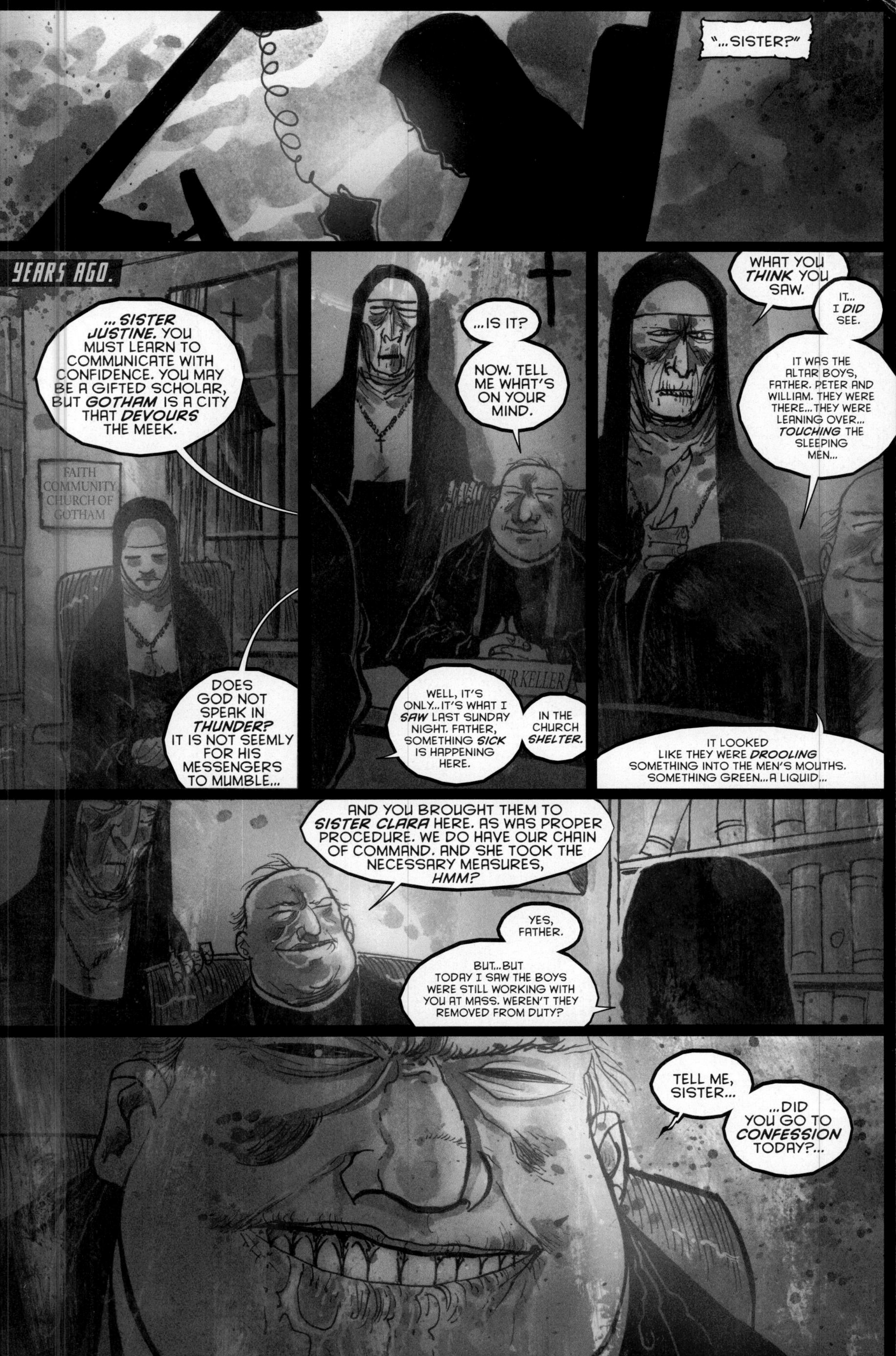
"...SISTER?"
YEARS AGO.
...SISTER JUSTINE. YOU MUST LEARN TO COMMUNICATE WITH CONFIDENCE. YOU MAY BE A GIFTED SCHOLAR, BUT GOTHAM IS A CITY THAT DEVOURS THE MEEK.
FAITH COMMUNITY CHURCH OF GOTHAM
DOES GOD NOT SPEAK IN THUNDER? IT IS NOT SEEMLY FOR HIS MESSENGERS TO MUMBLE...
...IS IT?
NOW. TELL ME WHAT'S ON YOUR MIND.
WELL, IT'S ONLY...IT'S WHAT I SAW LAST SUNDAY NIGHT. FATHER, SOMETHING SICK IS HAPPENING HERE.
IN THE CHURCH SHELTER.
WHAT YOU THINK YOU SAW.
IT... I DID SEE.
IT WAS THE ALTAR BOYS, FATHER. PETER AND WILLIAM. THEY WERE THERE... THEY WERE LEANING OVER... TOUCHING THE SLEEPING MEN...
IT LOOKED LIKE THEY WERE DROOLING SOMETHING INTO THE MEN'S MOUTHS. SOMETHING GREEN...A LIQUID...
AND YOU BROUGHT THEM TO SISTER CLARA HERE. AS WAS PROPER PROCEDURE. WE DO HAVE OUR CHAIN OF COMMAND. AND SHE TOOK THE NECESSARY MEASURES, HMM?
YES, FATHER.
BUT...BUT TODAY I SAW THE BOYS WERE STILL WORKING WITH YOU AT MASS. WEREN'T THEY REMOVED FROM DUTY?
TELL ME, SISTER...
...DID YOU GO TO CONFESSION TODAY?...

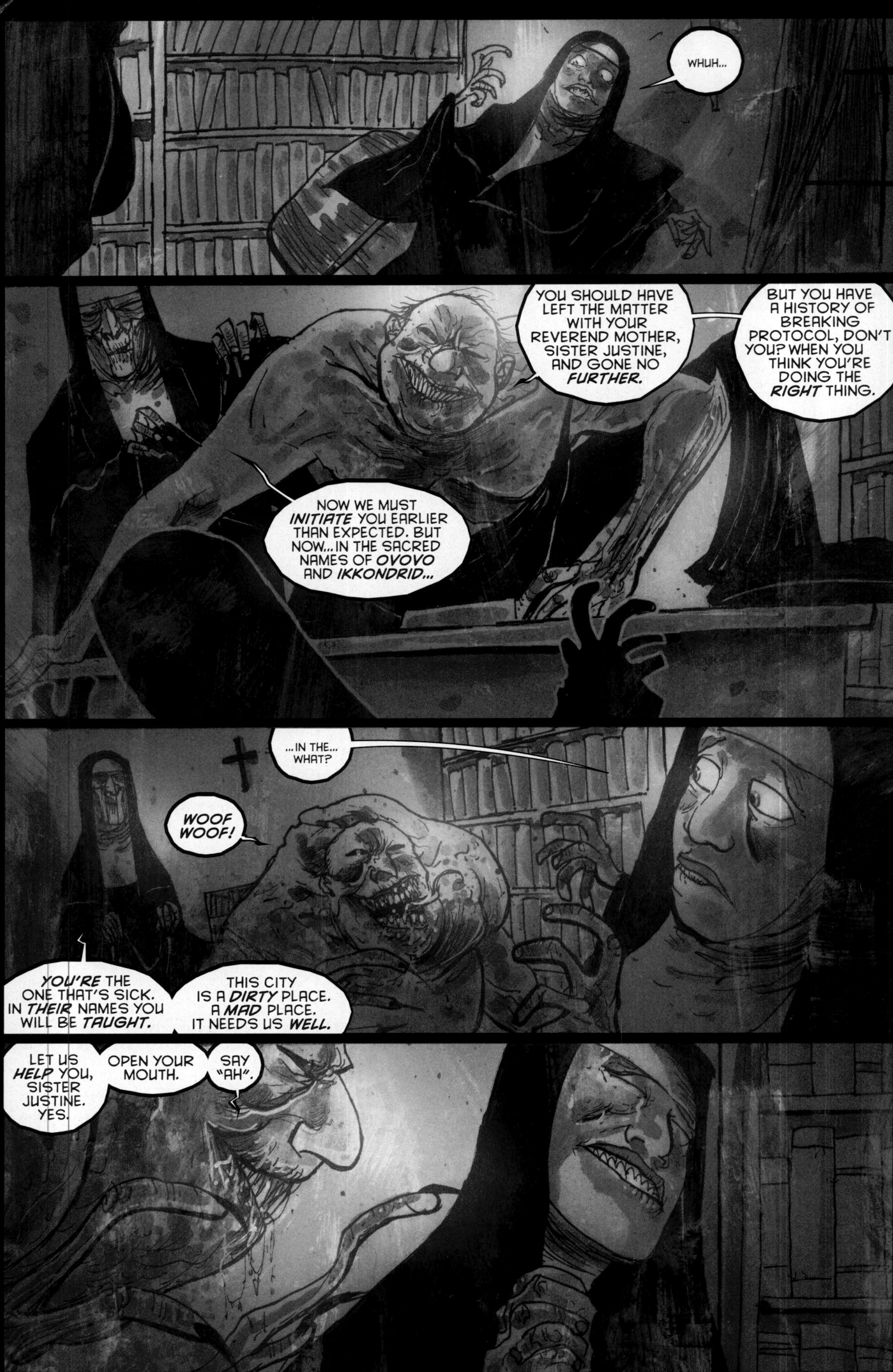
WHUH...
YOU SHOULD HAVE LEFT THE MATTER WITH YOUR REVEREND MOTHER, SISTER JUSTINE, AND GONE NO FURTHER.
BUT YOU HAVE A HISTORY OF BREAKING PROTOCOL, DON'T YOU? WHEN YOU THINK YOU'RE DOING THE RIGHT THING.
NOW WE MUST INITIATE YOU EARLIER THAN EXPECTED. BUT NOW...IN THE SACRED NAMES OF OVOVO AND IKKONDRID...
...IN THE... WHAT?
WOOF WOOF!
YOU'RE THE ONE THAT'S SICK. IN THEIR NAMES YOU WILL BE TAUGHT.
THIS CITY IS A DIRTY PLACE. A MAD PLACE. IT NEEDS US WELL.
LET US HELP YOU, SISTER JUSTINE. YES.
OPEN YOUR MOUTH.
SAY "AH".

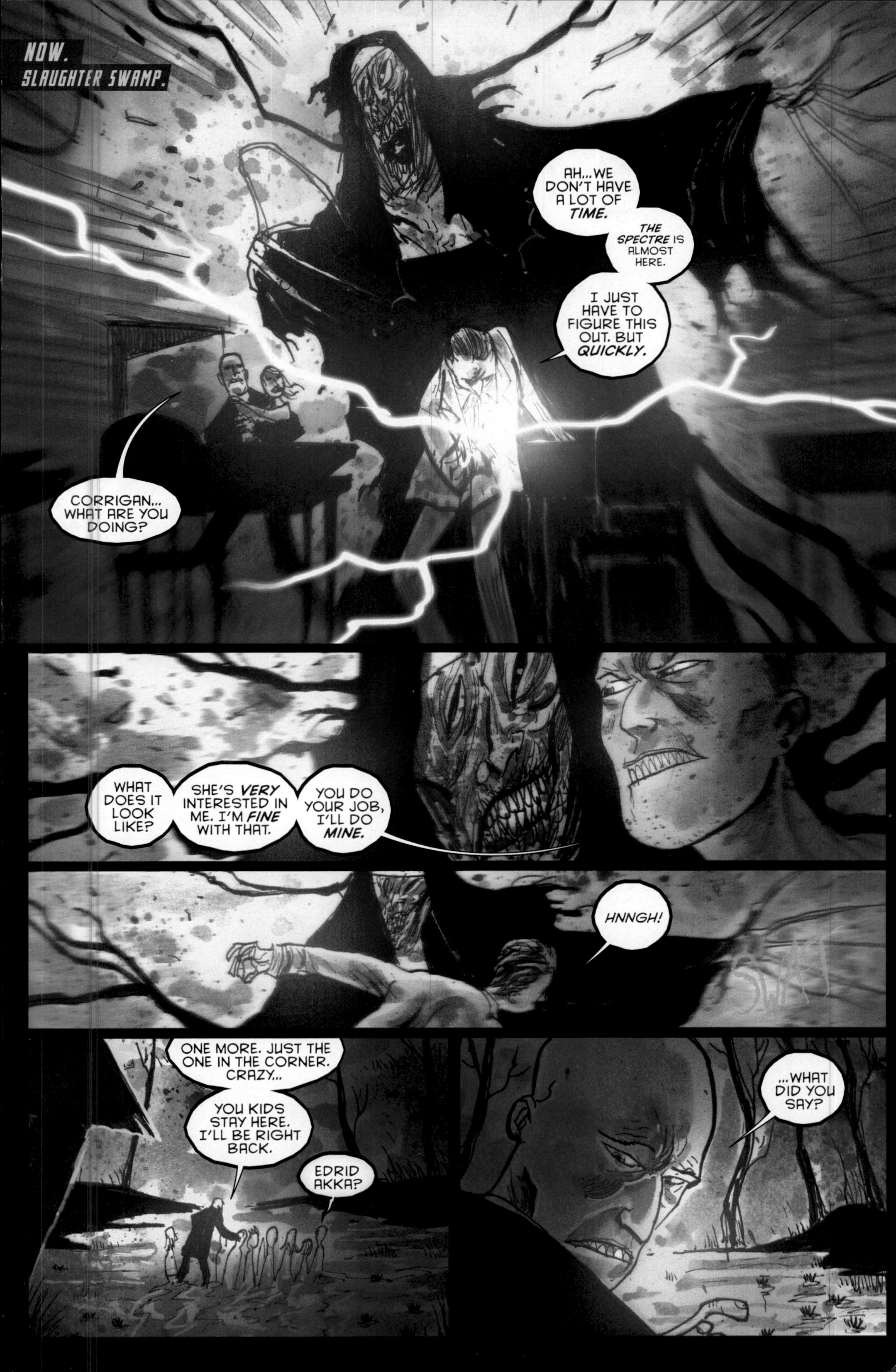
NOW.
SLAUGHTER SWAMP.
AH...WE DON'T HAVE A LOT OF TIME.
THE SPECTRE IS ALMOST HERE.
I JUST HAVE TO FIGURE THIS OUT. BUT QUICKLY.
CORRIGAN... WHAT ARE YOU DOING?
WHAT DOES IT LOOK LIKE?
SHE'S VERY INTERESTED IN ME. I'M FINE WITH THAT.
YOU DO YOUR JOB, I'LL DO MINE.
HNNGH!
ONE MORE. JUST THE ONE IN THE CORNER. CRAZY...
YOU KIDS STAY HERE. I'LL BE RIGHT BACK.
EDRID AKKA?
...WHAT DID YOU SAY?

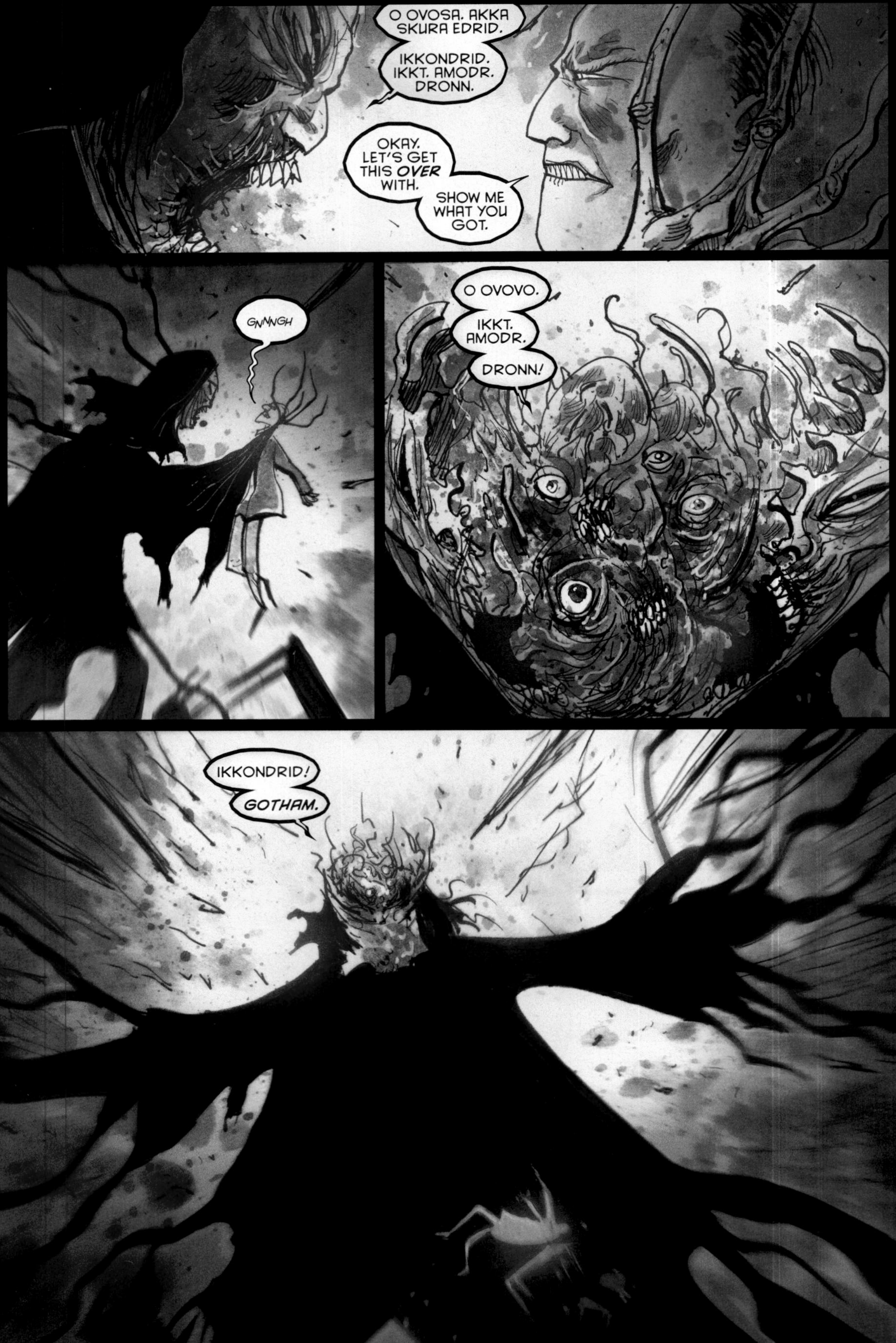
O OVOSA. AKKA SKURA EDRID.
IKKONDRID. IKKT. AMODR. DRONN.
OKAY. LET'S GET THIS OVER WITH.
SHOW ME WHAT YOU GOT.
GNNNGH
O OVOVO.
IKKT. AMODR.
DRONN!
IKKONDRID!
GOTHAM.

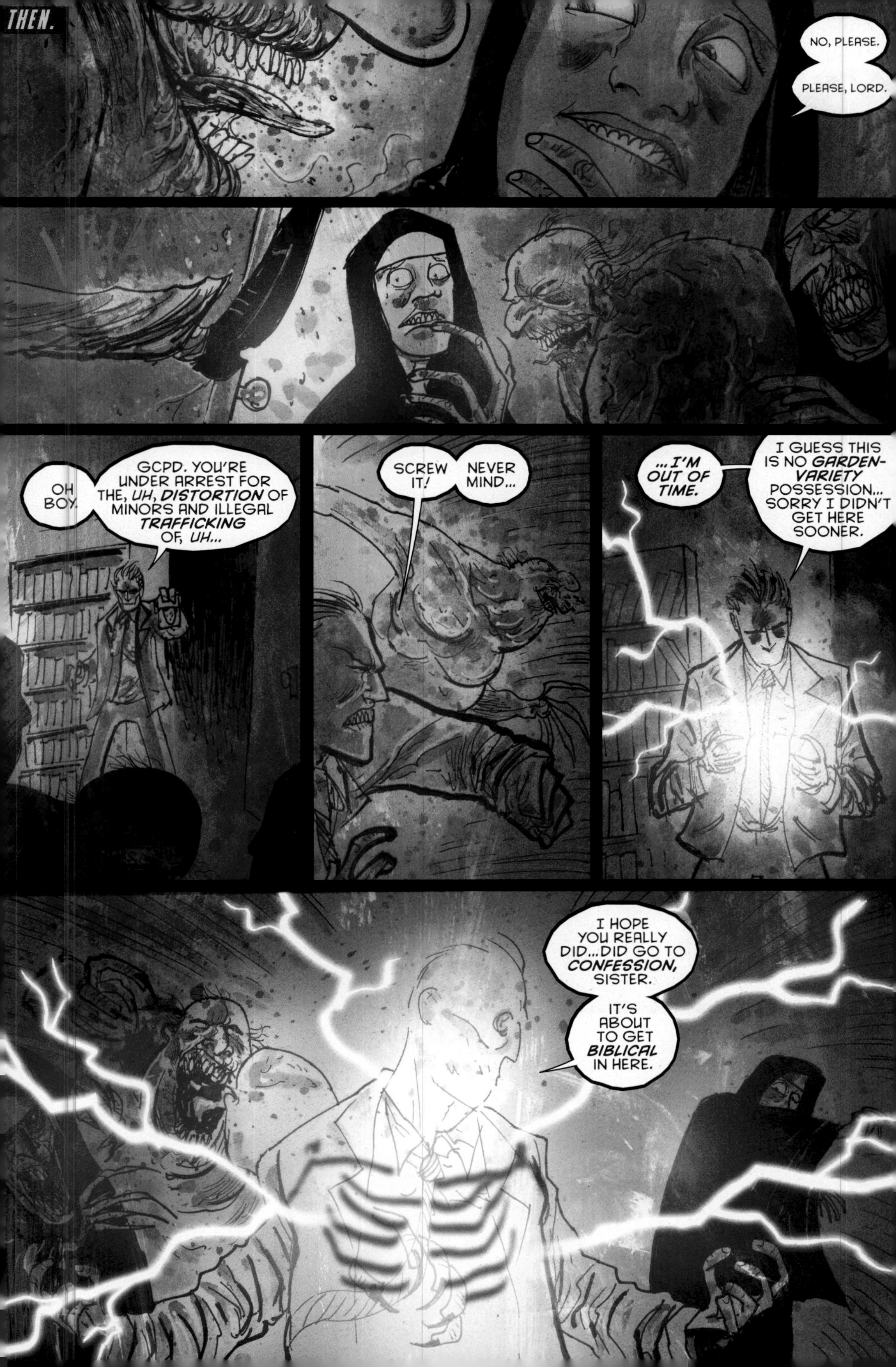
THEN.
NO, PLEASE.
PLEASE, LORD.
OH BOY.
GCPD. YOU'RE UNDER ARREST FOR THE, UH, DISTORTION OF MINORS AND ILLEGAL TRAFFICKING OF, UH...
SCREW IT!
NEVER MIND...
...I'M OUT OF TIME.
I GUESS THIS IS NO GARDEN-VARIETY POSSESSION... SORRY I DIDN'T GET HERE SOONER.
I HOPE YOU REALLY DID...DID GO TO CONFESSION, SISTER.
IT'S ABOUT TO GET BIBLICAL IN HERE.

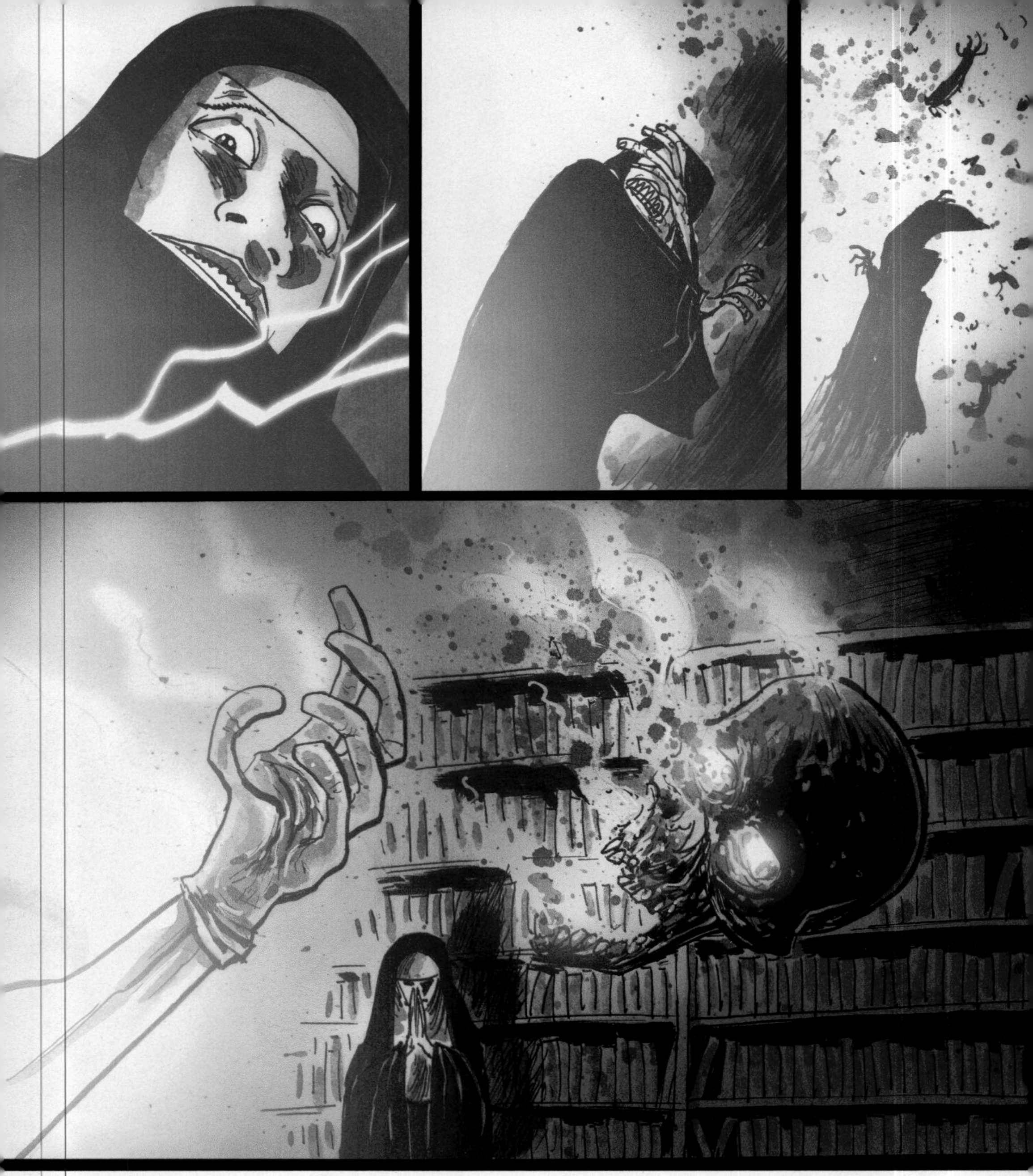

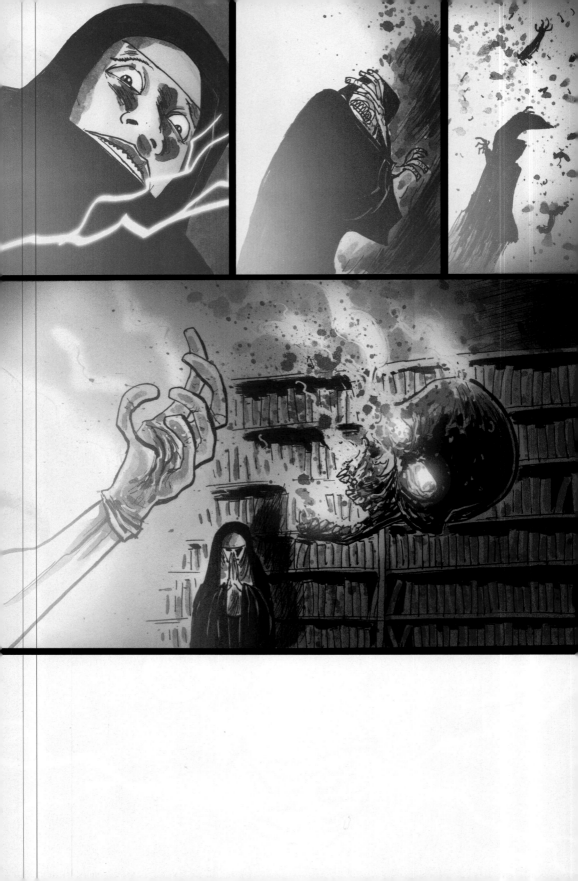

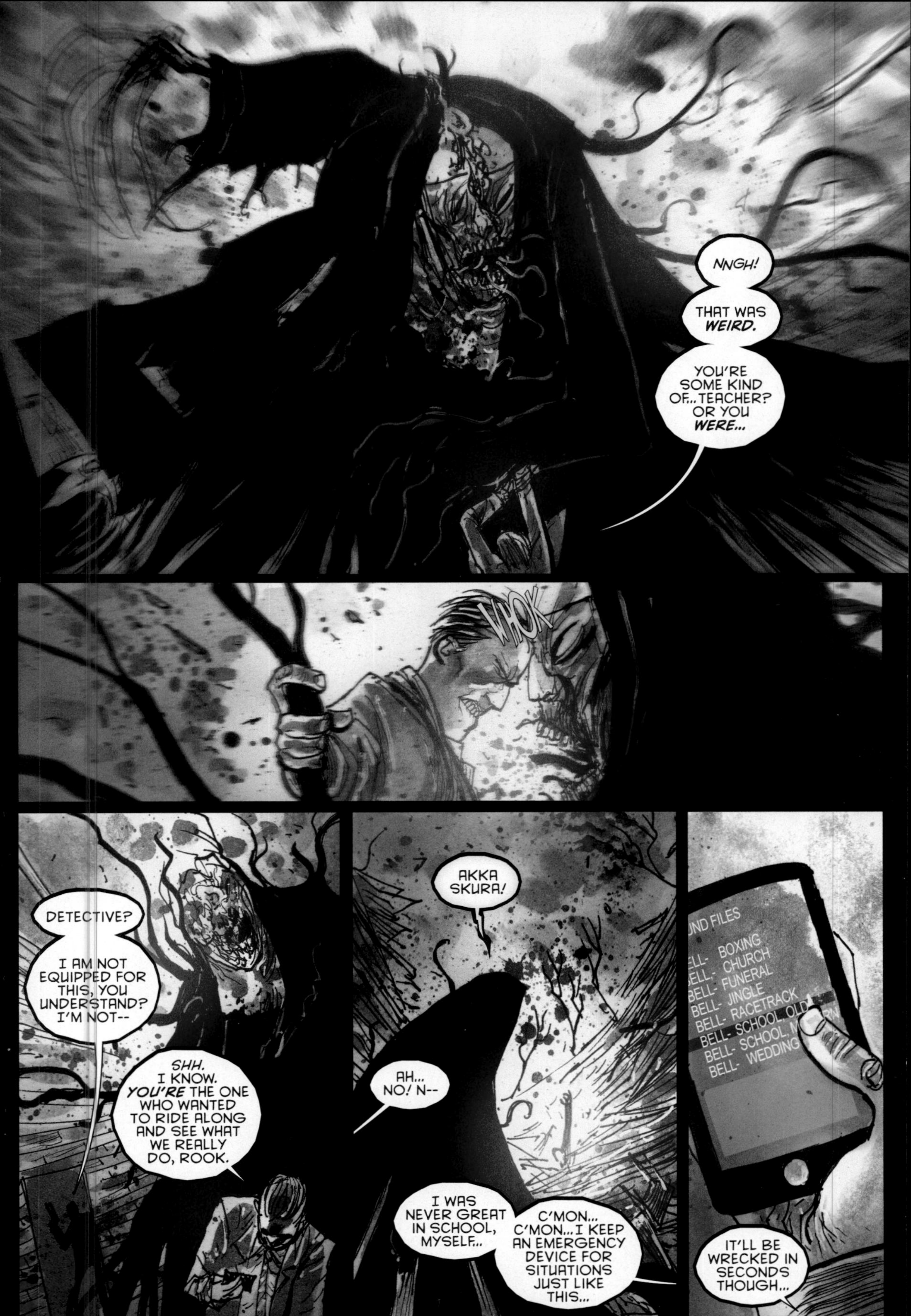
NNGH!
THAT WAS *WEIRD.*
YOU'RE SOME KIND OF... TEACHER? OR YOU *WERE...*
WHOK
DETECTIVE?
I AM NOT EQUIPPED FOR THIS, YOU UNDERSTAND? I'M NOT--
SHH. I KNOW. *YOU'RE* THE ONE WHO WANTED TO RIDE ALONG AND SEE WHAT WE REALLY DO, ROOK.
AKKA SKURA!
AH... NO! N--
I WAS NEVER GREAT IN SCHOOL, MYSELF...
C'MON... C'MON... I KEEP AN EMERGENCY DEVICE FOR SITUATIONS JUST LIKE THIS...
BELL- BOXING
BELL- FUNERAL
BELL- JINGLE
BELL- RACETRACK
IT'LL BE WRECKED IN SECONDS THOUGH...

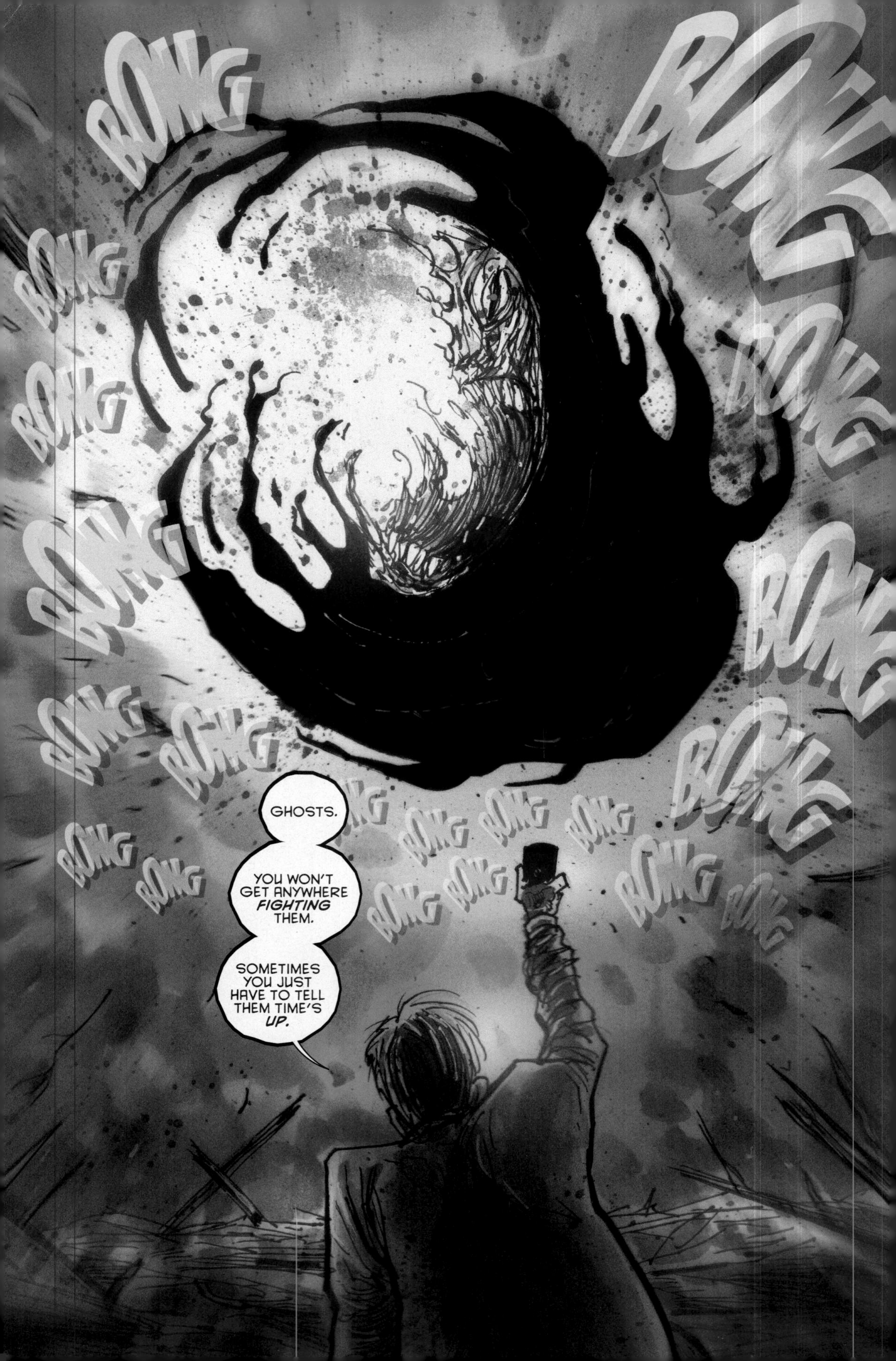
BONG
BONG
BONG
BONG
BONG
GHOSTS.
YOU WON'T GET ANYWHERE *FIGHTING* THEM.
SOMETIMES YOU JUST HAVE TO TELL THEM TIME'S *UP.*

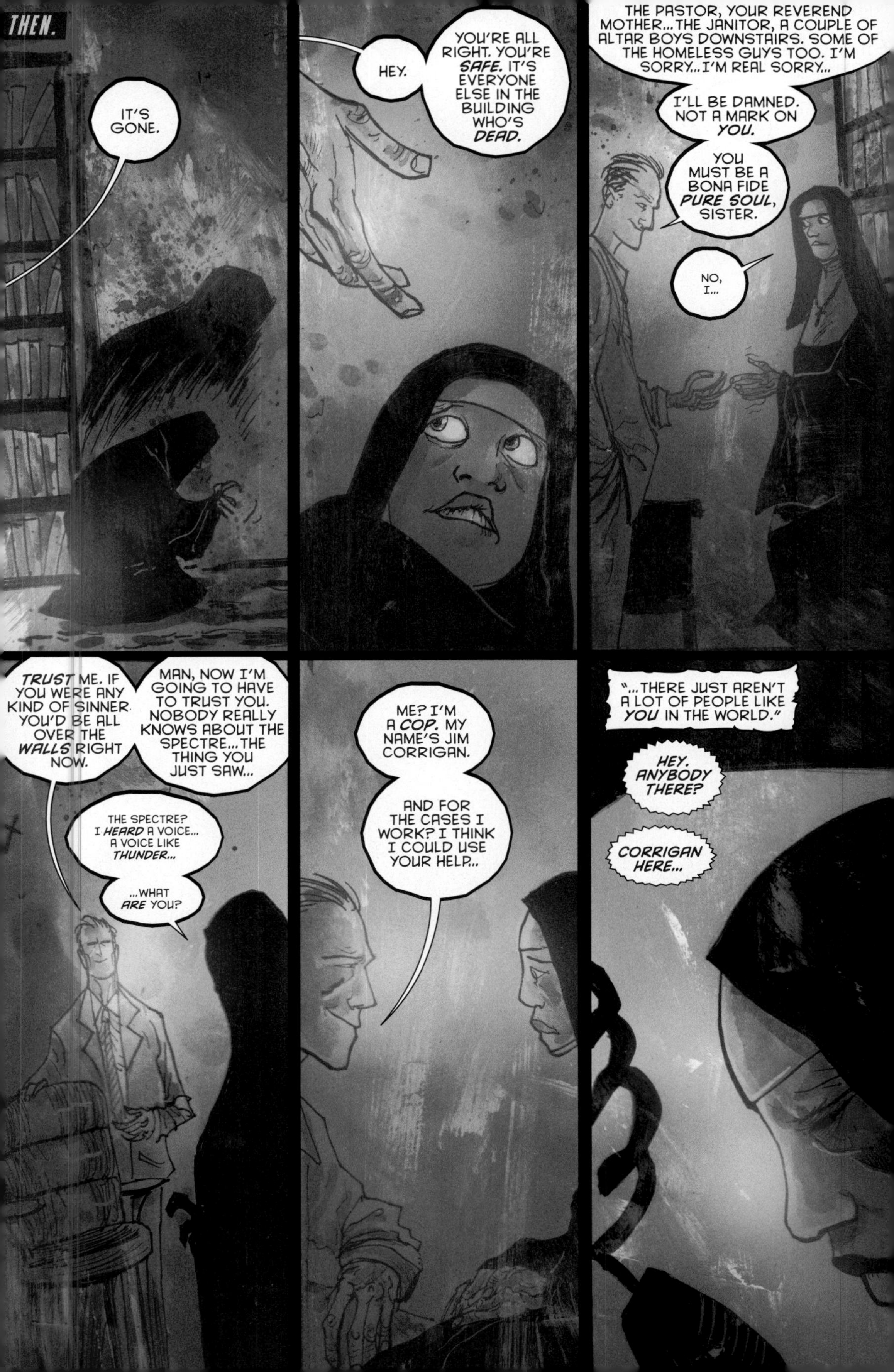
THEN.
IT'S GONE.
HEY.
YOU'RE ALL RIGHT. YOU'RE SAFE. IT'S EVERYONE ELSE IN THE BUILDING WHO'S DEAD.
THE PASTOR, YOUR REVEREND MOTHER... THE JANITOR, A COUPLE OF ALTAR BOYS DOWNSTAIRS. SOME OF THE HOMELESS GUYS TOO. I'M SORRY... I'M REAL SORRY...
I'LL BE DAMNED. NOT A MARK ON YOU.
YOU MUST BE A BONA FIDE PURE SOUL, SISTER.
NO, I...
TRUST ME. IF YOU WERE ANY KIND OF SINNER YOU'D BE ALL OVER THE WALLS RIGHT NOW.
MAN, NOW I'M GOING TO HAVE TO TRUST YOU. NOBODY REALLY KNOWS ABOUT THE SPECTRE... THE THING YOU JUST SAW...
THE SPECTRE? I HEARD A VOICE... A VOICE LIKE THUNDER...
...WHAT ARE YOU?
ME? I'M A COP. MY NAME'S JIM CORRIGAN.
AND FOR THE CASES I WORK? I THINK I COULD USE YOUR HELP...
"...THERE JUST AREN'T A LOT OF PEOPLE LIKE YOU IN THE WORLD."
HEY. ANYBODY THERE?
CORRIGAN HERE...

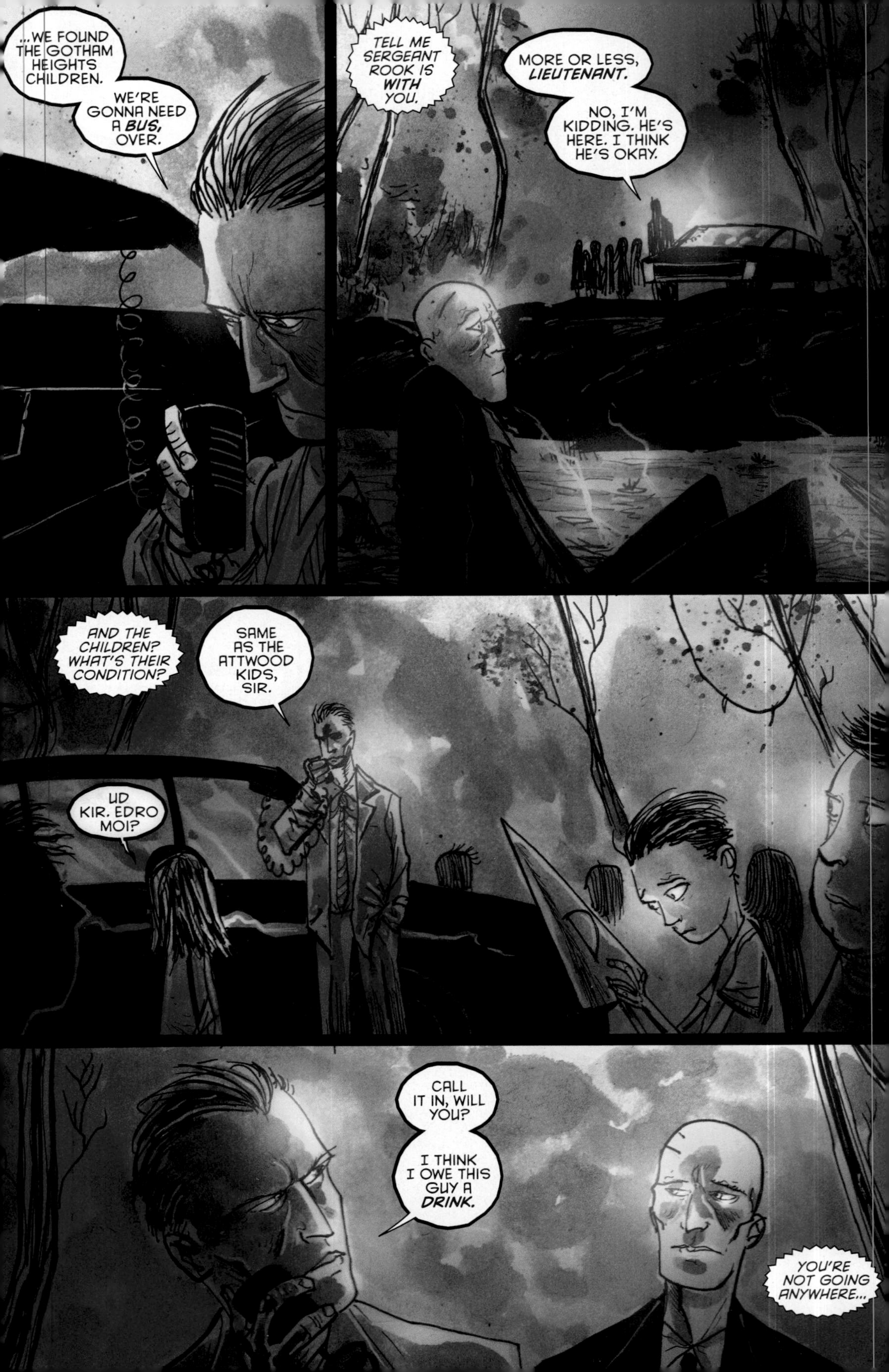
...WE FOUND THE GOTHAM HEIGHTS CHILDREN.
WE'RE GONNA NEED A BUS, OVER.
TELL ME SERGEANT ROOK IS WITH YOU.
MORE OR LESS, LIEUTENANT.
NO, I'M KIDDING. HE'S HERE. I THINK HE'S OKAY.
AND THE CHILDREN? WHAT'S THEIR CONDITION?
SAME AS THE ATTWOOD KIDS, SIR.
UD KIR. EDRO MOI?
CALL IT IN, WILL YOU?
I THINK I OWE THIS GUY A DRINK.
YOU'RE NOT GOING ANYWHERE...

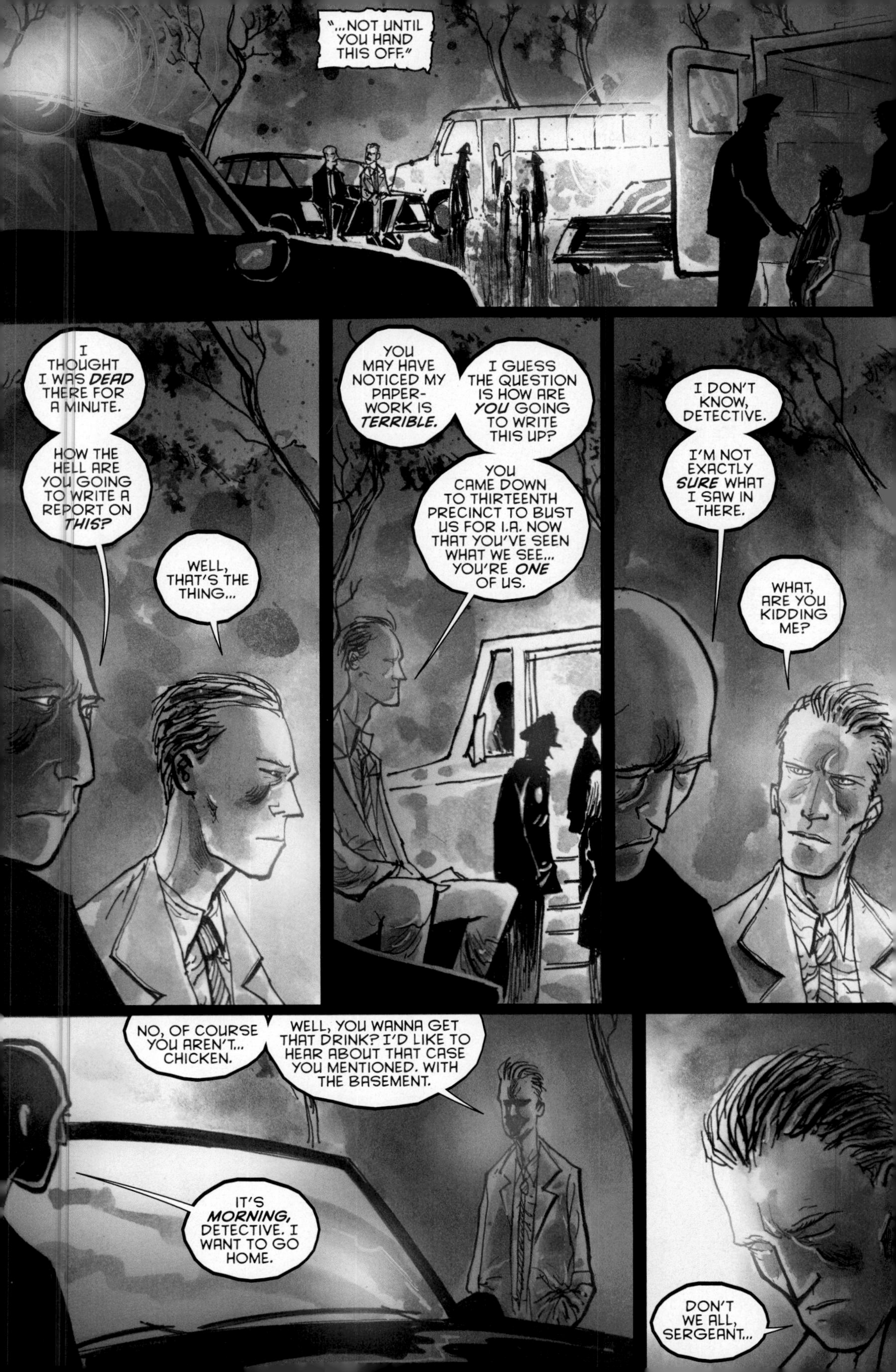
"...NOT UNTIL YOU HAND THIS OFF."
I THOUGHT I WAS DEAD THERE FOR A MINUTE.
HOW THE HELL ARE YOU GOING TO WRITE A REPORT ON THIS?
WELL, THAT'S THE THING...
YOU MAY HAVE NOTICED MY PAPER-WORK IS TERRIBLE.
I GUESS THE QUESTION IS HOW ARE YOU GOING TO WRITE THIS UP?
YOU CAME DOWN TO THIRTEENTH PRECINCT TO BUST US FOR I.A. NOW THAT YOU'VE SEEN WHAT WE SEE... YOU'RE ONE OF US.
I DON'T KNOW, DETECTIVE.
I'M NOT EXACTLY SURE WHAT I SAW IN THERE.
WHAT, ARE YOU KIDDING ME?
NO, OF COURSE YOU AREN'T... CHICKEN.
WELL, YOU WANNA GET THAT DRINK? I'D LIKE TO HEAR ABOUT THAT CASE YOU MENTIONED. WITH THE BASEMENT.
IT'S MORNING, DETECTIVE. I WANT TO GO HOME.
DON'T WE ALL, SERGEANT...

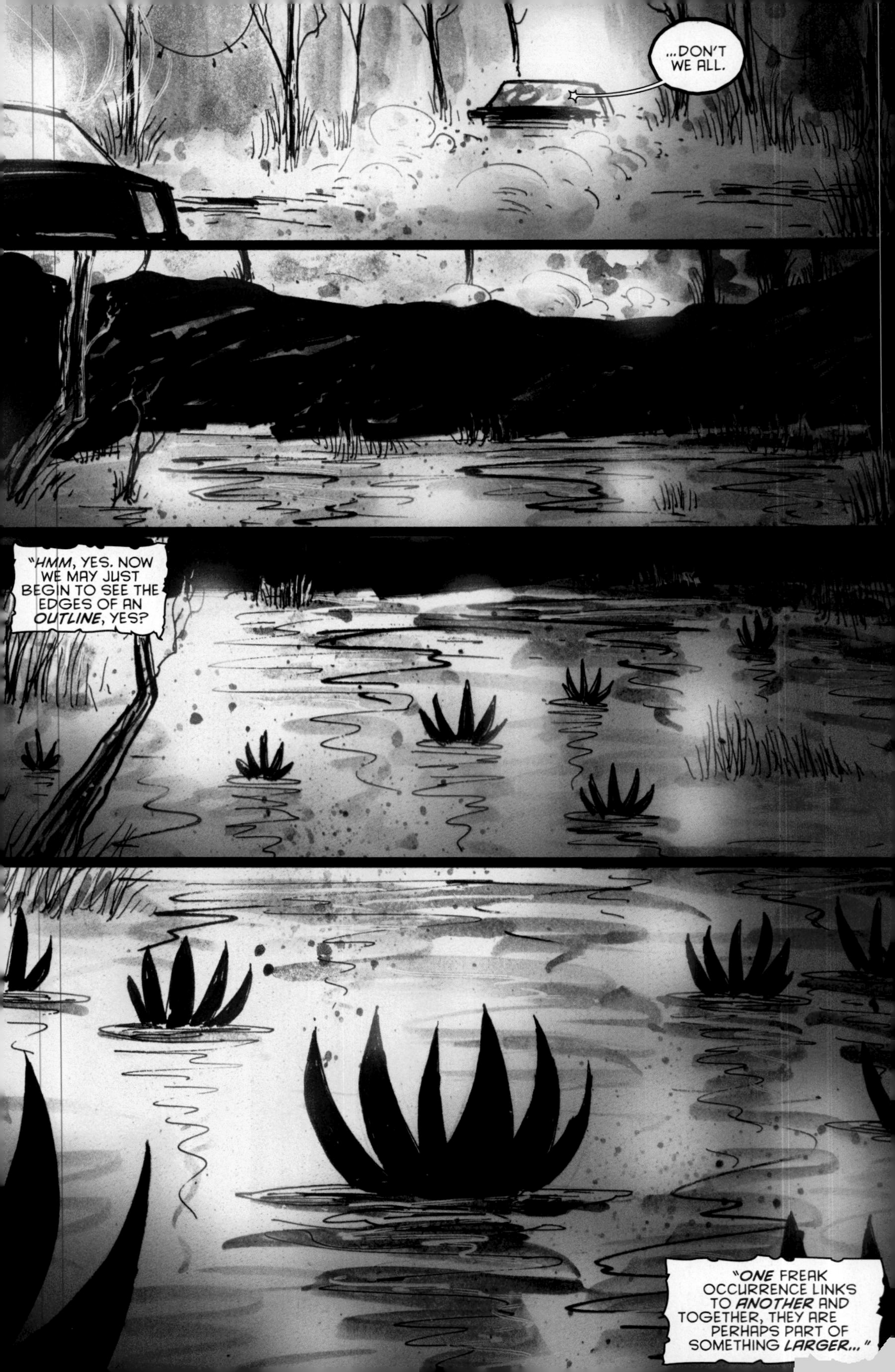
...DON'T WE ALL.
"HMM, YES. NOW WE MAY JUST BEGIN TO SEE THE EDGES OF AN OUTLINE, YES?
"ONE FREAK OCCURRENCE LINKS TO ANOTHER AND TOGETHER, THEY ARE PERHAPS PART OF SOMETHING LARGER..."

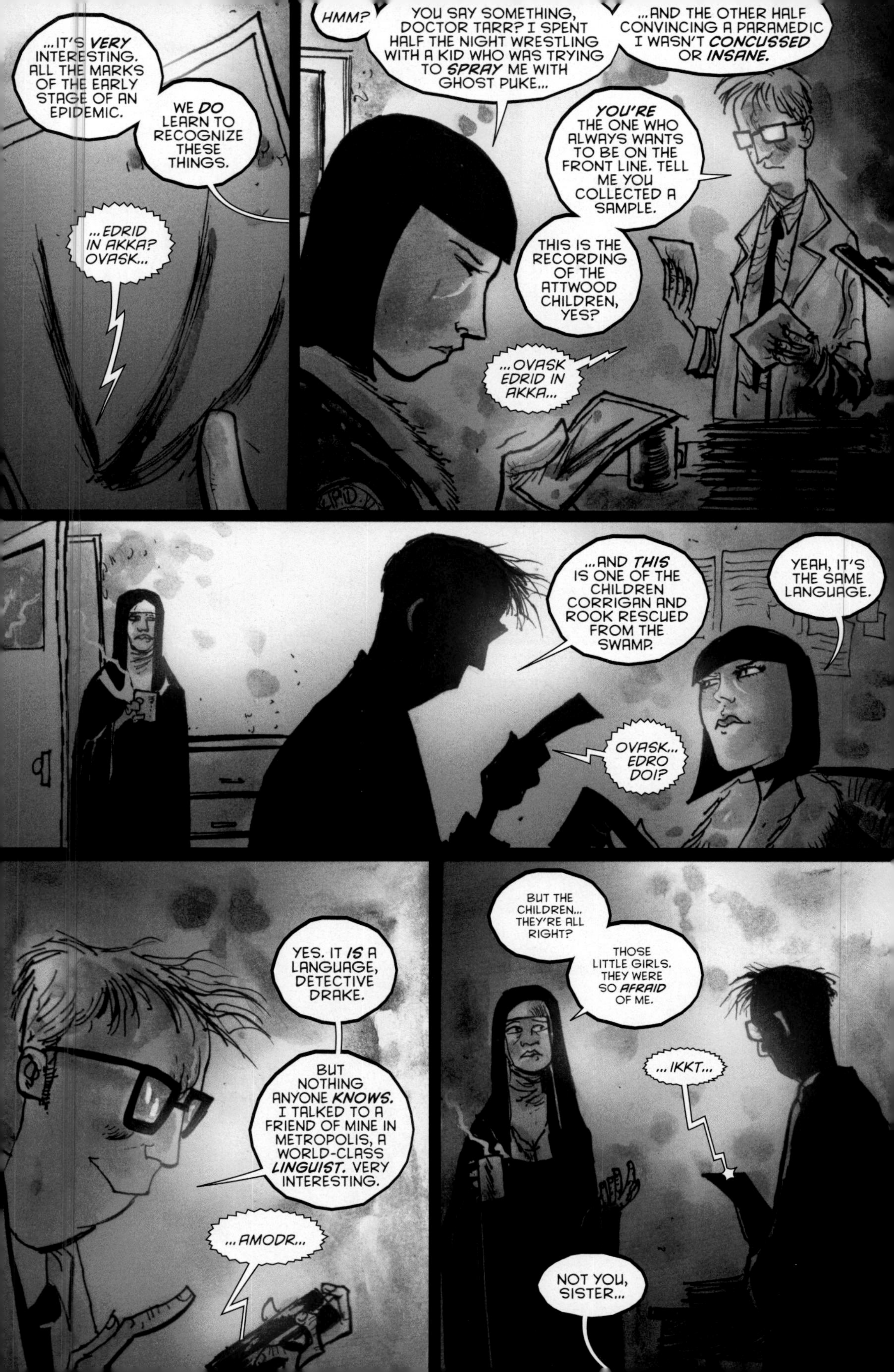
...IT'S VERY INTERESTING. ALL THE MARKS OF THE EARLY STAGE OF AN EPIDEMIC.
WE DO LEARN TO RECOGNIZE THESE THINGS.
...EDRID IN AKKA? OVASK...
HMM?
YOU SAY SOMETHING, DOCTOR TARR? I SPENT HALF THE NIGHT WRESTLING WITH A KID WHO WAS TRYING TO SPRAY ME WITH GHOST PUKE...
...AND THE OTHER HALF CONVINCING A PARAMEDIC I WASN'T CONCUSSED OR INSANE.
YOU'RE THE ONE WHO ALWAYS WANTS TO BE ON THE FRONT LINE. TELL ME YOU COLLECTED A SAMPLE.
THIS IS THE RECORDING OF THE ATTWOOD CHILDREN, YES?
...OVASK EDRID IN AKKA...
...AND THIS IS ONE OF THE CHILDREN CORRIGAN AND ROOK RESCUED FROM THE SWAMP.
YEAH, IT'S THE SAME LANGUAGE.
OVASK... EDRO DOI?
YES. IT IS A LANGUAGE, DETECTIVE DRAKE.
BUT NOTHING ANYONE KNOWS. I TALKED TO A FRIEND OF MINE IN METROPOLIS, A WORLD-CLASS LINGUIST. VERY INTERESTING.
...AMODR...
BUT THE CHILDREN... THEY'RE ALL RIGHT?
THOSE LITTLE GIRLS. THEY WERE SO AFRAID OF ME.
...IKKT...
NOT YOU, SISTER...

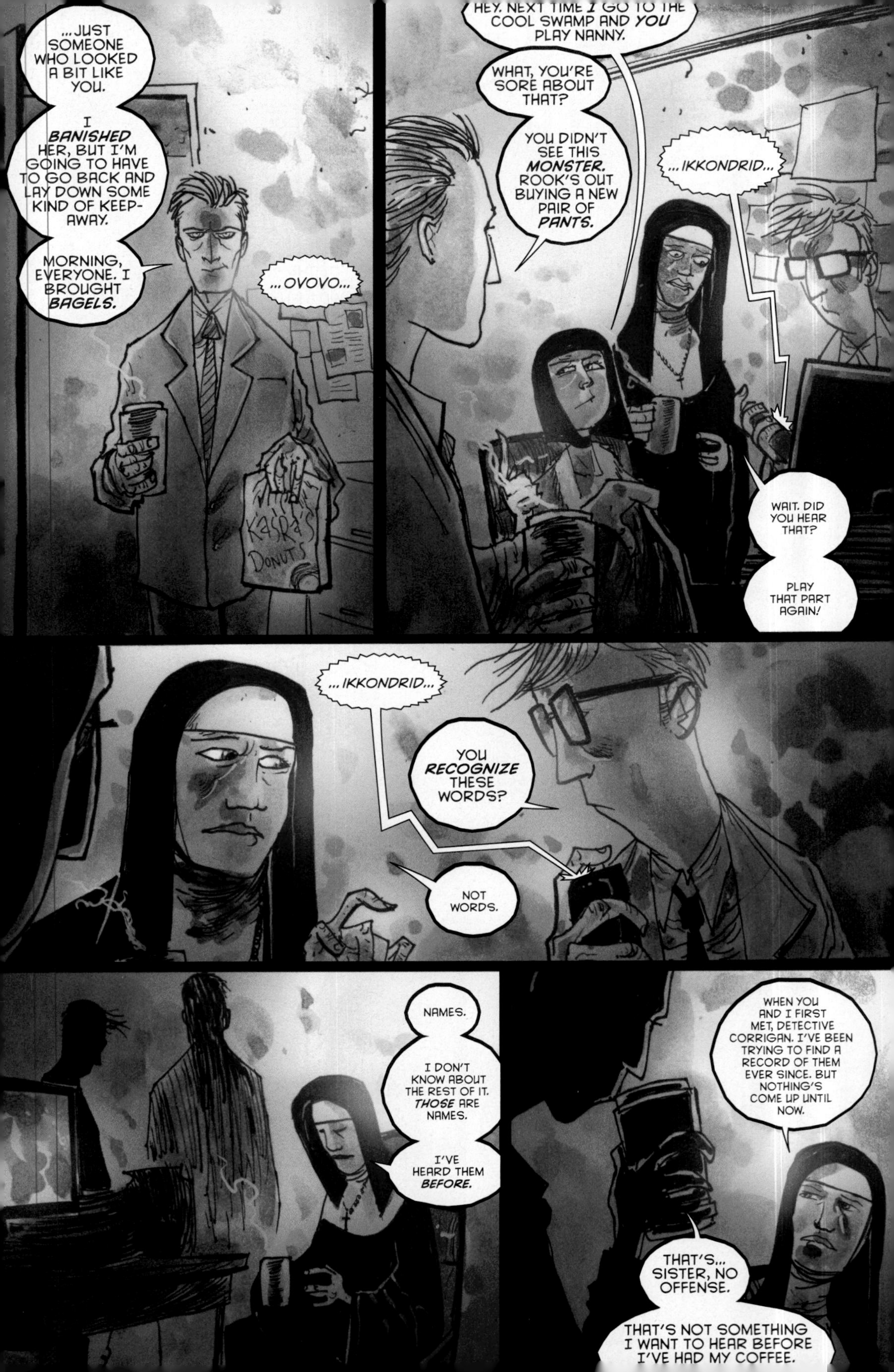

...JUST SOMEONE WHO LOOKED A BIT LIKE YOU.
I BANISHED HER, BUT I'M GOING TO HAVE TO GO BACK AND LAY DOWN SOME KIND OF KEEP-AWAY.
MORNING, EVERYONE. I BROUGHT BAGELS.
...OVOVO...
KASRA'S DONUTS
HEY. NEXT TIME I GO TO THE COOL SWAMP AND YOU PLAY NANNY.
WHAT, YOU'RE SORE ABOUT THAT?
YOU DIDN'T SEE THIS MONSTER. ROOK'S OUT BUYING A NEW PAIR OF PANTS.
...IKKONDRID...
WAIT. DID YOU HEAR THAT?
PLAY THAT PART AGAIN!
...IKKONDRID...
YOU RECOGNIZE THESE WORDS?
NOT WORDS.
NAMES.
I DON'T KNOW ABOUT THE REST OF IT. THOSE ARE NAMES.
I'VE HEARD THEM BEFORE.
WHEN YOU AND I FIRST MET, DETECTIVE CORRIGAN. I'VE BEEN TRYING TO FIND A RECORD OF THEM EVER SINCE. BUT NOTHING'S COME UP UNTIL NOW.
THAT'S... SISTER, NO OFFENSE.
THAT'S NOT SOMETHING I WANT TO HEAR BEFORE I'VE HAD MY COFFEE.

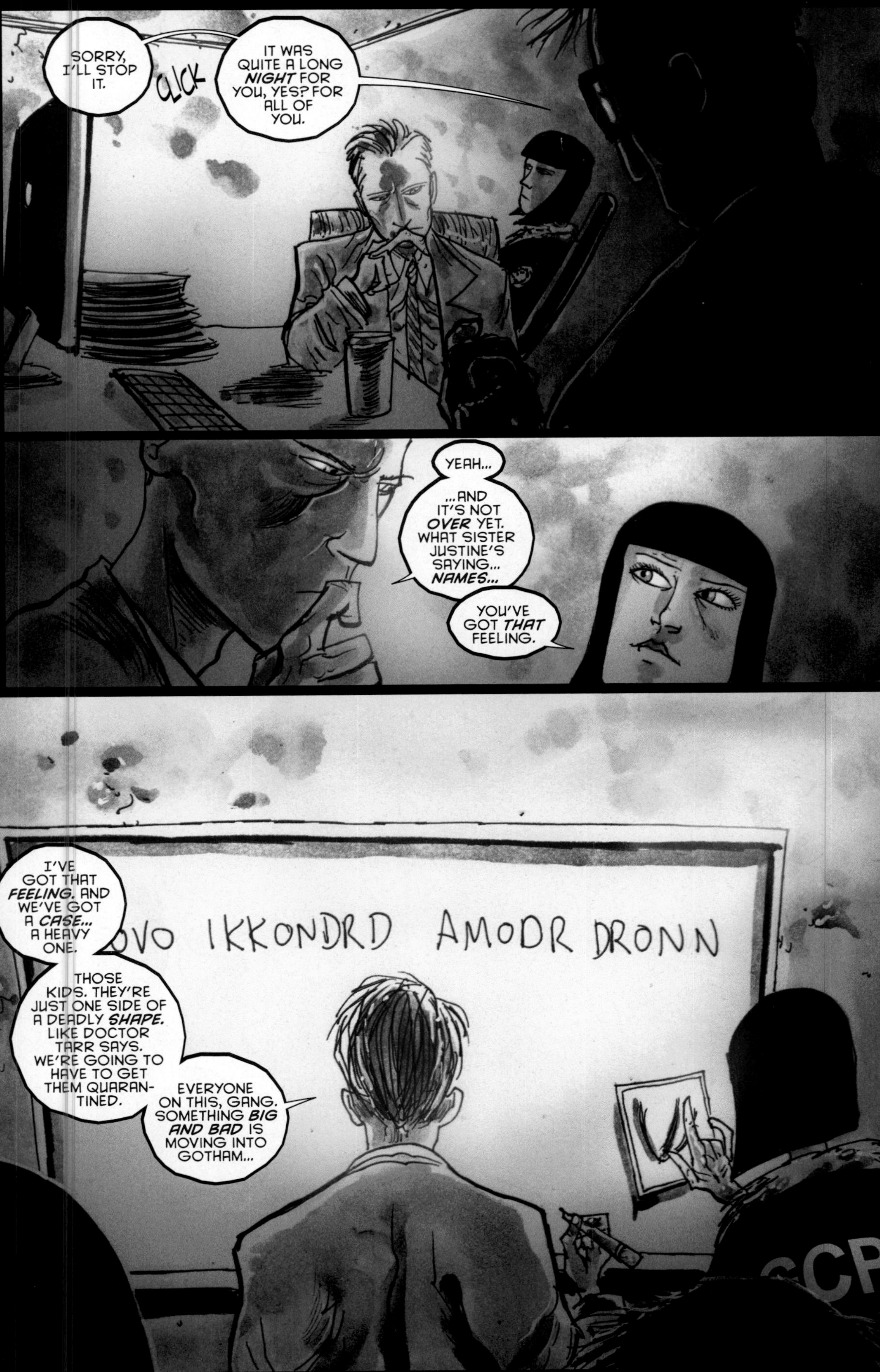
SORRY, I'LL STOP IT.
CLICK
IT WAS QUITE A LONG NIGHT FOR YOU, YES? FOR ALL OF YOU.
YEAH...
...AND IT'S NOT OVER YET. WHAT SISTER JUSTINE'S SAYING... NAMES...
YOU'VE GOT THAT FEELING.
I'VE GOT THAT FEELING. AND WE'VE GOT A CASE... A HEAVY ONE.
OVO IKKONDRD AMODR DRONN
THOSE KIDS. THEY'RE JUST ONE SIDE OF A DEADLY SHAPE. LIKE DOCTOR TARR SAYS. WE'RE GOING TO HAVE TO GET THEM QUARANTINED.
EVERYONE ON THIS, GANG. SOMETHING BIG AND BAD IS MOVING INTO GOTHAM...
GCPD

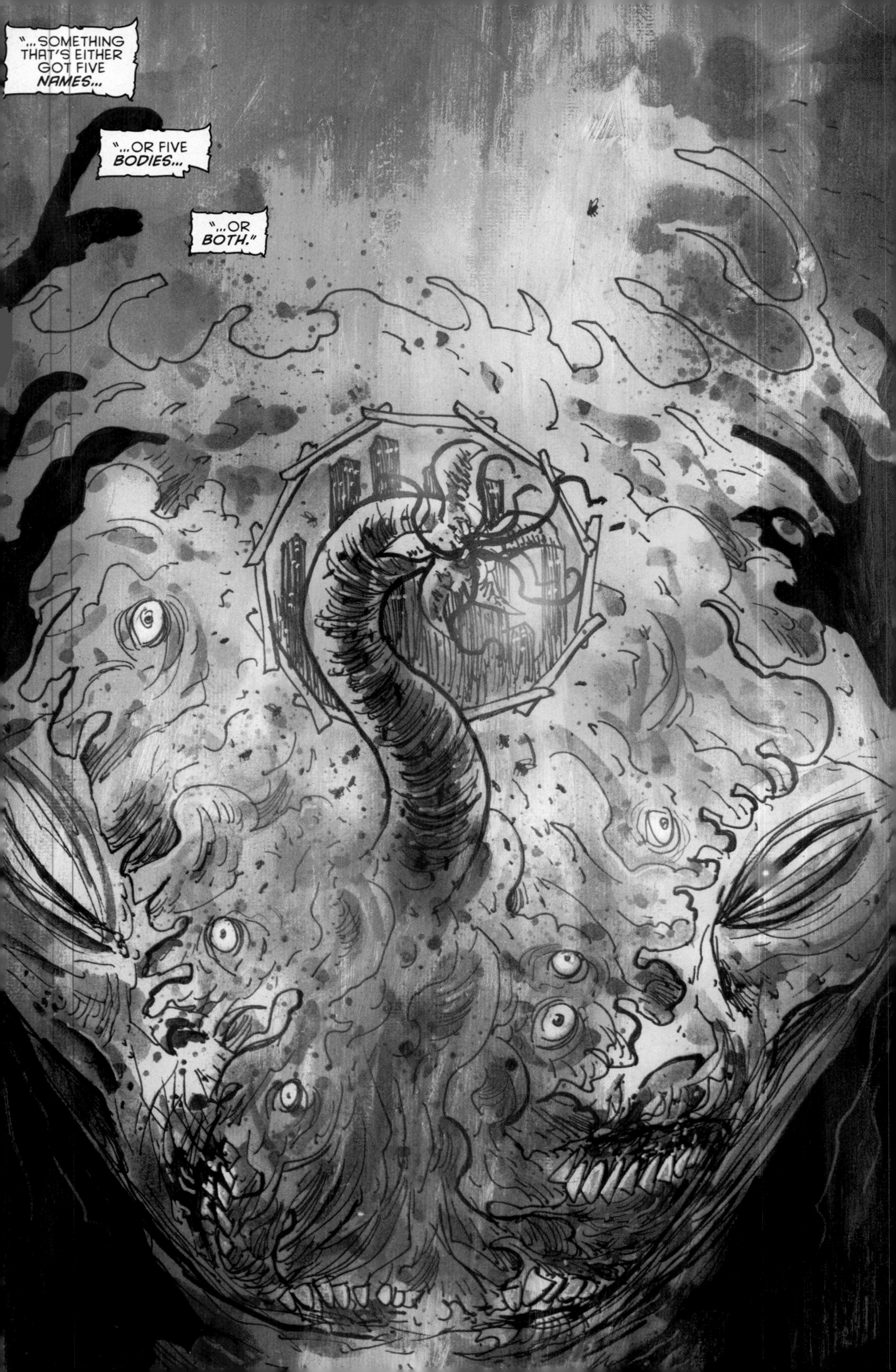
"...SOMETHING THAT'S EITHER GOT FIVE *NAMES*...
"...OR FIVE *BODIES*...
"...OR *BOTH*."

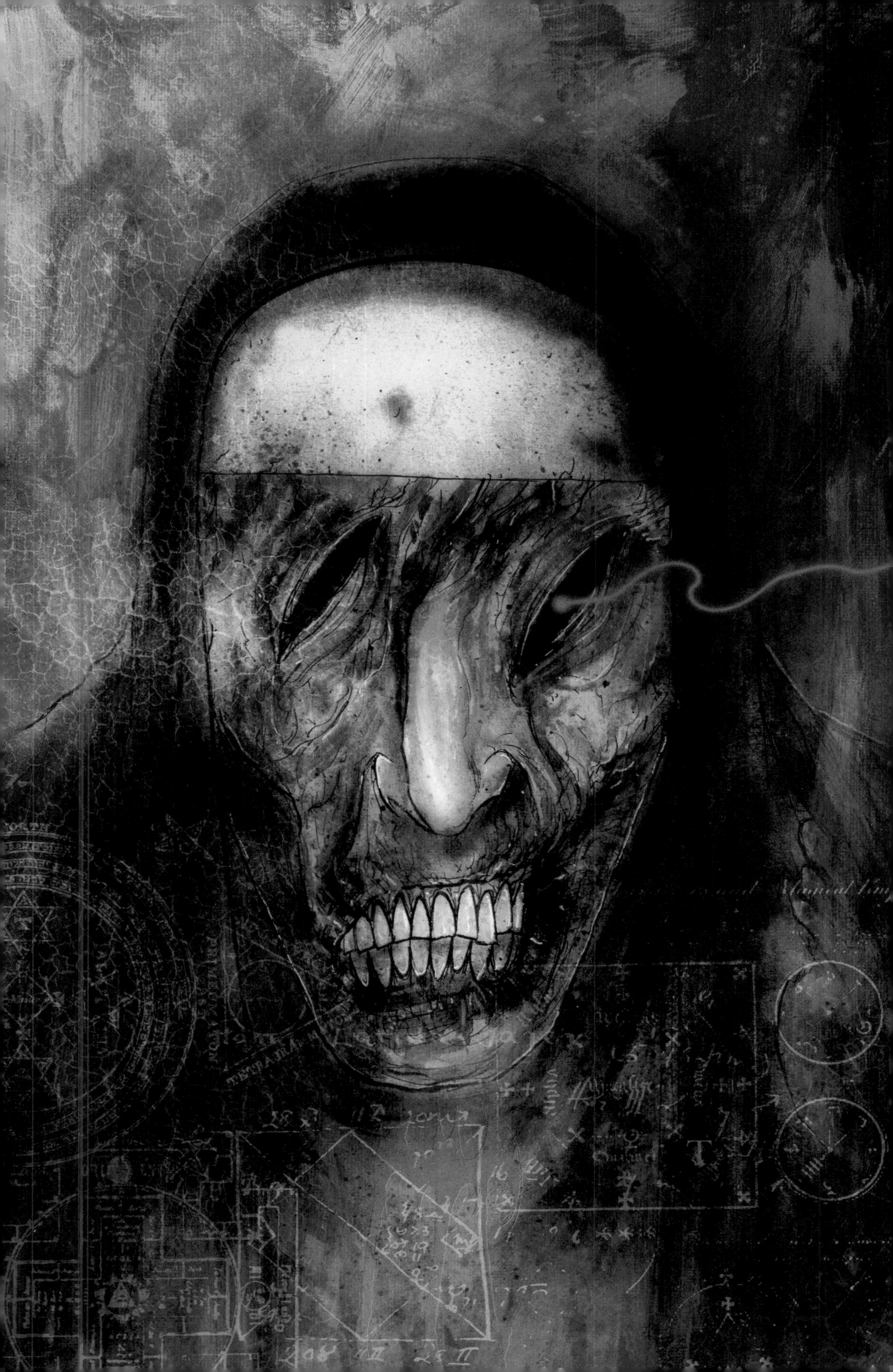

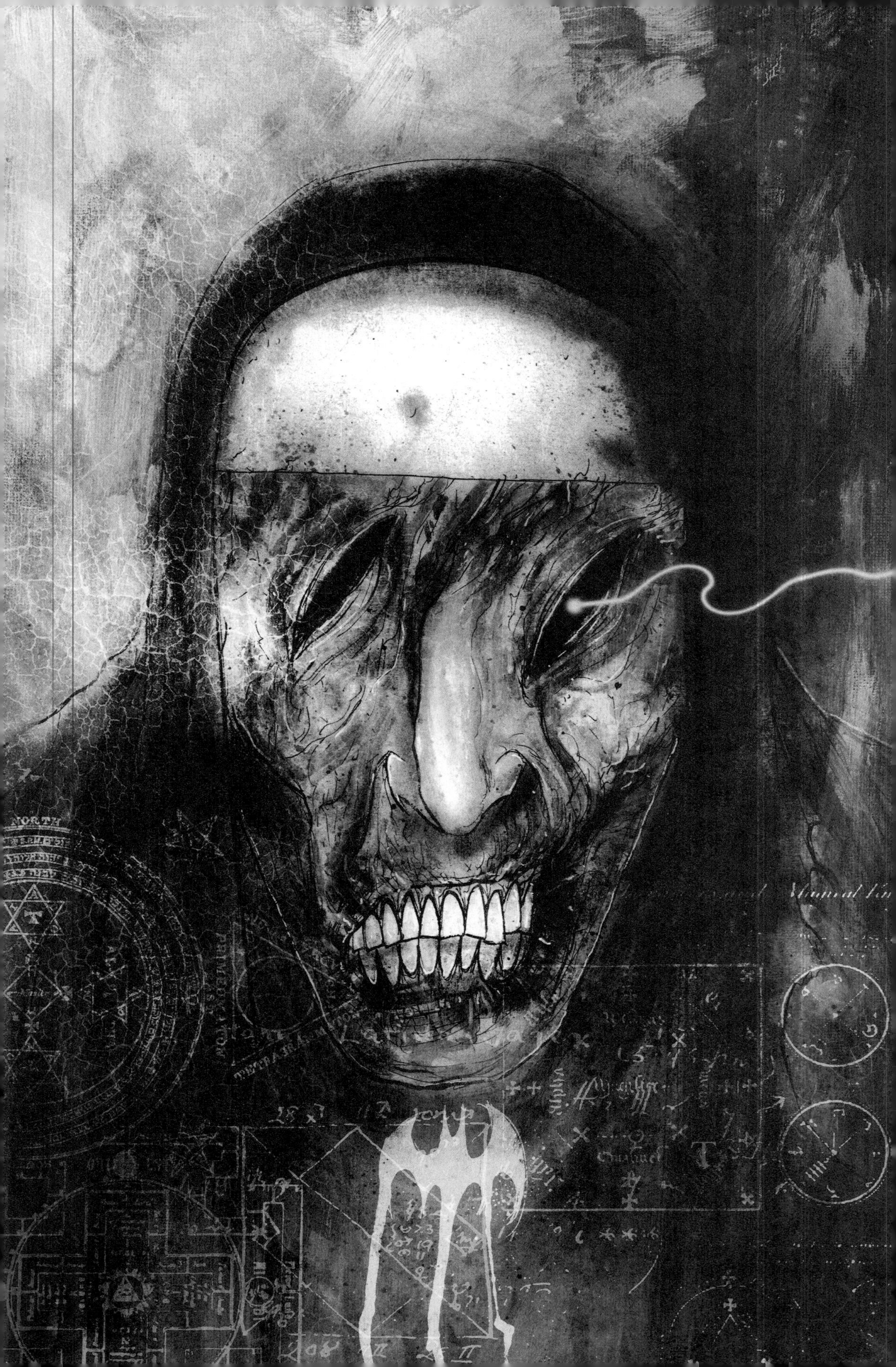

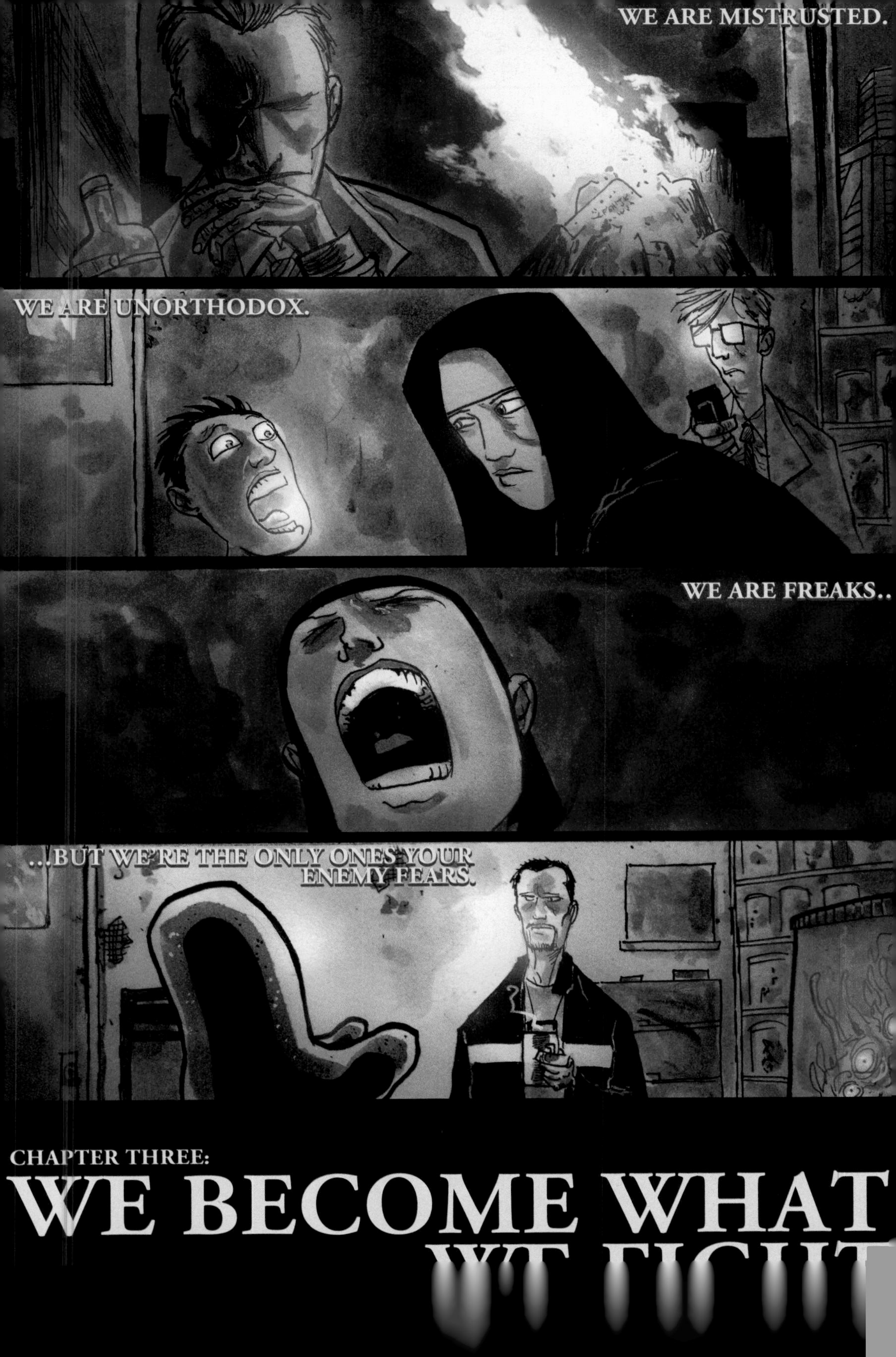
WE ARE MISTRUSTED.
WE ARE UNORTHODOX.
WE ARE FREAKS..
...BUT WE'RE THE ONLY ONES YOUR ENEMY FEARS.

CHAPTER THREE:

WE BECOME WHAT WE FIGHT

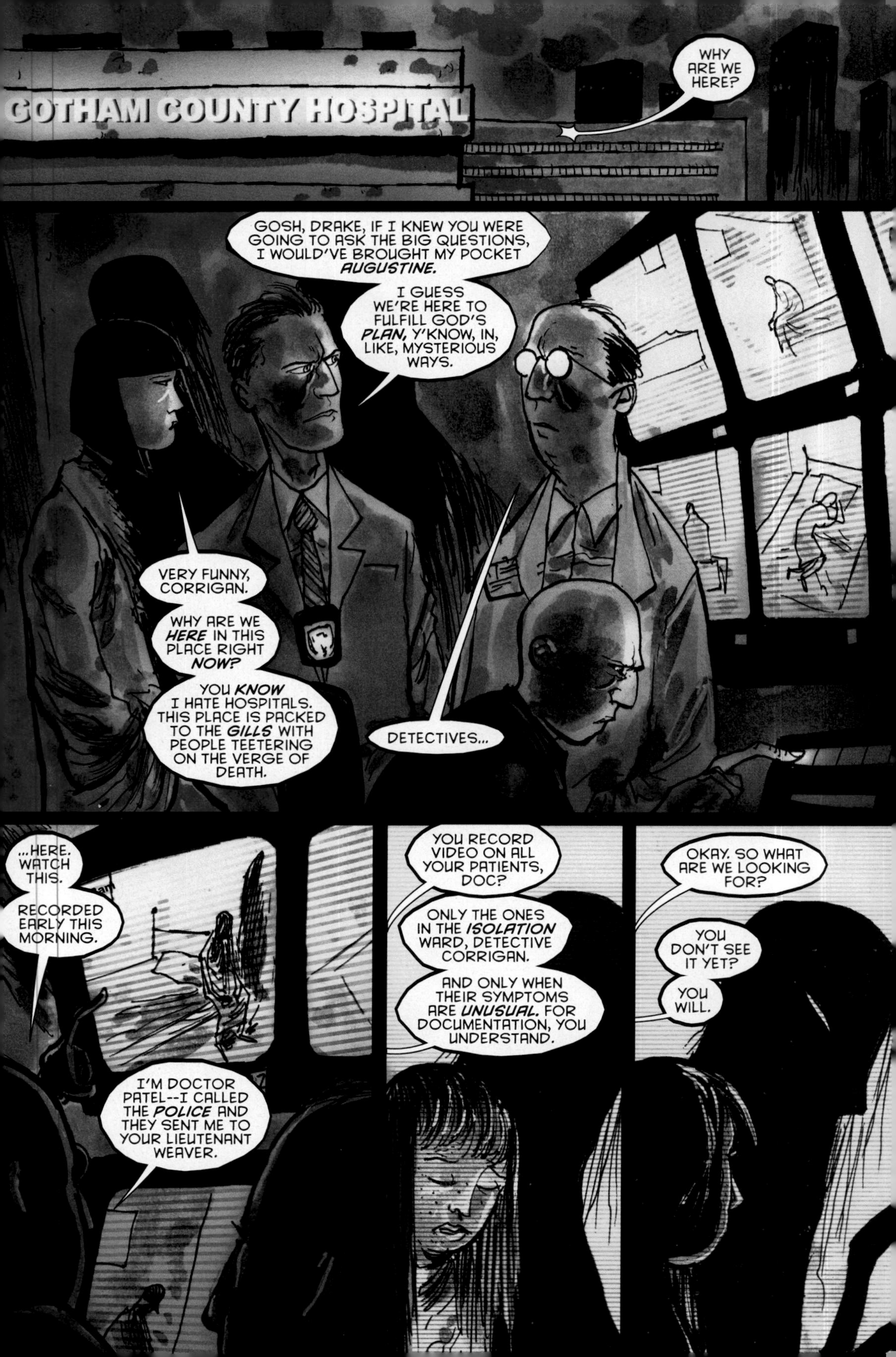
GOTHAM COUNTY HOSPITAL
WHY ARE WE HERE?
GOSH, DRAKE, IF I KNEW YOU WERE GOING TO ASK THE BIG QUESTIONS, I WOULD'VE BROUGHT MY POCKET AUGUSTINE.
I GUESS WE'RE HERE TO FULFILL GOD'S PLAN, Y'KNOW, IN, LIKE, MYSTERIOUS WAYS.
VERY FUNNY, CORRIGAN.
WHY ARE WE HERE IN THIS PLACE RIGHT NOW?
YOU KNOW I HATE HOSPITALS. THIS PLACE IS PACKED TO THE GILLS WITH PEOPLE TEETERING ON THE VERGE OF DEATH.
DETECTIVES...
...HERE. WATCH THIS.
RECORDED EARLY THIS MORNING.
I'M DOCTOR PATEL--I CALLED THE POLICE AND THEY SENT ME TO YOUR LIEUTENANT WEAVER.
YOU RECORD VIDEO ON ALL YOUR PATIENTS, DOC?
ONLY THE ONES IN THE ISOLATION WARD, DETECTIVE CORRIGAN.
AND ONLY WHEN THEIR SYMPTOMS ARE UNUSUAL. FOR DOCUMENTATION, YOU UNDERSTAND.
OKAY. SO WHAT ARE WE LOOKING FOR?
YOU DON'T SEE IT YET?
YOU WILL.

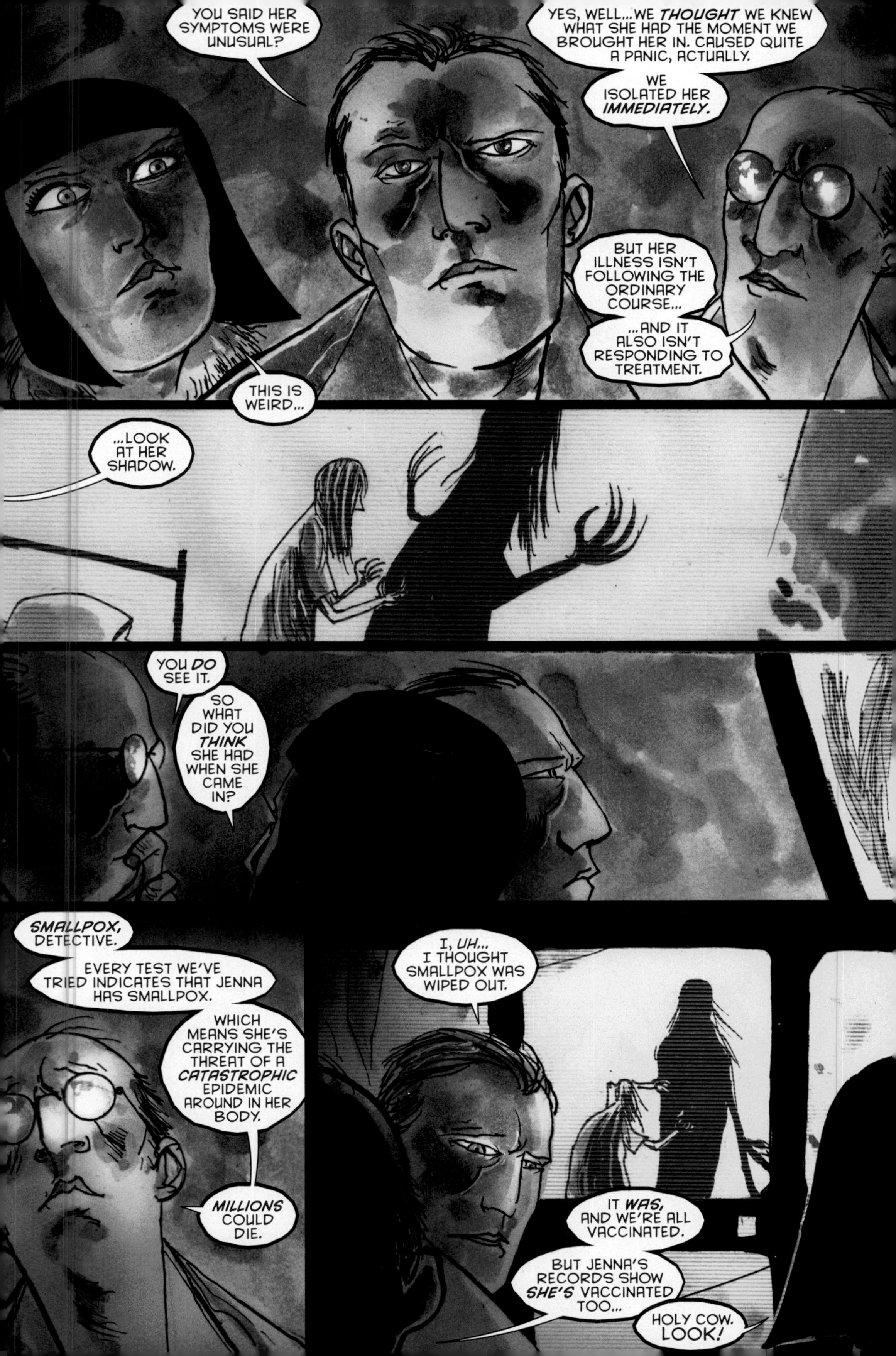
YOU SAID HER SYMPTOMS WERE UNUSUAL?
YES, WELL...WE THOUGHT WE KNEW WHAT SHE HAD THE MOMENT WE BROUGHT HER IN. CAUSED QUITE A PANIC, ACTUALLY.
WE ISOLATED HER IMMEDIATELY.
BUT HER ILLNESS ISN'T FOLLOWING THE ORDINARY COURSE...
...AND IT ALSO ISN'T RESPONDING TO TREATMENT.
THIS IS WEIRD...
...LOOK AT HER SHADOW.
YOU DO SEE IT.
SO WHAT DID YOU THINK SHE HAD WHEN SHE CAME IN?
SMALLPOX, DETECTIVE.
EVERY TEST WE'VE TRIED INDICATES THAT JENNA HAS SMALLPOX.
WHICH MEANS SHE'S CARRYING THE THREAT OF A CATASTROPHIC EPIDEMIC AROUND IN HER BODY.
MILLIONS COULD DIE.
I, UH... I THOUGHT SMALLPOX WAS WIPED OUT.
IT WAS, AND WE'RE ALL VACCINATED.
BUT JENNA'S RECORDS SHOW SHE'S VACCINATED TOO...
HOLY COW. LOOK!

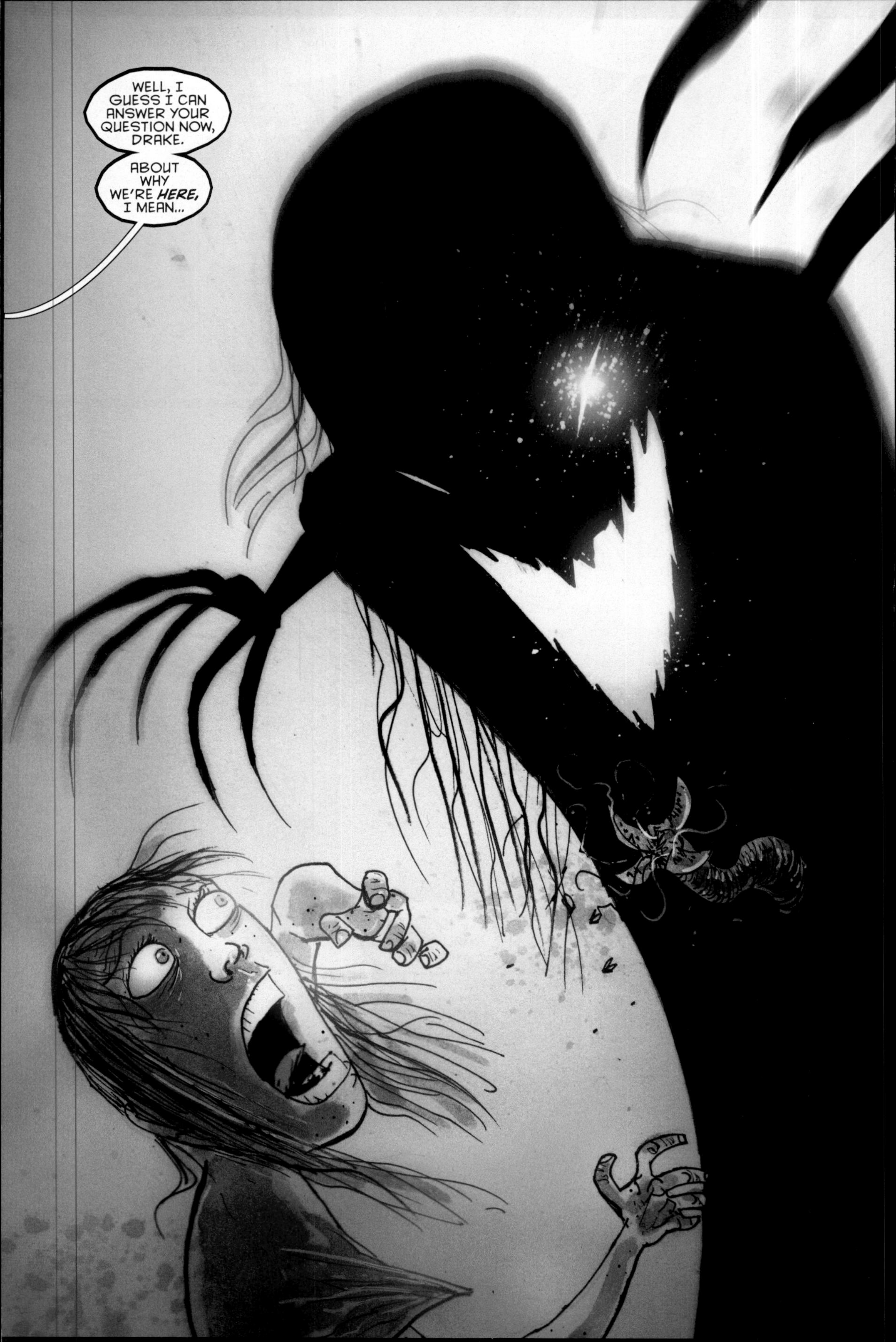
WELL, I GUESS I CAN ANSWER YOUR QUESTION NOW, DRAKE.
ABOUT WHY WE'RE *HERE,* I MEAN...

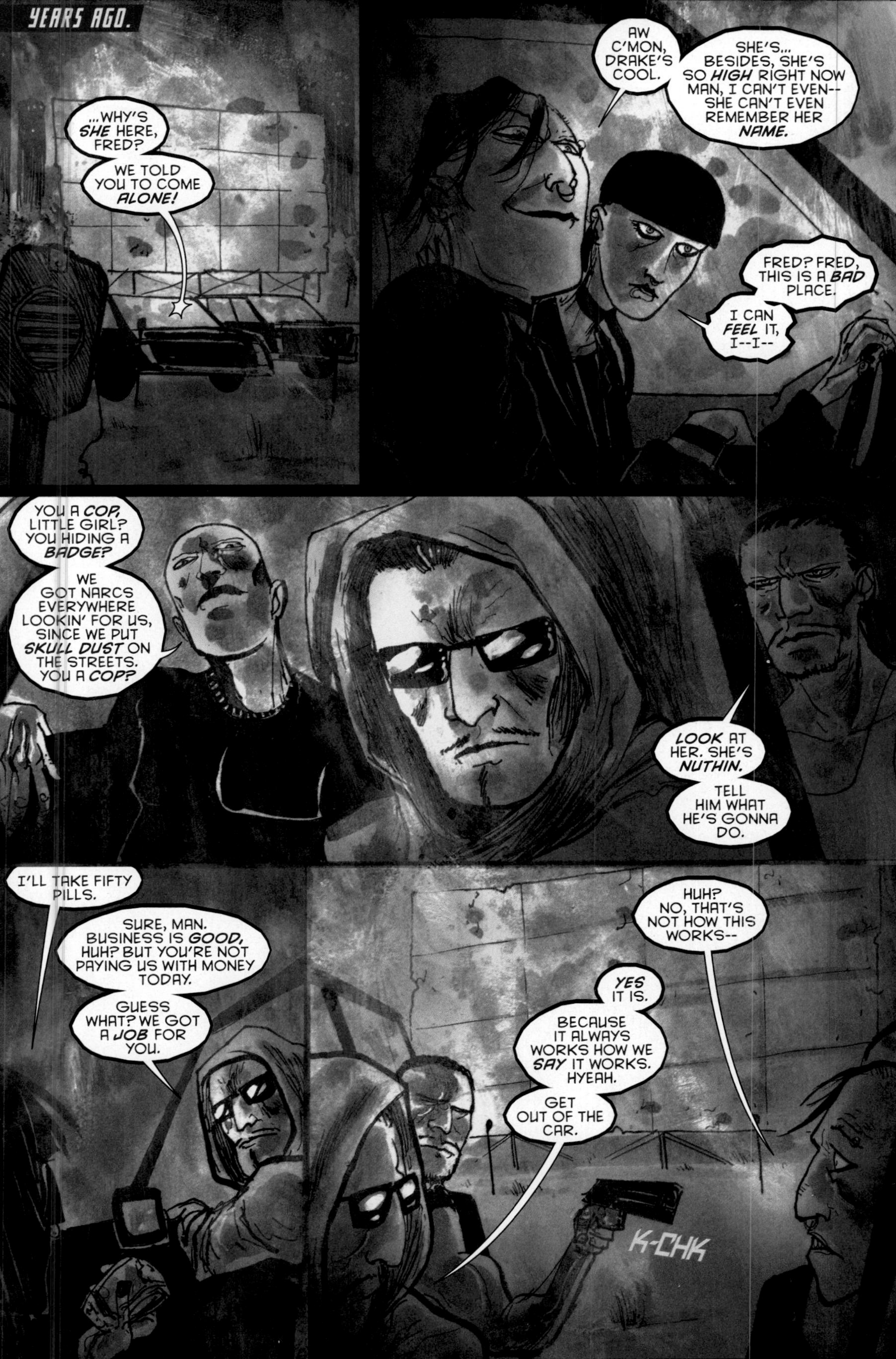
YEARS AGO.
...WHY'S SHE HERE, FRED?
WE TOLD YOU TO COME ALONE!
AW C'MON, DRAKE'S COOL.
SHE'S... BESIDES, SHE'S SO HIGH RIGHT NOW MAN, I CAN'T EVEN-- SHE CAN'T EVEN REMEMBER HER NAME.
FRED? FRED, THIS IS A BAD PLACE.
I CAN FEEL IT, I--I--
YOU A COP, LITTLE GIRL? YOU HIDING A BADGE?
WE GOT NARCS EVERYWHERE LOOKIN' FOR US, SINCE WE PUT SKULL DUST ON THE STREETS. YOU A COP?
LOOK AT HER. SHE'S NUTHIN.
TELL HIM WHAT HE'S GONNA DO.
I'LL TAKE FIFTY PILLS.
SURE, MAN. BUSINESS IS GOOD, HUH? BUT YOU'RE NOT PAYING US WITH MONEY TODAY.
GUESS WHAT? WE GOT A JOB FOR YOU.
HUH? NO, THAT'S NOT HOW THIS WORKS--
YES IT IS.
BECAUSE IT ALWAYS WORKS HOW WE SAY IT WORKS. HYEAH.
GET OUT OF THE CAR.
K-CHK

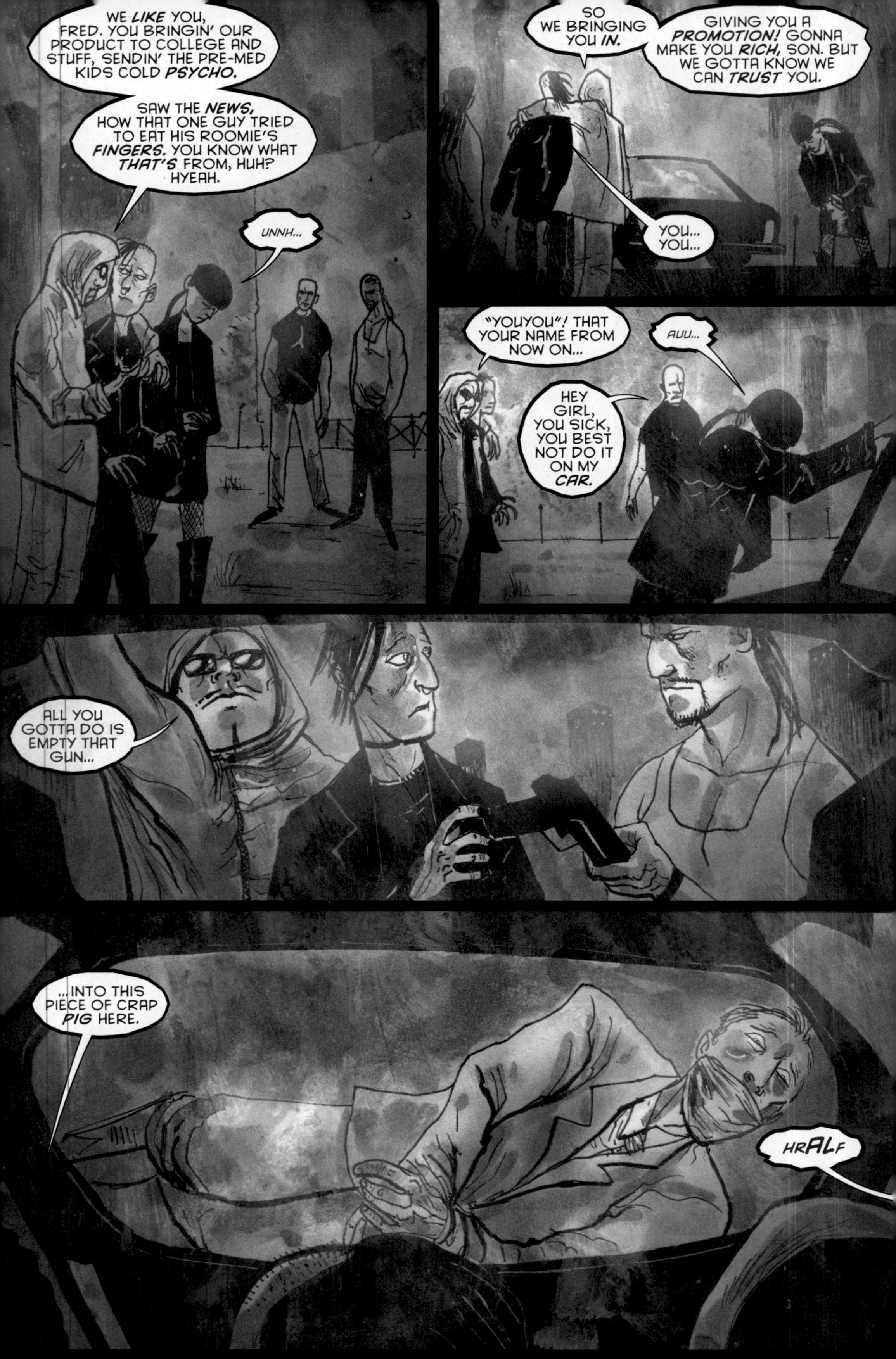
WE LIKE YOU, FRED. YOU BRINGIN' OUR PRODUCT TO COLLEGE AND STUFF, SENDIN' THE PRE-MED KIDS COLD PSYCHO.
SAW THE NEWS, HOW THAT ONE GUY TRIED TO EAT HIS ROOMIE'S FINGERS. YOU KNOW WHAT THAT'S FROM, HUH? HYEAH.
UNNH...
SO WE BRINGING YOU IN.
GIVING YOU A PROMOTION! GONNA MAKE YOU RICH, SON. BUT WE GOTTA KNOW WE CAN TRUST YOU.
YOU... YOU...
"YOUYOU"! THAT YOUR NAME FROM NOW ON...
AUU...
HEY GIRL, YOU SICK, YOU BEST NOT DO IT ON MY CAR.
ALL YOU GOTTA DO IS EMPTY THAT GUN...
...INTO THIS PIECE OF CRAP PIG HERE.
HRALF

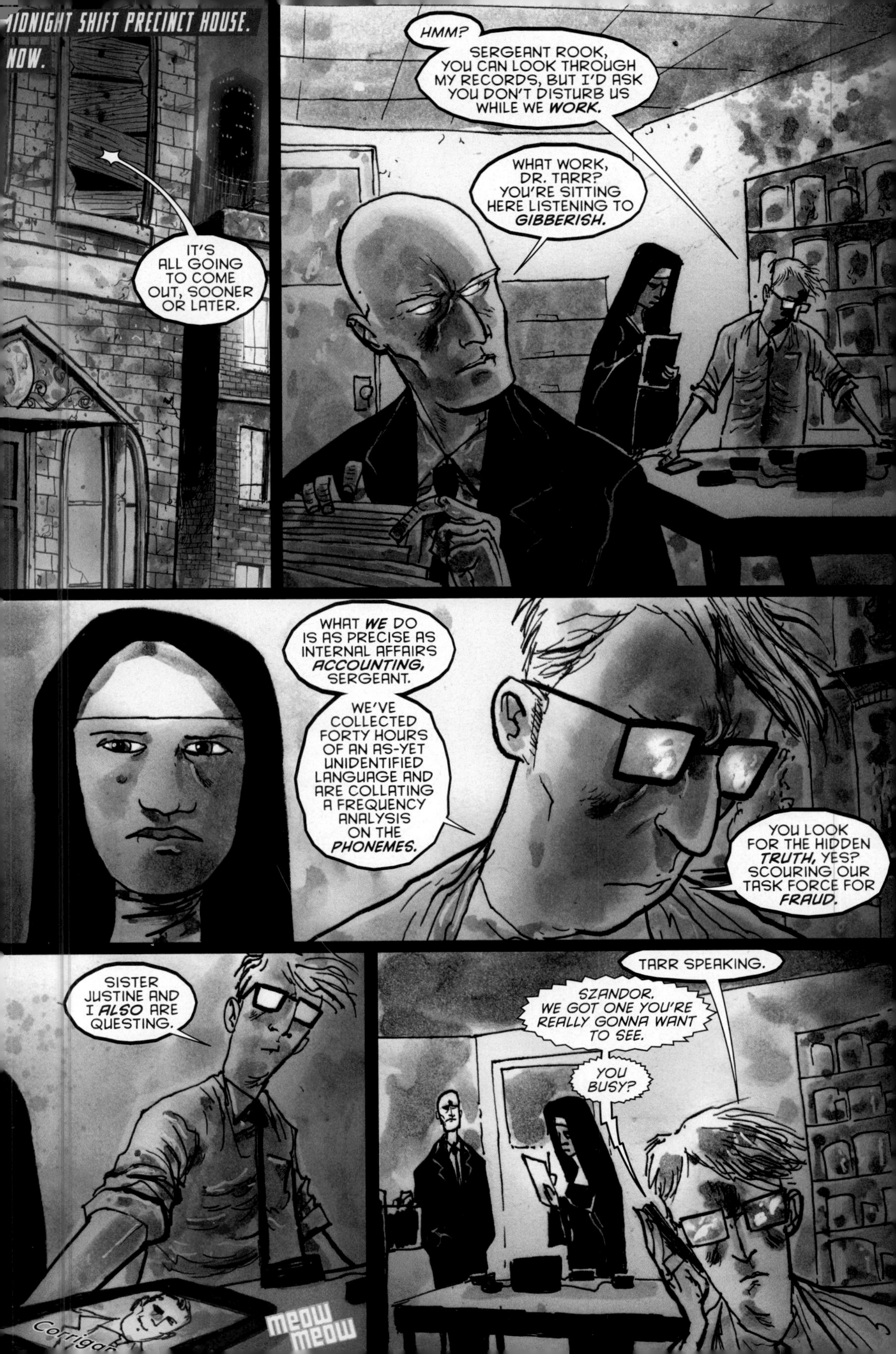

MIDNIGHT SHIFT PRECINCT HOUSE.
NOW.
IT'S ALL GOING TO COME OUT, SOONER OR LATER.
HMM?
SERGEANT ROOK, YOU CAN LOOK THROUGH MY RECORDS, BUT I'D ASK YOU DON'T DISTURB US WHILE WE WORK.
WHAT WORK, DR. TARR? YOU'RE SITTING HERE LISTENING TO GIBBERISH.
WHAT WE DO IS AS PRECISE AS INTERNAL AFFAIRS ACCOUNTING, SERGEANT.
WE'VE COLLECTED FORTY HOURS OF AN AS-YET UNIDENTIFIED LANGUAGE AND ARE COLLATING A FREQUENCY ANALYSIS ON THE PHONEMES.
YOU LOOK FOR THE HIDDEN TRUTH, YES? SCOURING OUR TASK FORCE FOR FRAUD.
SISTER JUSTINE AND I ALSO ARE QUESTING.
Corrigan
MEOW MEOW
TARR SPEAKING.
SZANDOR. WE GOT ONE YOU'RE REALLY GONNA WANT TO SEE.
YOU BUSY?

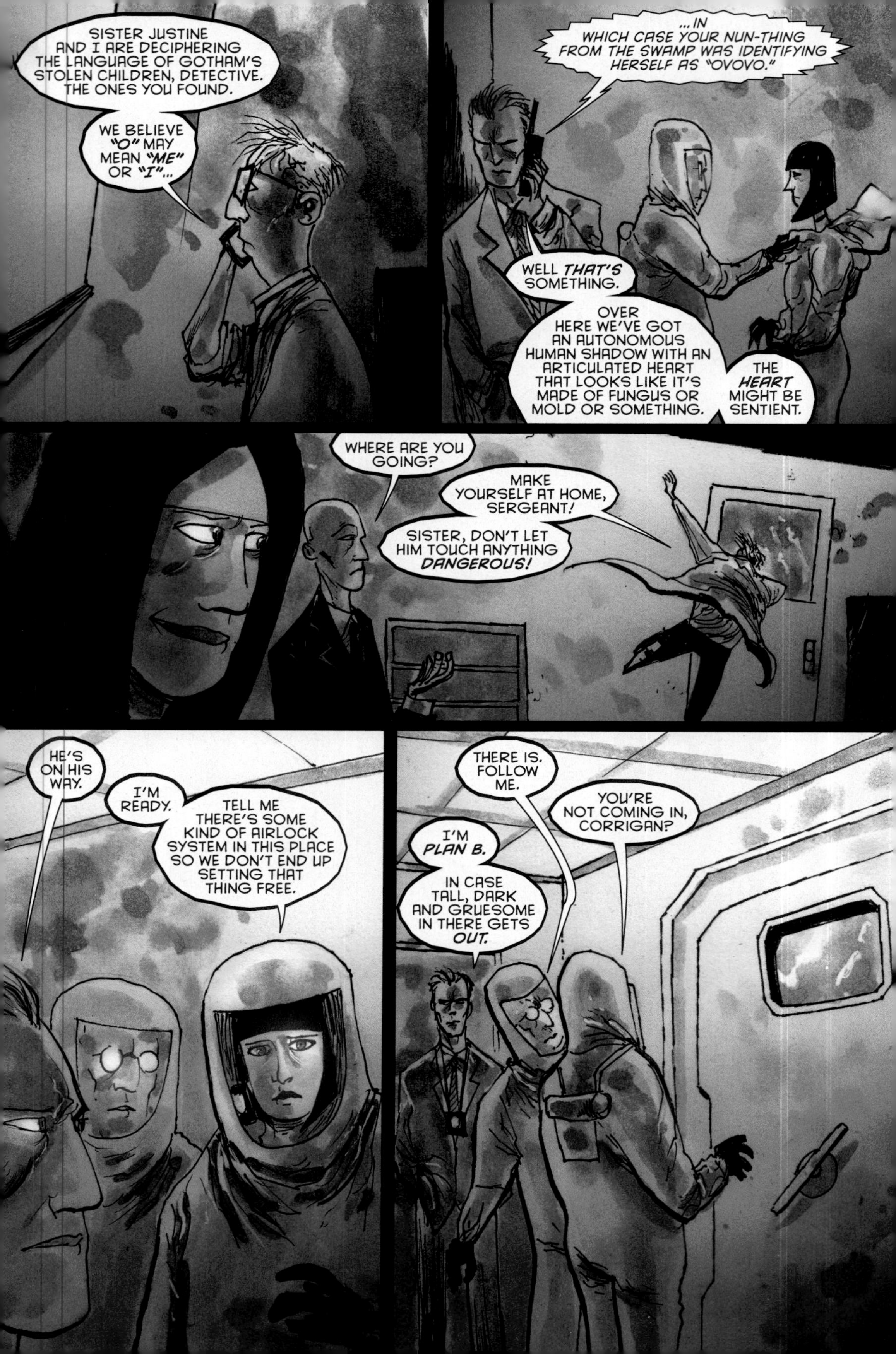
SISTER JUSTINE AND I ARE DECIPHERING THE LANGUAGE OF GOTHAM'S STOLEN CHILDREN, DETECTIVE. THE ONES YOU FOUND.
WE BELIEVE "O" MAY MEAN "ME" OR "I"...
...IN WHICH CASE YOUR NUN-THING FROM THE SWAMP WAS IDENTIFYING HERSELF AS "OVOVO."
WELL THAT'S SOMETHING.
OVER HERE WE'VE GOT AN AUTONOMOUS HUMAN SHADOW WITH AN ARTICULATED HEART THAT LOOKS LIKE IT'S MADE OF FUNGUS OR MOLD OR SOMETHING.
THE HEART MIGHT BE SENTIENT.
WHERE ARE YOU GOING?
MAKE YOURSELF AT HOME, SERGEANT!
SISTER, DON'T LET HIM TOUCH ANYTHING DANGEROUS!
HE'S ON HIS WAY.
I'M READY.
TELL ME THERE'S SOME KIND OF AIRLOCK SYSTEM IN THIS PLACE SO WE DON'T END UP SETTING THAT THING FREE.
THERE IS. FOLLOW ME.
YOU'RE NOT COMING IN, CORRIGAN?
I'M PLAN B.
IN CASE TALL, DARK AND GRUESOME IN THERE GETS OUT.

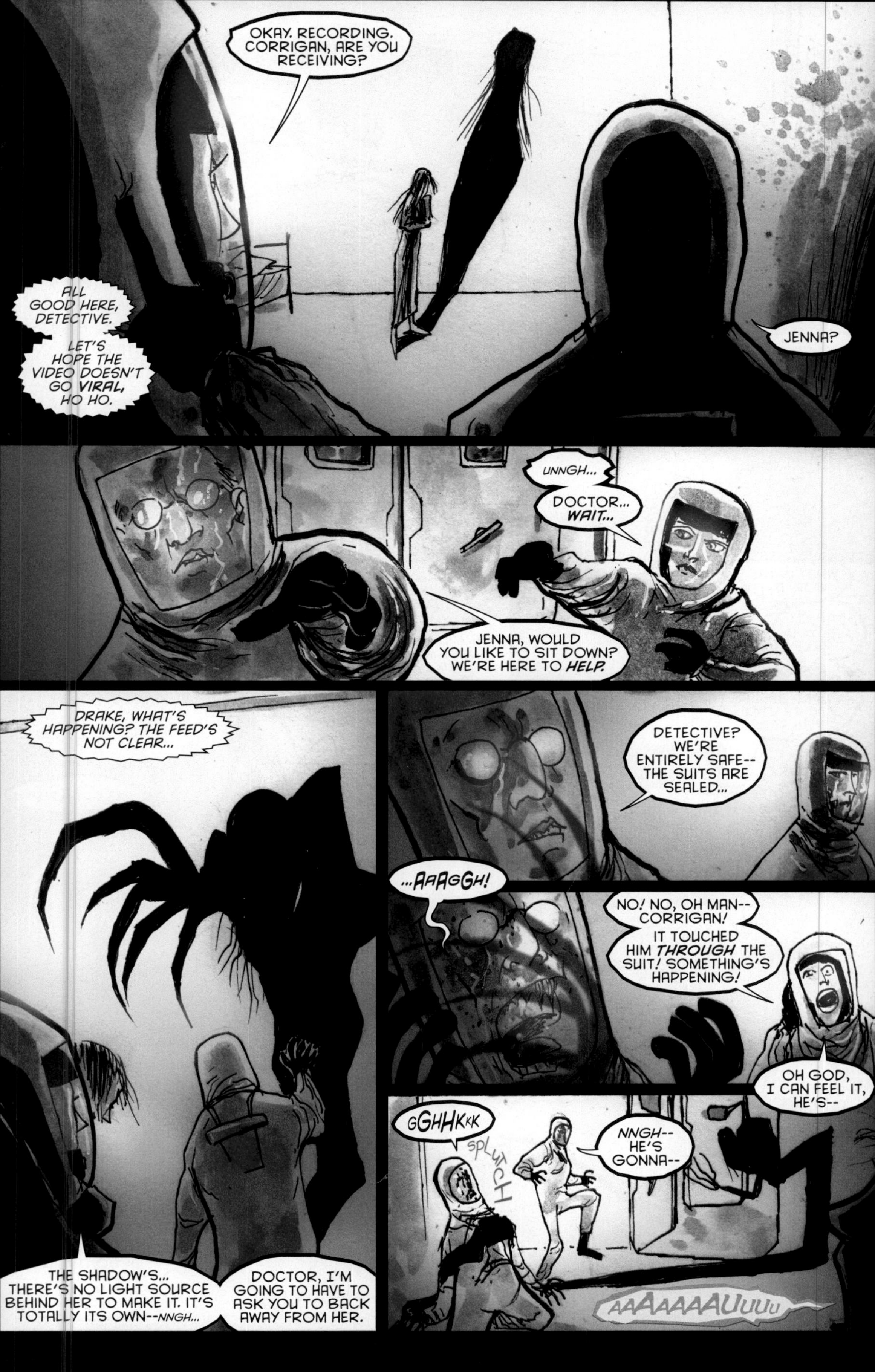
OKAY. RECORDING. CORRIGAN, ARE YOU RECEIVING?
ALL GOOD HERE, DETECTIVE.
LET'S HOPE THE VIDEO DOESN'T GO VIRAL, HO HO.
JENNA?
UNNGH...
DOCTOR... WAIT...
JENNA, WOULD YOU LIKE TO SIT DOWN? WE'RE HERE TO HELP.
DRAKE, WHAT'S HAPPENING? THE FEED'S NOT CLEAR...
THE SHADOW'S... THERE'S NO LIGHT SOURCE BEHIND HER TO MAKE IT. IT'S TOTALLY ITS OWN--NNGH...
DOCTOR, I'M GOING TO HAVE TO ASK YOU TO BACK AWAY FROM HER.
DETECTIVE? WE'RE ENTIRELY SAFE-- THE SUITS ARE SEALED...
...AAAGGH!
NO! NO, OH MAN-- CORRIGAN!
IT TOUCHED HIM THROUGH THE SUIT! SOMETHING'S HAPPENING!
OH GOD, I CAN FEEL IT, HE'S--
GGHHKKK
SPLUTCH
NNGH-- HE'S GONNA--
AAAAAAAUUUU

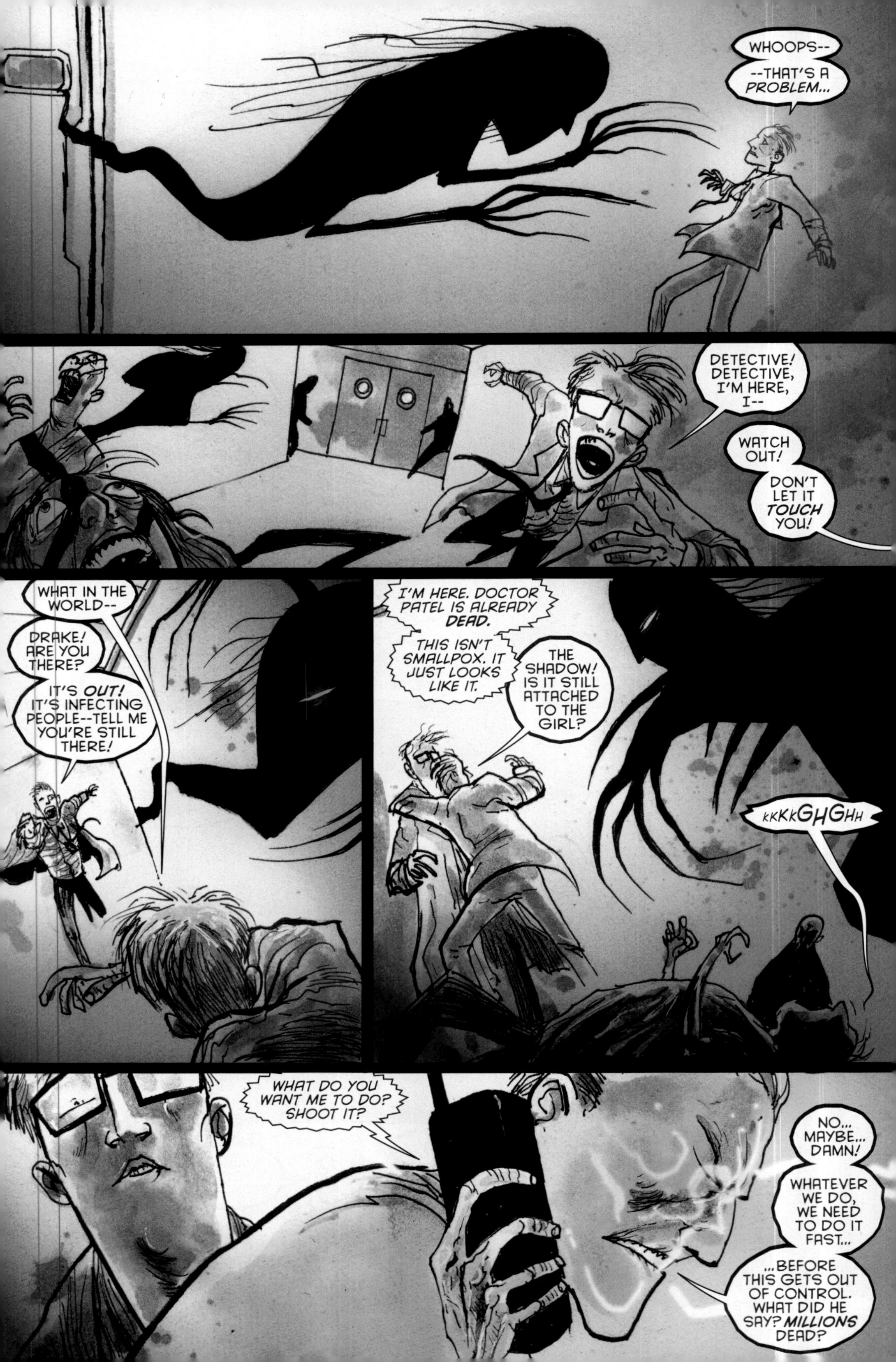
WHOOPS--
--THAT'S A *PROBLEM*...
DETECTIVE! DETECTIVE, I'M HERE, I--
WATCH OUT!
DON'T LET IT *TOUCH* YOU!
WHAT IN THE WORLD--
DRAKE! ARE YOU THERE?
IT'S *OUT!* IT'S INFECTING PEOPLE--TELL ME YOU'RE STILL THERE!
I'M HERE. DOCTOR PATEL IS ALREADY *DEAD.*
THIS ISN'T SMALLPOX. IT JUST LOOKS LIKE IT.
THE SHADOW! IS IT STILL ATTACHED TO THE GIRL?
KKKKGHGHH
WHAT DO YOU WANT ME TO DO? SHOOT IT?
NO... MAYBE... DAMN!
WHATEVER WE DO, WE NEED TO DO IT FAST...
...BEFORE THIS GETS OUT OF CONTROL. WHAT DID HE SAY? *MILLIONS* DEAD?

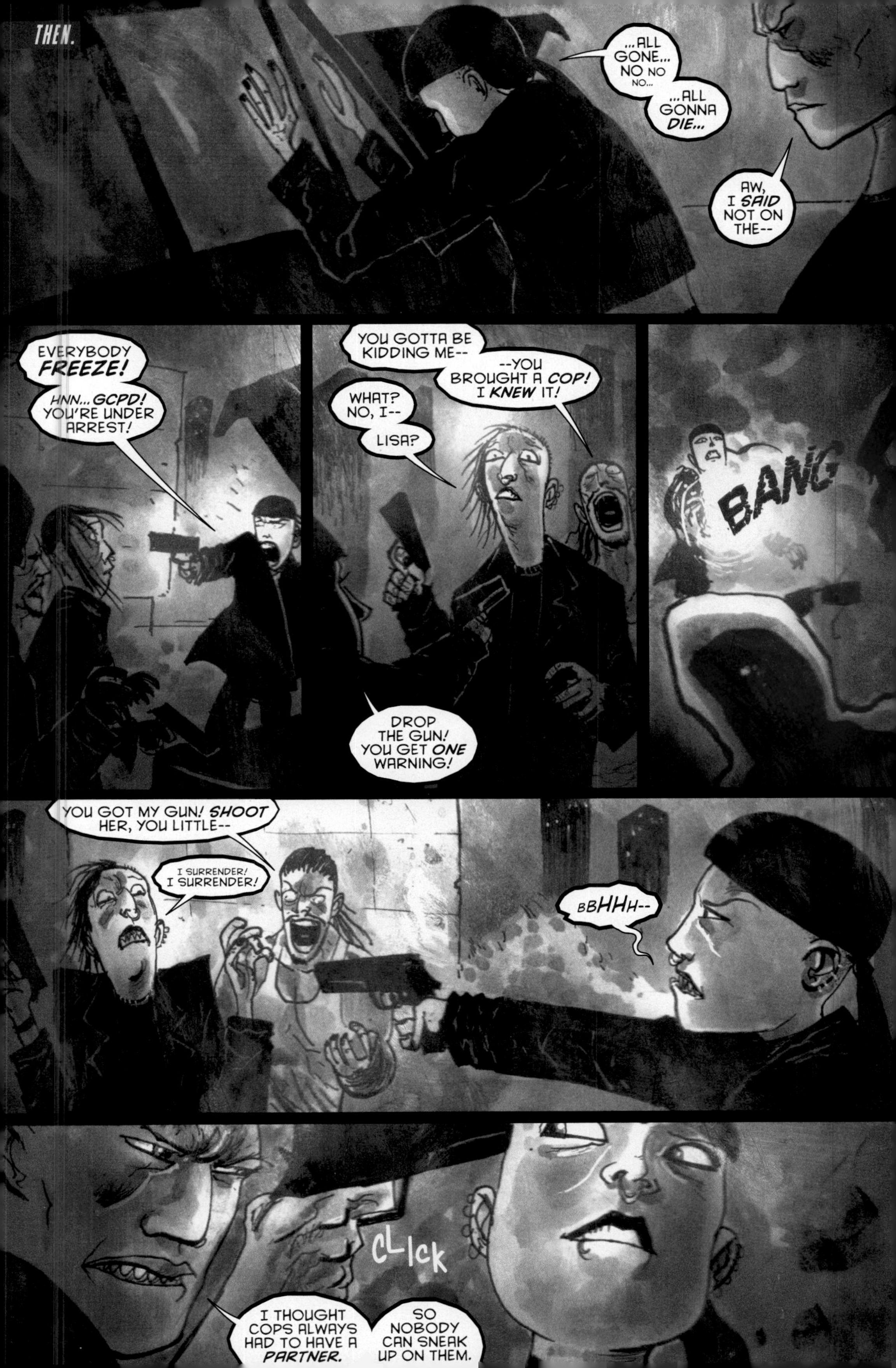

THEN.
...ALL GONE... NO NO NO...
...ALL GONNA DIE...
AW, I SAID NOT ON THE--
EVERYBODY FREEZE!
HNN... GCPD! YOU'RE UNDER ARREST!
YOU GOTTA BE KIDDING ME--
--YOU BROUGHT A COP! I KNEW IT!
WHAT? NO, I--
LISA?
DROP THE GUN! YOU GET ONE WARNING!
BANG
YOU GOT MY GUN! SHOOT HER, YOU LITTLE--
I SURRENDER! I SURRENDER!
BBHHH--
CLICK
I THOUGHT COPS ALWAYS HAD TO HAVE A PARTNER.
SO NOBODY CAN SNEAK UP ON THEM.

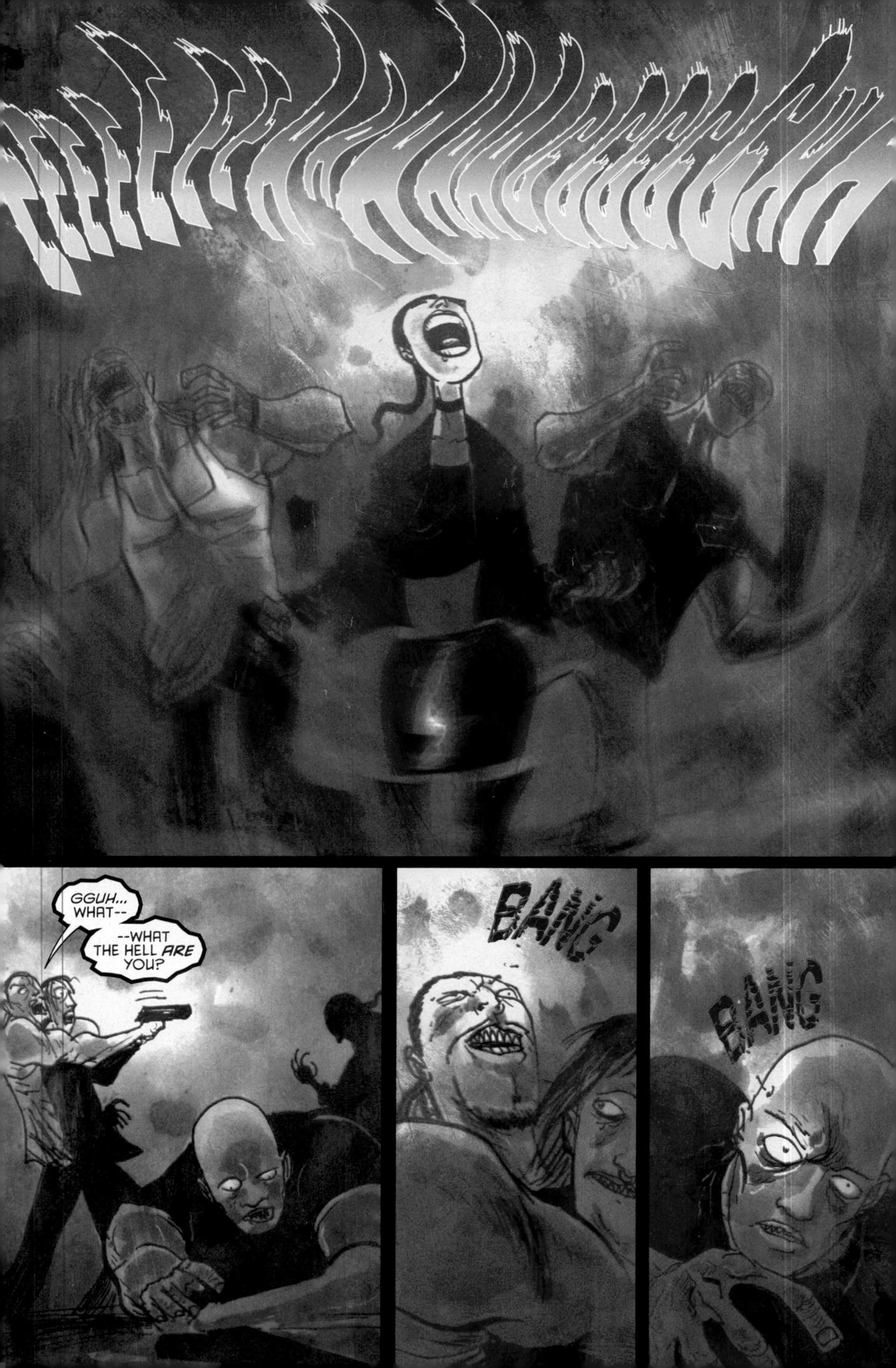
GGUH... WHAT--
--WHAT THE HELL *ARE* YOU?
BANG
BANG

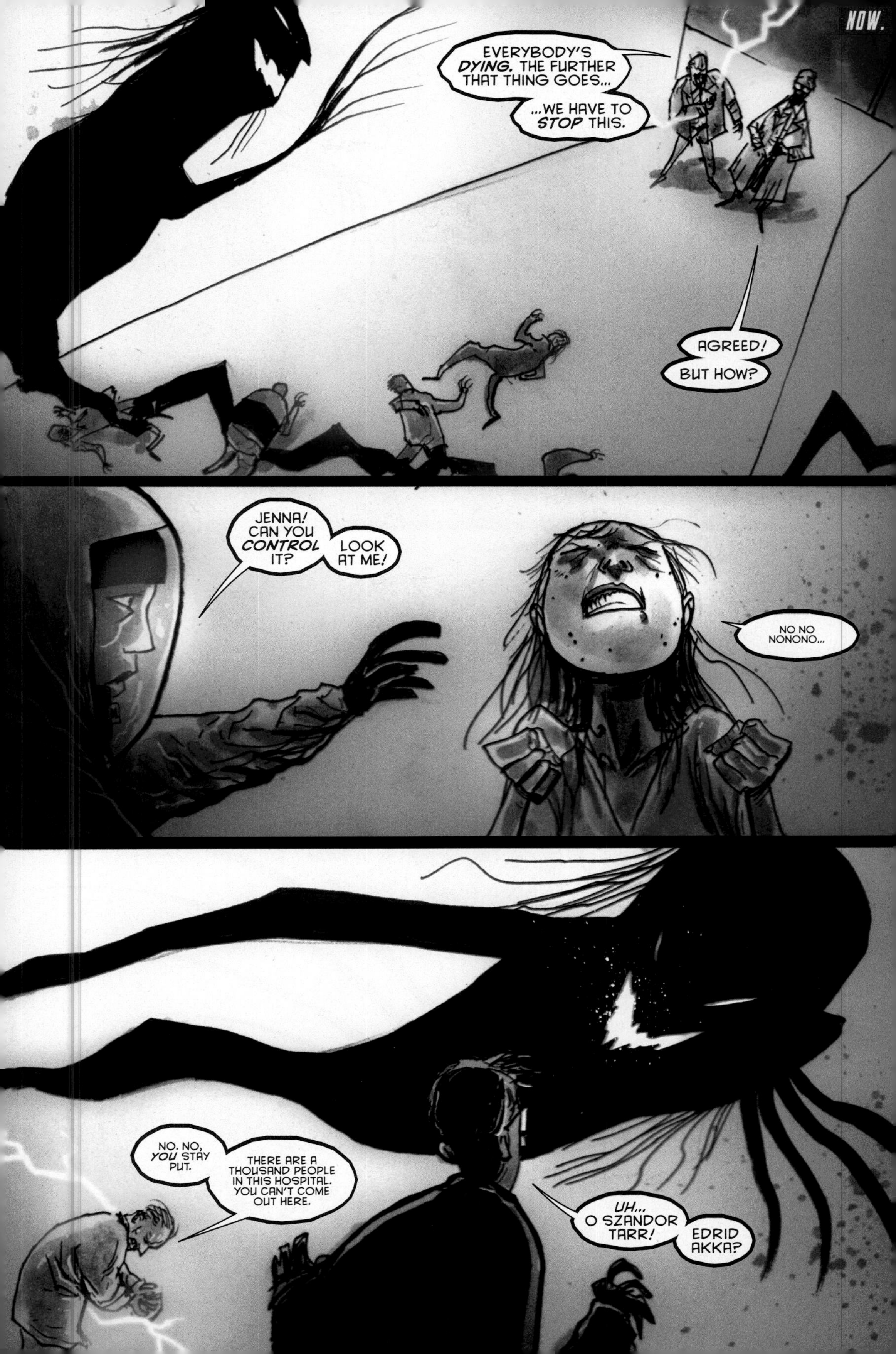
NOW.
EVERYBODY'S DYING. THE FURTHER THAT THING GOES...
...WE HAVE TO STOP THIS.
AGREED!
BUT HOW?
JENNA! CAN YOU CONTROL IT?
LOOK AT ME!
NO NO NONONO...
NO. NO, YOU STAY PUT.
THERE ARE A THOUSAND PEOPLE IN THIS HOSPITAL. YOU CAN'T COME OUT HERE.
UH... O SZANDOR TARR!
EDRID AKKA?

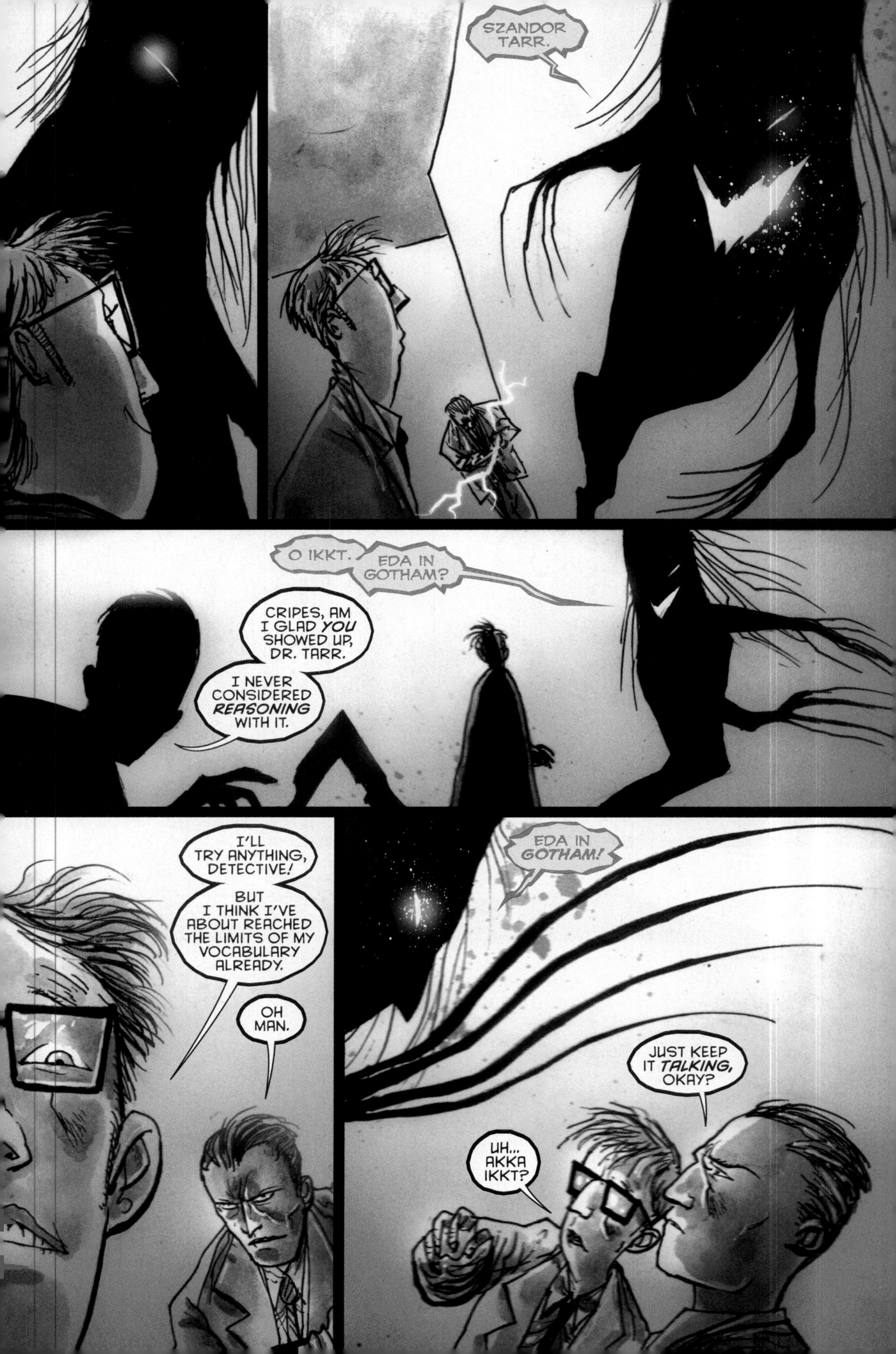
SZANDOR TARR.
O IKKT.
EDA IN GOTHAM?
CRIPES, AM I GLAD *YOU* SHOWED UP, DR. TARR.
I NEVER CONSIDERED ***REASONING*** WITH IT.
I'LL TRY ANYTHING, DETECTIVE!
BUT I THINK I'VE ABOUT REACHED THE LIMITS OF MY VOCABULARY ALREADY.
OH MAN.
EDA IN ***GOTHAM!***
JUST KEEP IT *TALKING*, OKAY?
UH... AKKA IKKT?

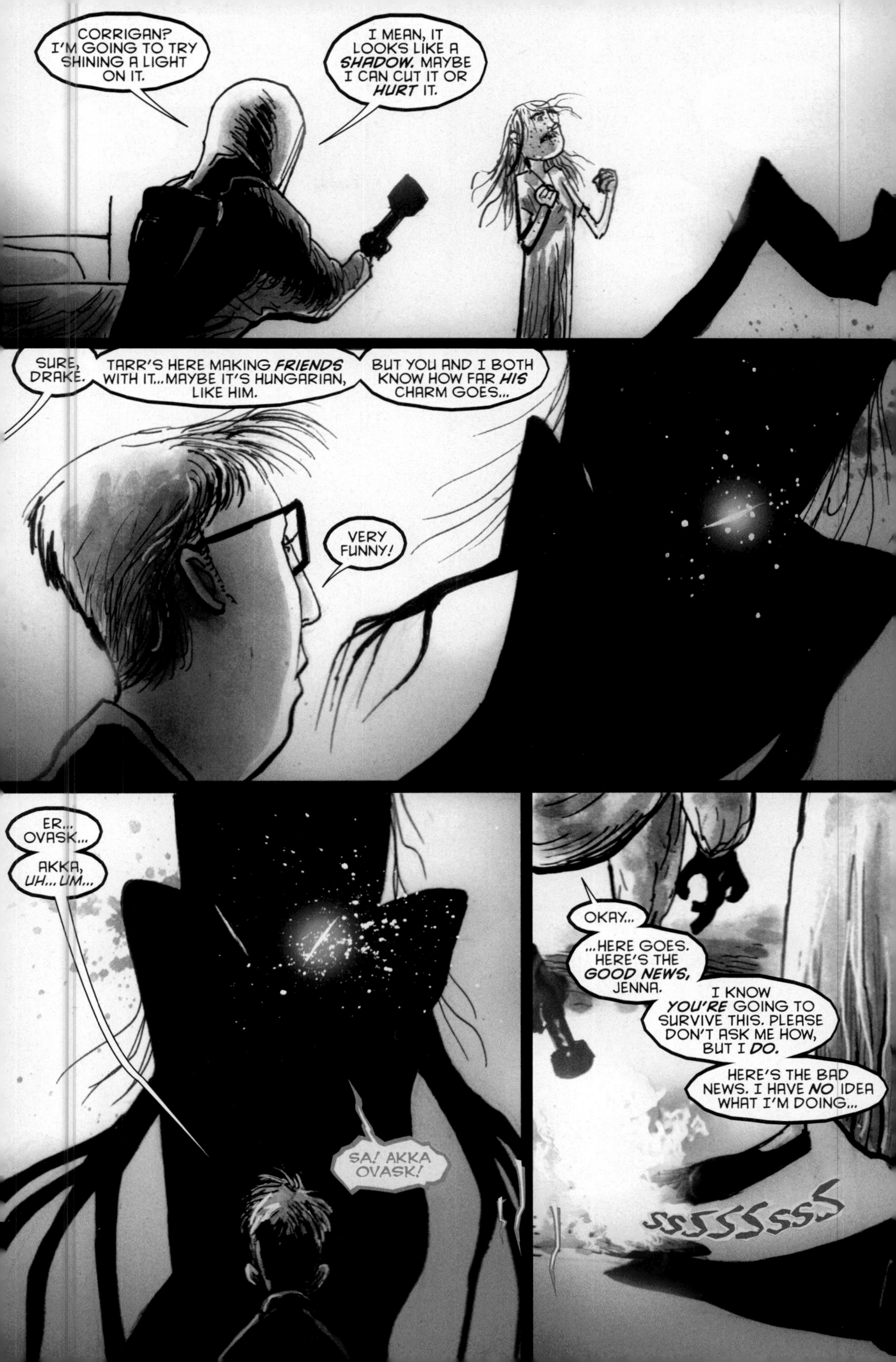
CORRIGAN? I'M GOING TO TRY SHINING A LIGHT ON IT.
I MEAN, IT LOOKS LIKE A SHADOW. MAYBE I CAN CUT IT OR HURT IT.
SURE, DRAKE.
TARR'S HERE MAKING FRIENDS WITH IT...MAYBE IT'S HUNGARIAN, LIKE HIM.
BUT YOU AND I BOTH KNOW HOW FAR HIS CHARM GOES...
VERY FUNNY!
ER... OVASK...
AKKA, UH... UM...
SA! AKKA OVASK!
OKAY...
...HERE GOES. HERE'S THE GOOD NEWS, JENNA.
I KNOW YOU'RE GOING TO SURVIVE THIS. PLEASE DON'T ASK ME HOW, BUT I DO.
HERE'S THE BAD NEWS. I HAVE NO IDEA WHAT I'M DOING...
SSSSSSSSS

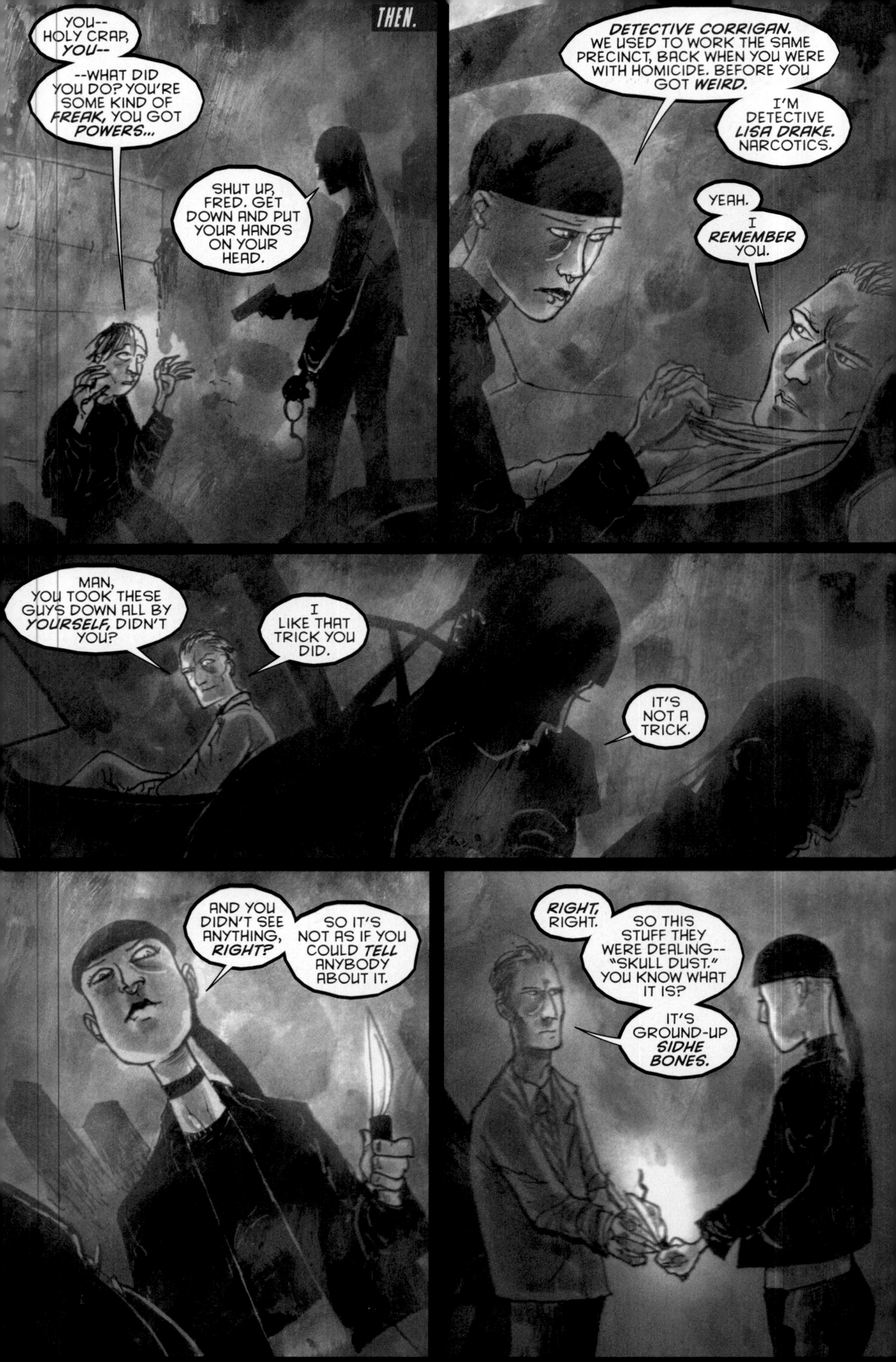
THEN.
YOU-- HOLY CRAP, *YOU--*
--WHAT DID YOU DO? YOU'RE SOME KIND OF *FREAK*, YOU GOT *POWERS...*
SHUT UP, FRED. GET DOWN AND PUT YOUR HANDS ON YOUR HEAD.
DETECTIVE CORRIGAN. WE USED TO WORK THE SAME PRECINCT, BACK WHEN YOU WERE WITH HOMICIDE. BEFORE YOU GOT *WEIRD.*
I'M DETECTIVE *LISA DRAKE.* NARCOTICS.
YEAH.
I *REMEMBER* YOU.
MAN, YOU TOOK THESE GUYS DOWN ALL BY *YOURSELF*, DIDN'T YOU?
I LIKE THAT TRICK YOU DID.
IT'S NOT A TRICK.
AND YOU DIDN'T SEE ANYTHING, *RIGHT?*
SO IT'S NOT AS IF YOU COULD *TELL* ANYBODY ABOUT IT.
RIGHT, RIGHT.
SO THIS STUFF THEY WERE DEALING-- "SKULL DUST." YOU KNOW WHAT IT IS?
IT'S GROUND-UP *SIDHE BONES.*

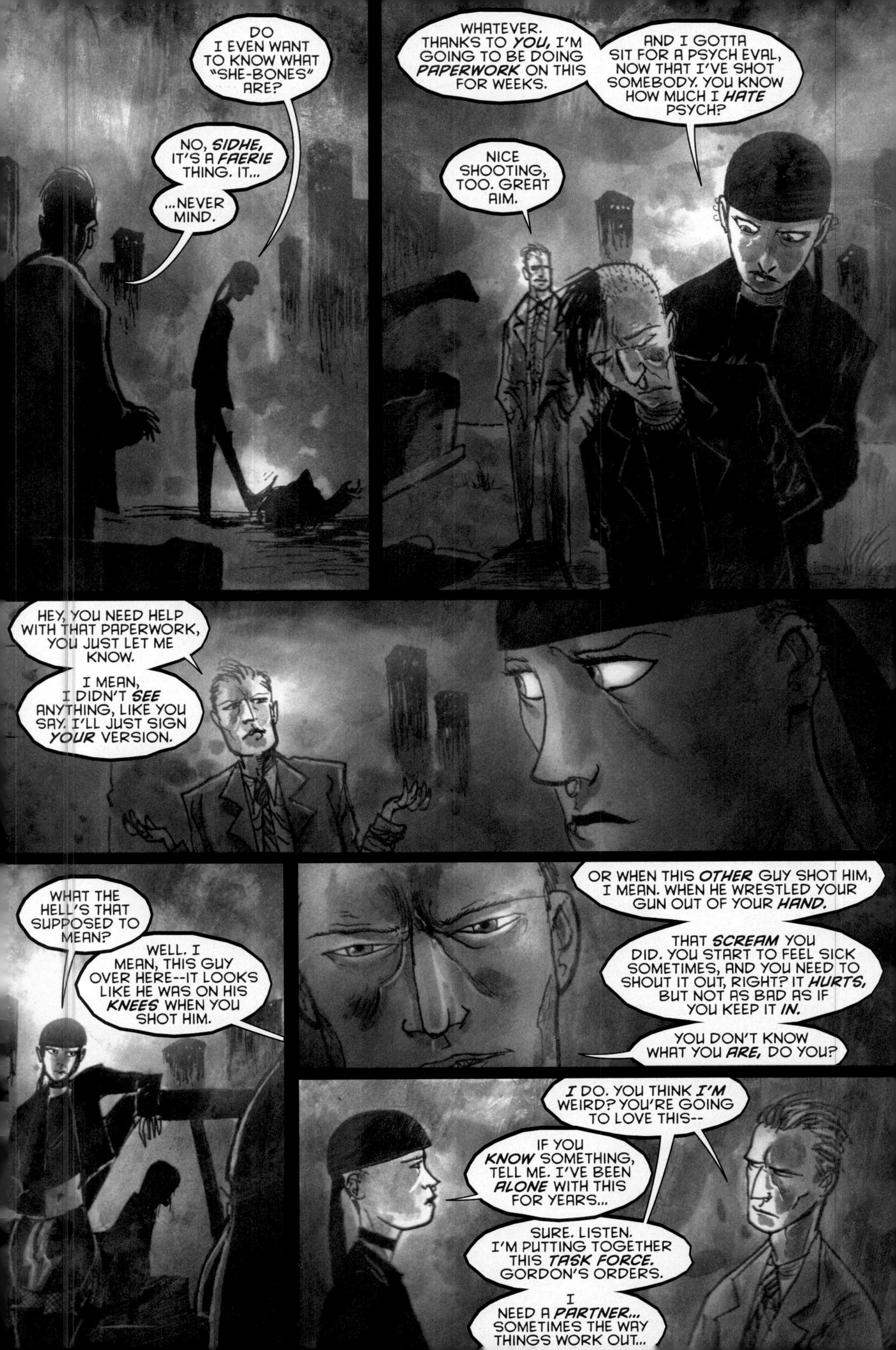

DO I EVEN WANT TO KNOW WHAT "SHE-BONES" ARE?
NO, SIDHE, IT'S A FAERIE THING. IT...
...NEVER MIND.
WHATEVER. THANKS TO YOU, I'M GOING TO BE DOING PAPERWORK ON THIS FOR WEEKS.
AND I GOTTA SIT FOR A PSYCH EVAL, NOW THAT I'VE SHOT SOMEBODY. YOU KNOW HOW MUCH I HATE PSYCH?
NICE SHOOTING, TOO. GREAT AIM.
HEY, YOU NEED HELP WITH THAT PAPERWORK, YOU JUST LET ME KNOW.
I MEAN, I DIDN'T SEE ANYTHING, LIKE YOU SAY. I'LL JUST SIGN YOUR VERSION.
WHAT THE HELL'S THAT SUPPOSED TO MEAN?
WELL. I MEAN, THIS GUY OVER HERE--IT LOOKS LIKE HE WAS ON HIS KNEES WHEN YOU SHOT HIM.
OR WHEN THIS OTHER GUY SHOT HIM, I MEAN. WHEN HE WRESTLED YOUR GUN OUT OF YOUR HAND.
THAT SCREAM YOU DID. YOU START TO FEEL SICK SOMETIMES, AND YOU NEED TO SHOUT IT OUT, RIGHT? IT HURTS, BUT NOT AS BAD AS IF YOU KEEP IT IN.
YOU DON'T KNOW WHAT YOU ARE, DO YOU?
I DO. YOU THINK I'M WEIRD? YOU'RE GOING TO LOVE THIS--
IF YOU KNOW SOMETHING, TELL ME. I'VE BEEN ALONE WITH THIS FOR YEARS...
SURE. LISTEN. I'M PUTTING TOGETHER THIS TASK FORCE. GORDON'S ORDERS.
I NEED A PARTNER... SOMETIMES THE WAY THINGS WORK OUT...

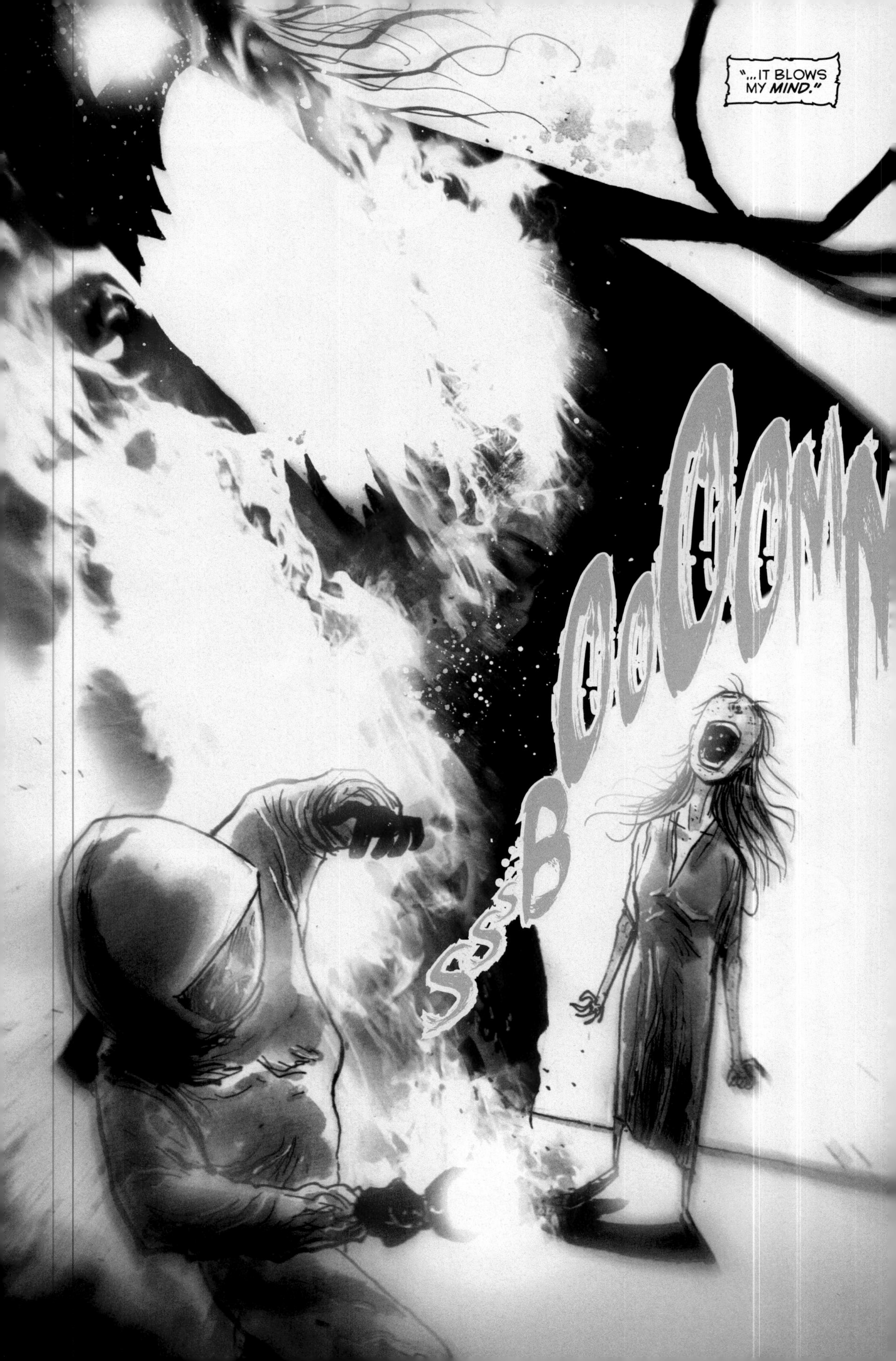
"...IT BLOWS MY MIND."
SSSBOOOOMM

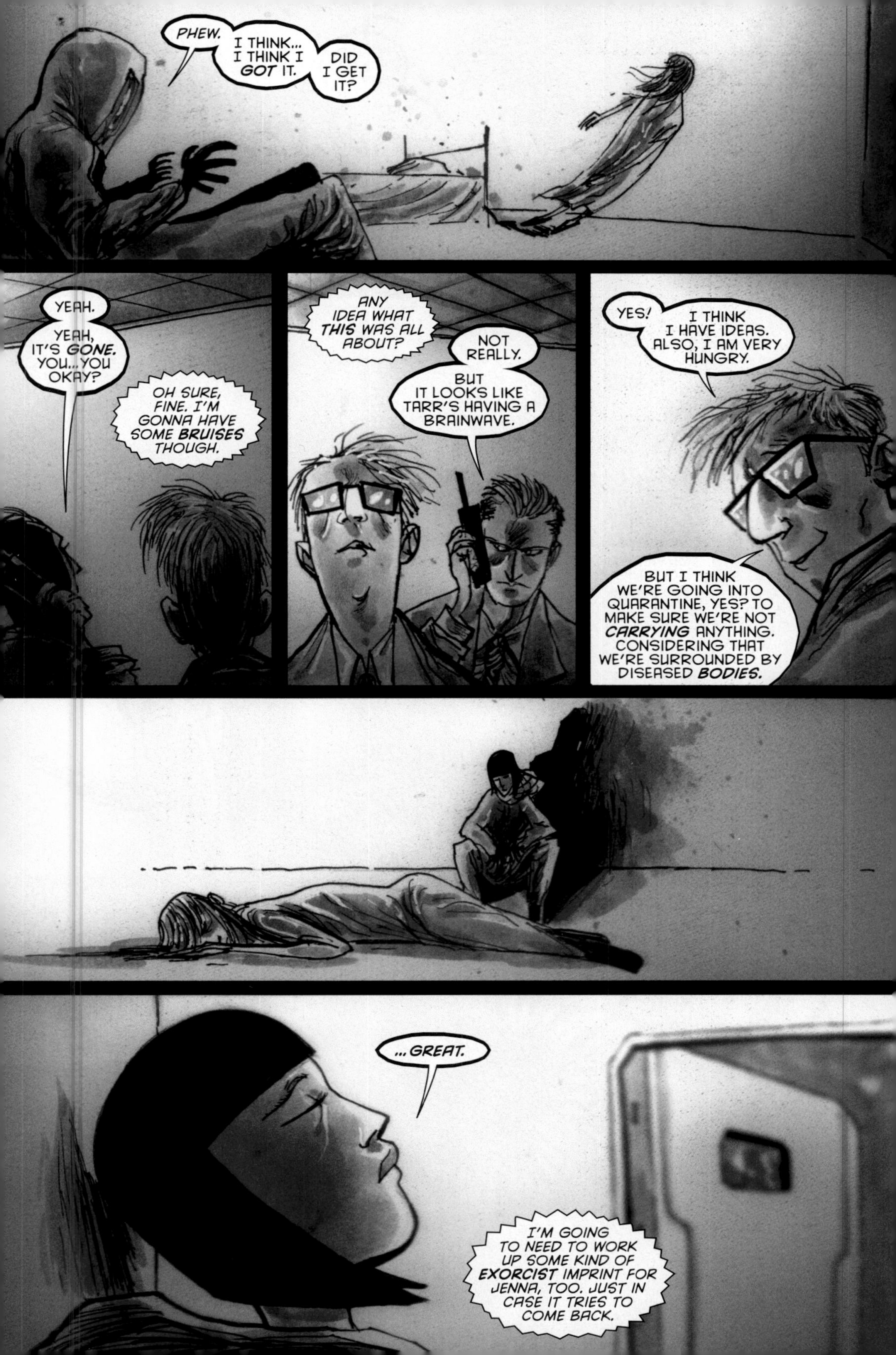
PHEW.
I THINK... I THINK I GOT IT.
DID I GET IT?
YEAH.
YEAH, IT'S GONE. YOU...YOU OKAY?
OH SURE, FINE. I'M GONNA HAVE SOME BRUISES THOUGH.
ANY IDEA WHAT THIS WAS ALL ABOUT?
NOT REALLY.
BUT IT LOOKS LIKE TARR'S HAVING A BRAINWAVE.
YES!
I THINK I HAVE IDEAS. ALSO, I AM VERY HUNGRY.
BUT I THINK WE'RE GOING INTO QUARANTINE, YES? TO MAKE SURE WE'RE NOT CARRYING ANYTHING. CONSIDERING THAT WE'RE SURROUNDED BY DISEASED BODIES.
...GREAT.
I'M GOING TO NEED TO WORK UP SOME KIND OF EXORCIST IMPRINT FOR JENNA, TOO. JUST IN CASE IT TRIES TO COME BACK.

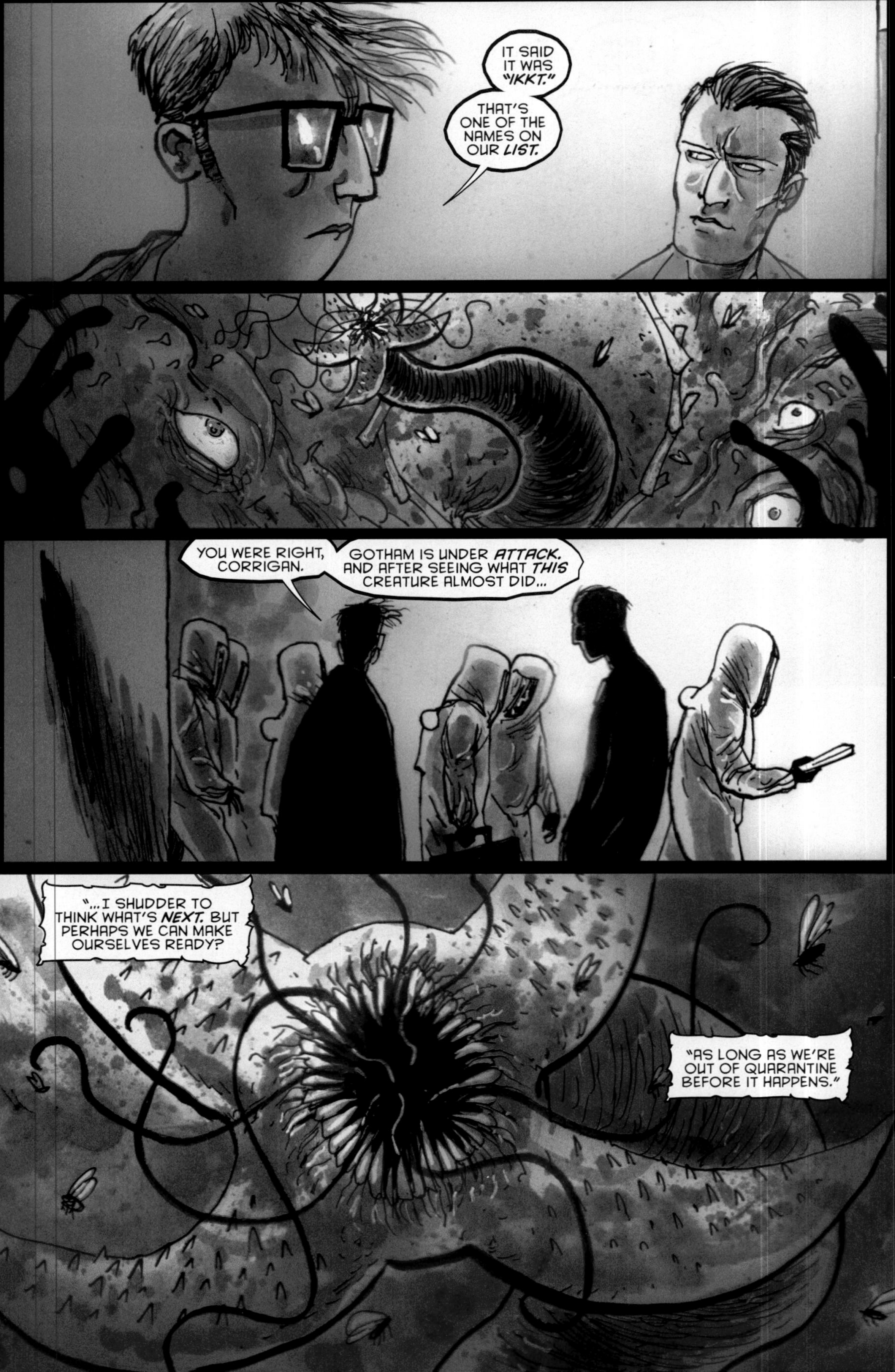
IT SAID IT WAS "IKKT."
THAT'S ONE OF THE NAMES ON OUR LIST.
YOU WERE RIGHT, CORRIGAN.
GOTHAM IS UNDER ATTACK. AND AFTER SEEING WHAT THIS CREATURE ALMOST DID...
"...I SHUDDER TO THINK WHAT'S NEXT. BUT PERHAPS WE CAN MAKE OURSELVES READY?
"AS LONG AS WE'RE OUT OF QUARANTINE BEFORE IT HAPPENS."

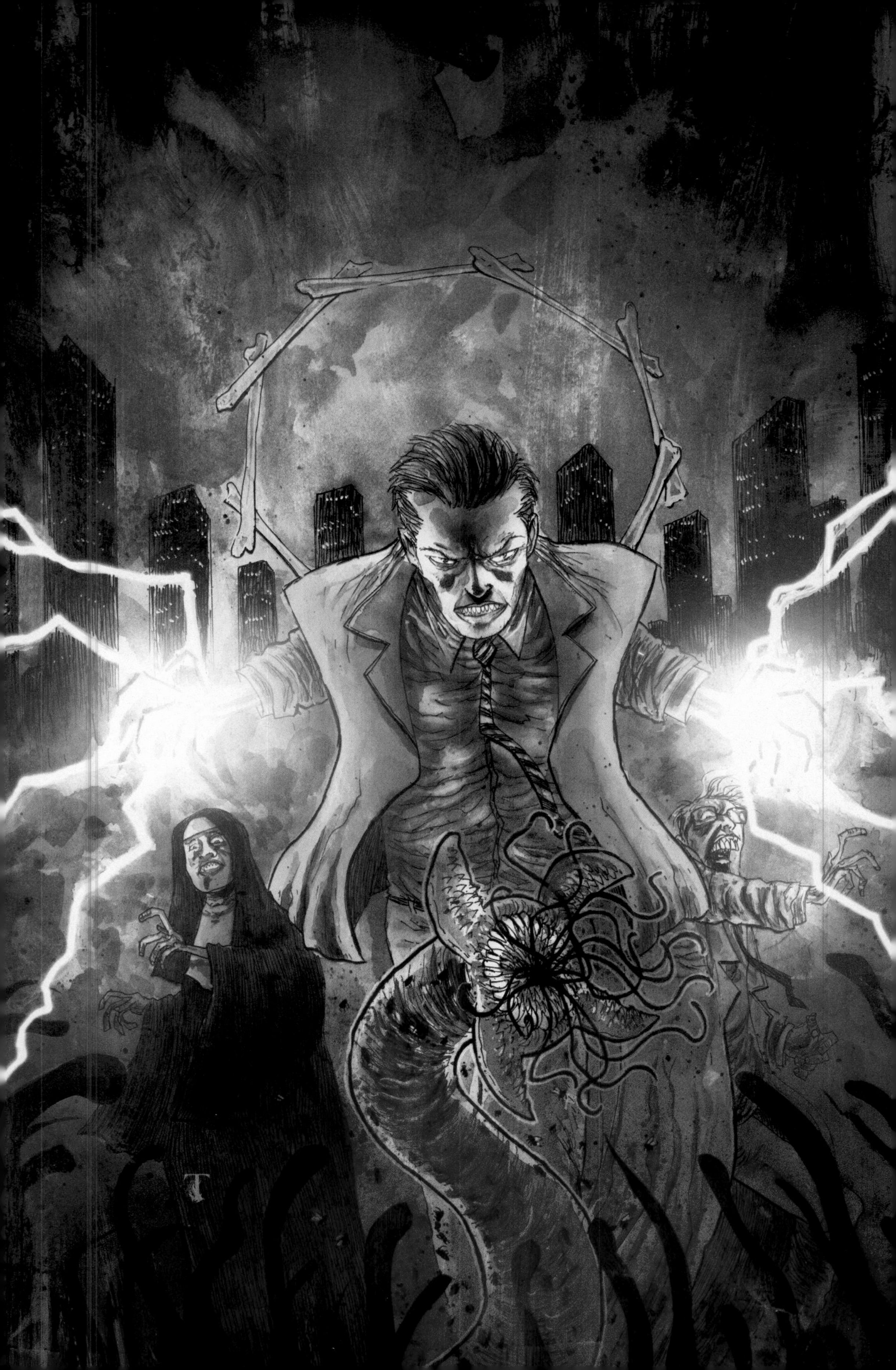

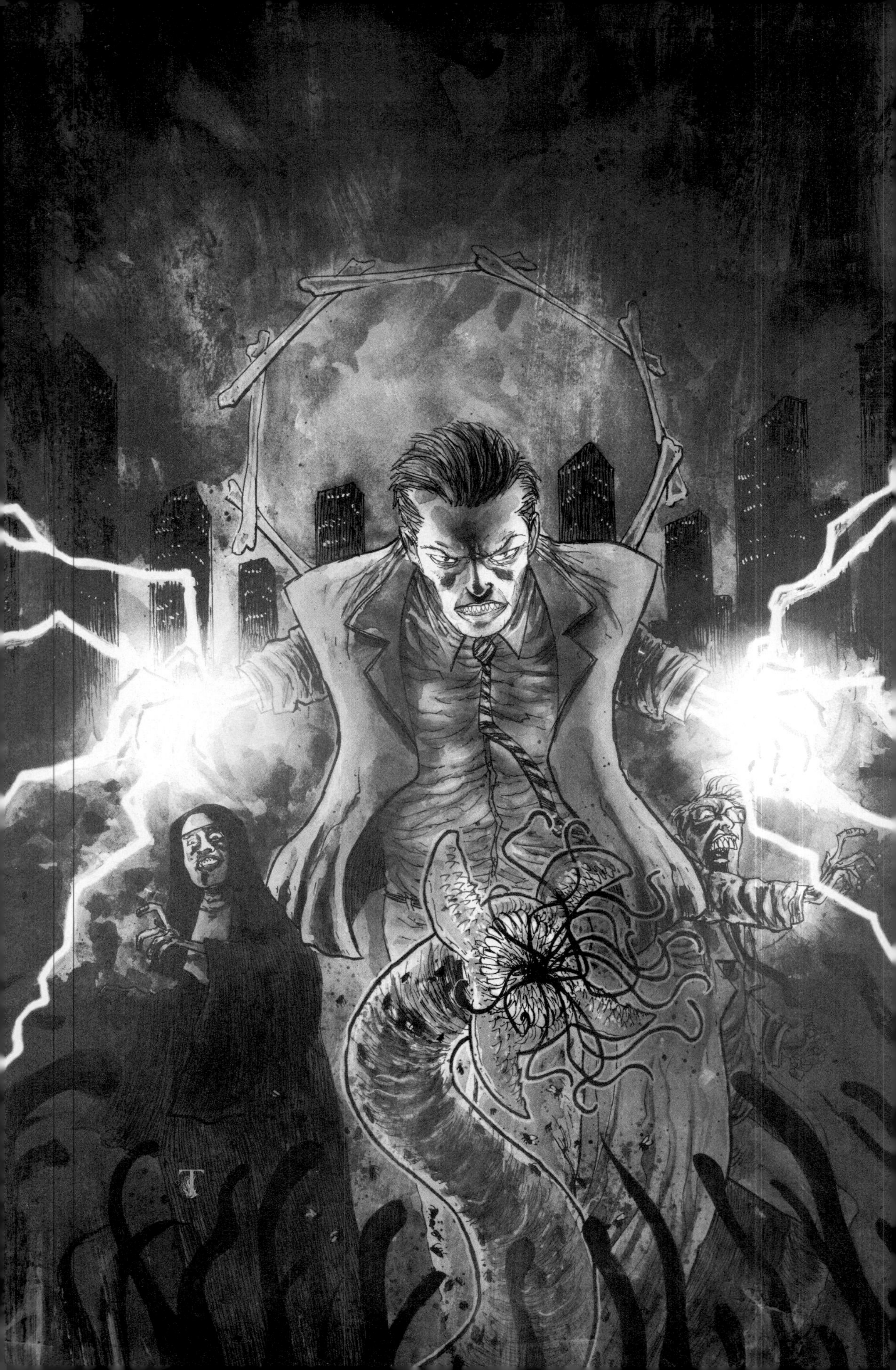

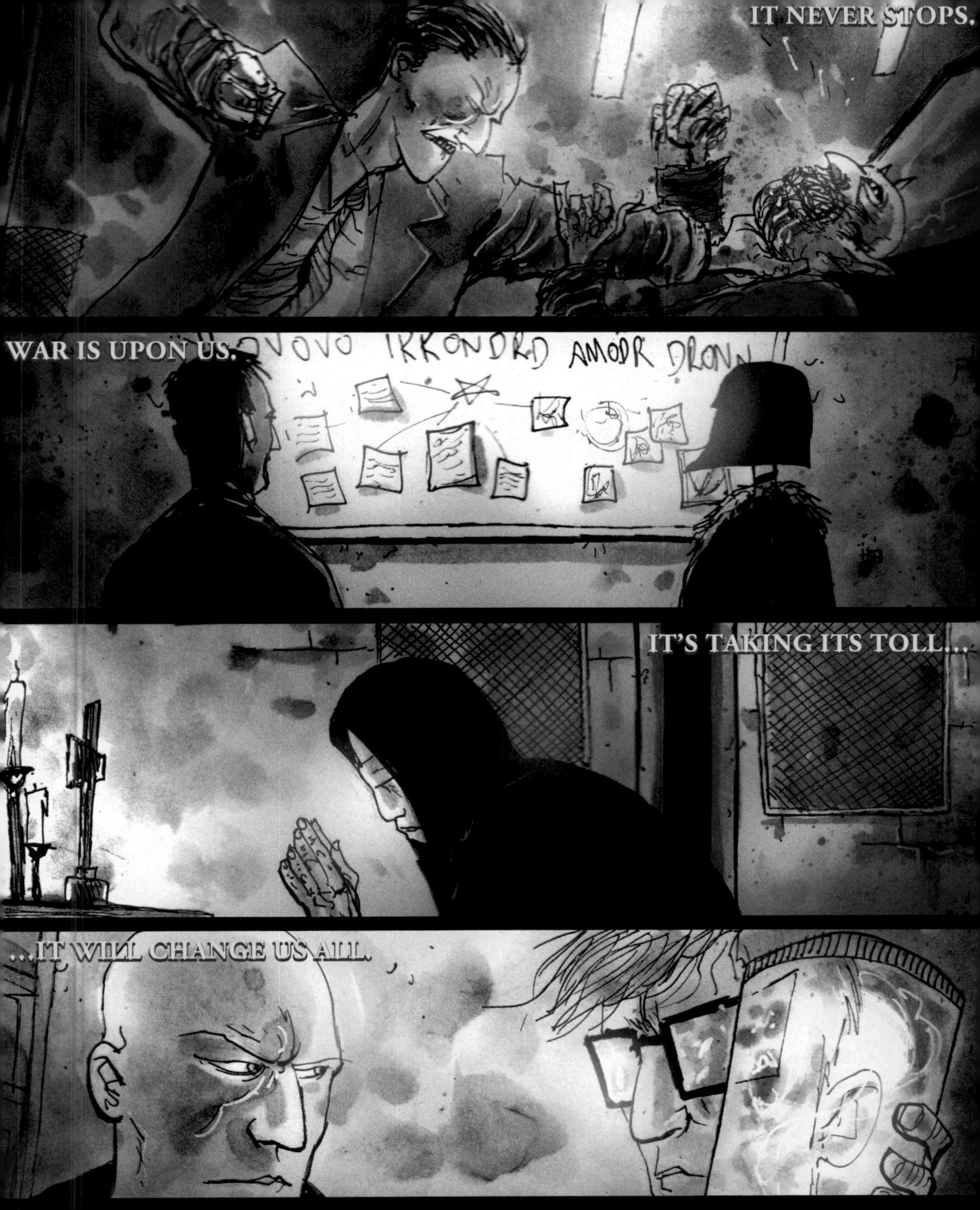
IT NEVER STOPS.
WAR IS UPON US.
IT'S TAKING ITS TOLL...
...IT WILL CHANGE US ALL.

CHAPTER FOUR:

WE FIGHT WHAT WE BECOME

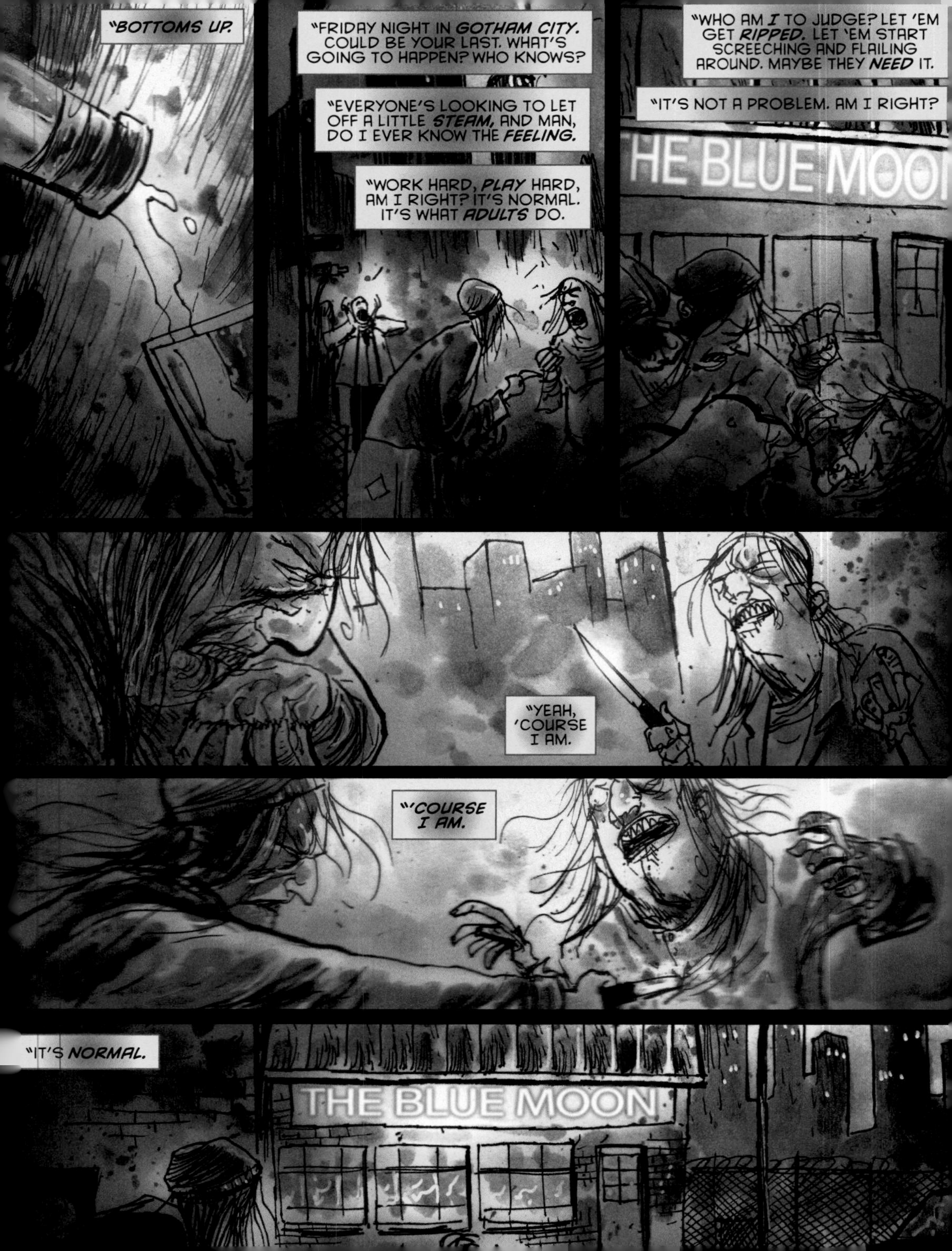
"BOTTOMS UP.
"FRIDAY NIGHT IN GOTHAM CITY. COULD BE YOUR LAST. WHAT'S GOING TO HAPPEN? WHO KNOWS?
"EVERYONE'S LOOKING TO LET OFF A LITTLE STEAM, AND MAN, DO I EVER KNOW THE FEELING.
"WORK HARD, PLAY HARD, AM I RIGHT? IT'S NORMAL. IT'S WHAT ADULTS DO.
"WHO AM I TO JUDGE? LET 'EM GET RIPPED. LET 'EM START SCREECHING AND FLAILING AROUND. MAYBE THEY NEED IT.
"IT'S NOT A PROBLEM. AM I RIGHT?
THE BLUE MOON
"YEAH, 'COURSE I AM.
"'COURSE I AM.
"IT'S NORMAL.
THE BLUE MOON

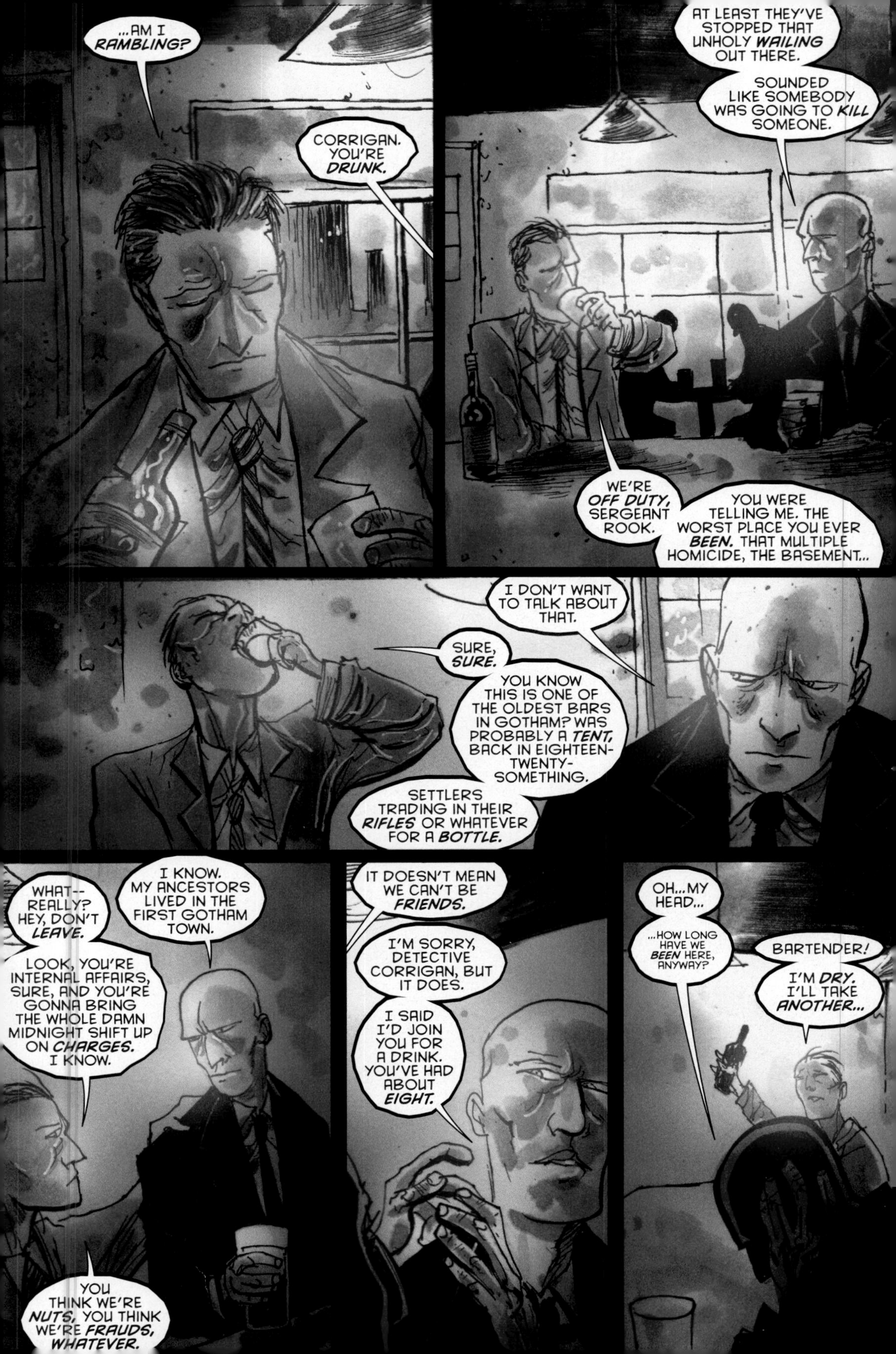
...AM I RAMBLING?
CORRIGAN. YOU'RE DRUNK.
AT LEAST THEY'VE STOPPED THAT UNHOLY WAILING OUT THERE.
SOUNDED LIKE SOMEBODY WAS GOING TO KILL SOMEONE.
WE'RE OFF DUTY, SERGEANT ROOK.
YOU WERE TELLING ME. THE WORST PLACE YOU EVER BEEN. THAT MULTIPLE HOMICIDE, THE BASEMENT...
I DON'T WANT TO TALK ABOUT THAT.
SURE, SURE.
YOU KNOW THIS IS ONE OF THE OLDEST BARS IN GOTHAM? WAS PROBABLY A TENT, BACK IN EIGHTEEN-TWENTY-SOMETHING.
SETTLERS TRADING IN THEIR RIFLES OR WHATEVER FOR A BOTTLE.
I KNOW. MY ANCESTORS LIVED IN THE FIRST GOTHAM TOWN.
WHAT--REALLY? HEY, DON'T LEAVE.
LOOK, YOU'RE INTERNAL AFFAIRS, SURE, AND YOU'RE GONNA BRING THE WHOLE DAMN MIDNIGHT SHIFT UP ON CHARGES. I KNOW.
YOU THINK WE'RE NUTS, YOU THINK WE'RE FRAUDS, WHATEVER.
IT DOESN'T MEAN WE CAN'T BE FRIENDS.
I'M SORRY, DETECTIVE CORRIGAN, BUT IT DOES.
I SAID I'D JOIN YOU FOR A DRINK. YOU'VE HAD ABOUT EIGHT.
OH...MY HEAD...
...HOW LONG HAVE WE BEEN HERE, ANYWAY?
BARTENDER!
I'M DRY. I'LL TAKE ANOTHER...

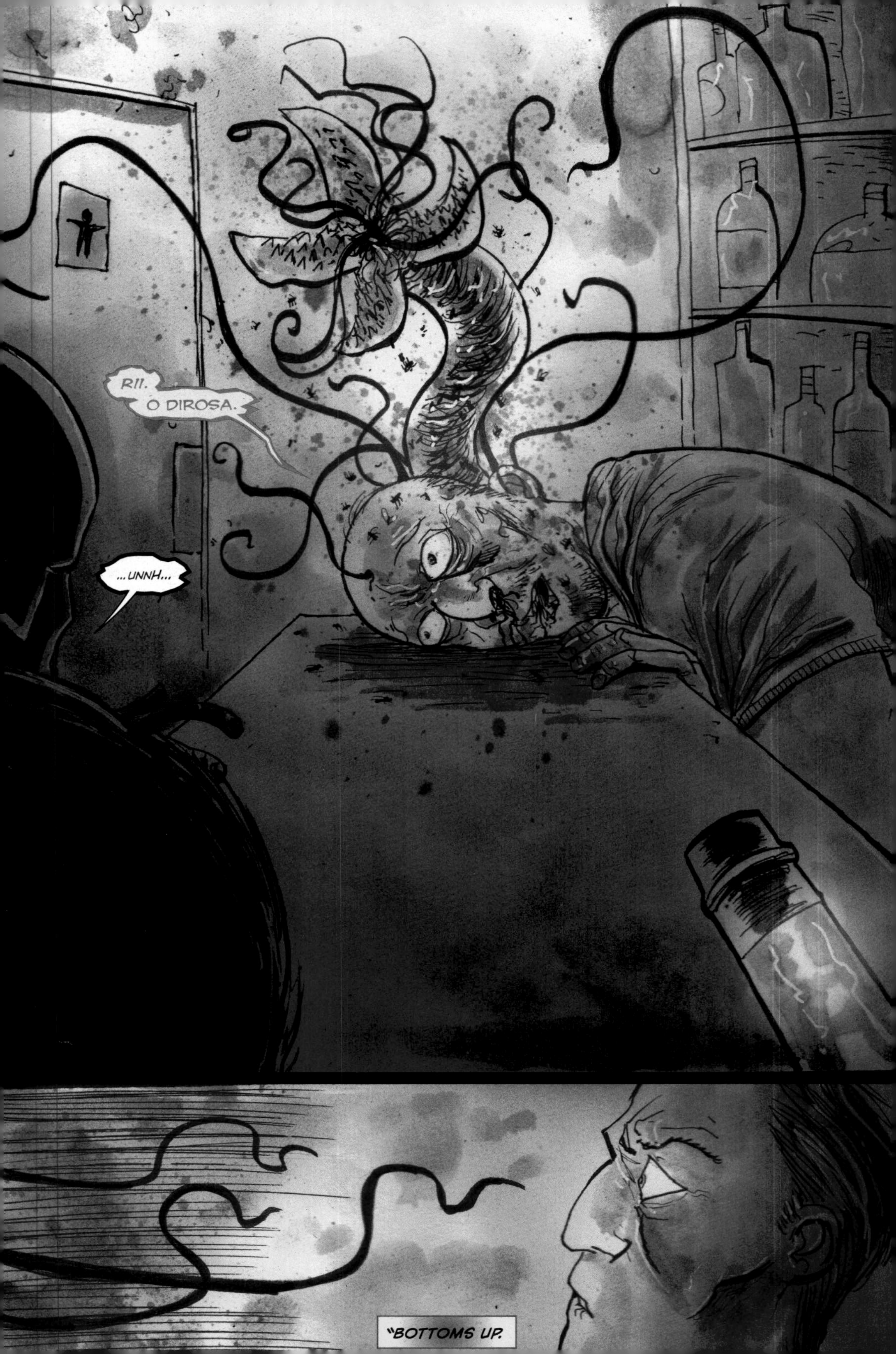
RII.
O DIROSA.
...UNNH...
"BOTTOMS UP.

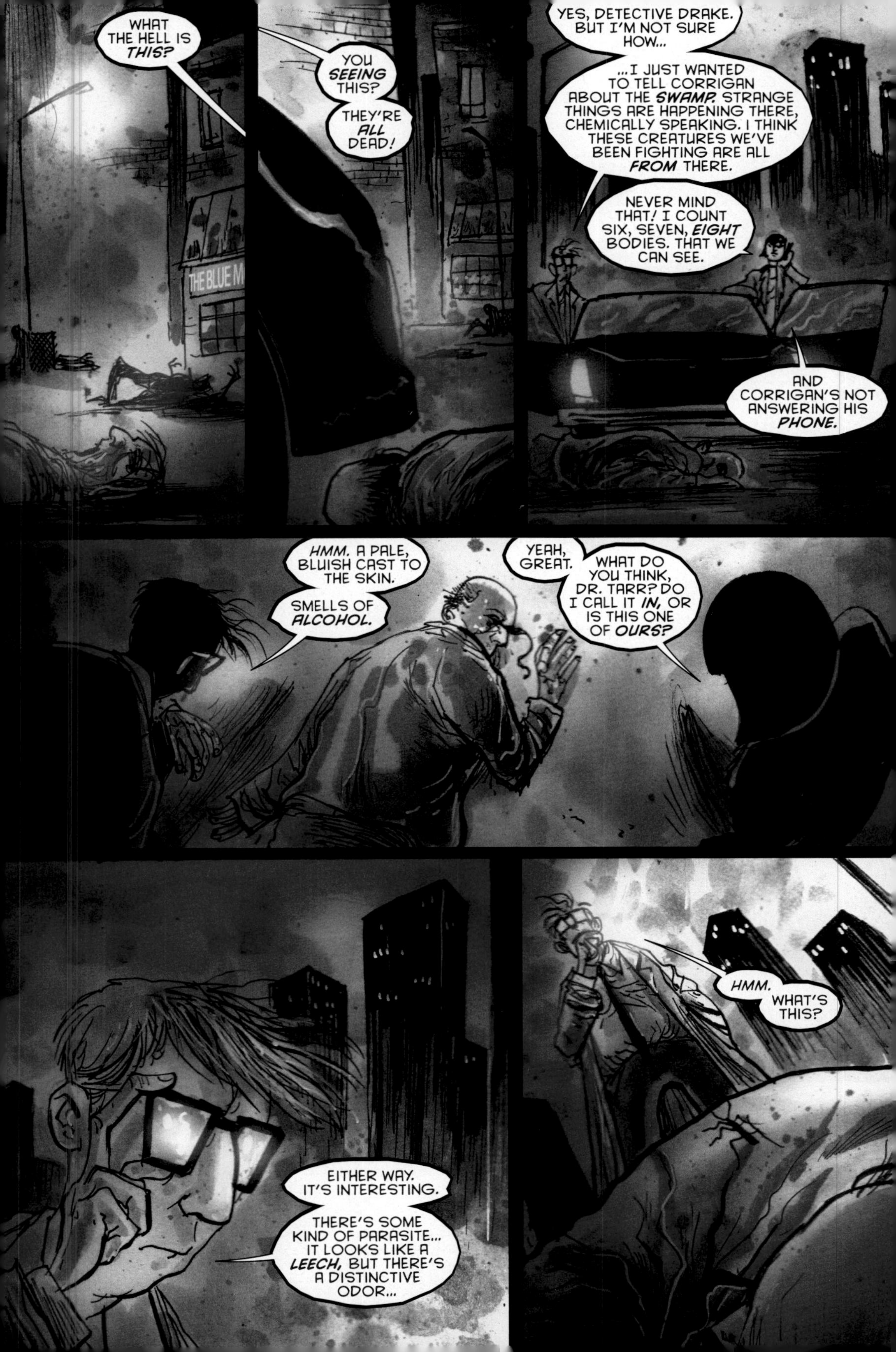
WHAT THE HELL IS THIS?
THE BLUE M
YOU SEEING THIS?
THEY'RE ALL DEAD!
YES, DETECTIVE DRAKE. BUT I'M NOT SURE HOW...
...I JUST WANTED TO TELL CORRIGAN ABOUT THE SWAMP. STRANGE THINGS ARE HAPPENING THERE, CHEMICALLY SPEAKING. I THINK THESE CREATURES WE'VE BEEN FIGHTING ARE ALL FROM THERE.
NEVER MIND THAT! I COUNT SIX, SEVEN, EIGHT BODIES. THAT WE CAN SEE.
AND CORRIGAN'S NOT ANSWERING HIS PHONE.
HMM. A PALE, BLUISH CAST TO THE SKIN.
SMELLS OF ALCOHOL.
YEAH, GREAT.
WHAT DO YOU THINK, DR. TARR? DO I CALL IT IN, OR IS THIS ONE OF OURS?
EITHER WAY. IT'S INTERESTING.
THERE'S SOME KIND OF PARASITE... IT LOOKS LIKE A LEECH, BUT THERE'S A DISTINCTIVE ODOR...
HMM.
WHAT'S THIS?

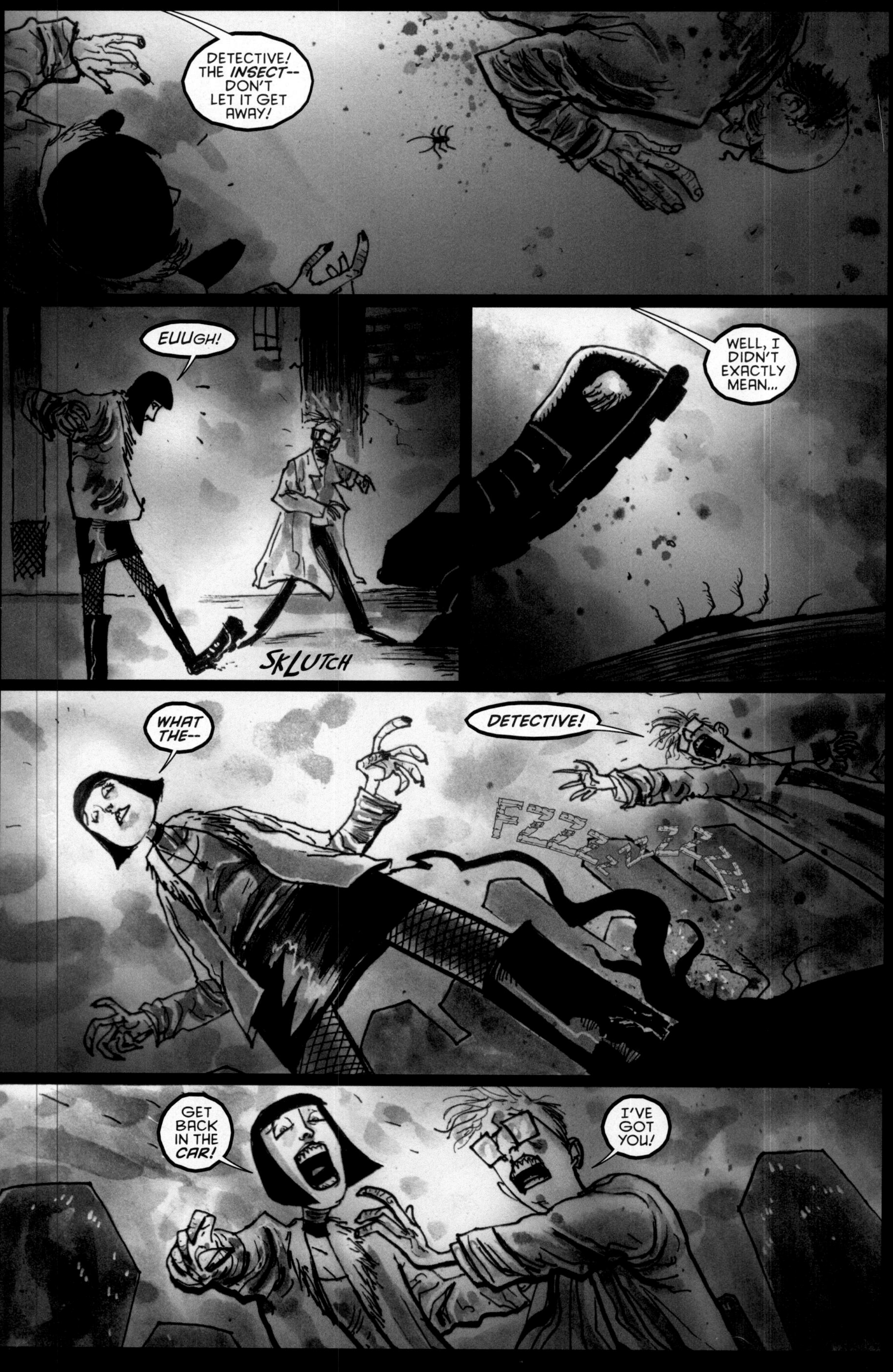
DETECTIVE! THE *INSECT*-- DON'T LET IT GET AWAY!
EUUGH!
SKLUTCH
WELL, I DIDN'T EXACTLY MEAN...
WHAT THE--
DETECTIVE!
FZZZzzzZZZzzz
GET BACK IN THE *CAR*!
I'VE GOT YOU!

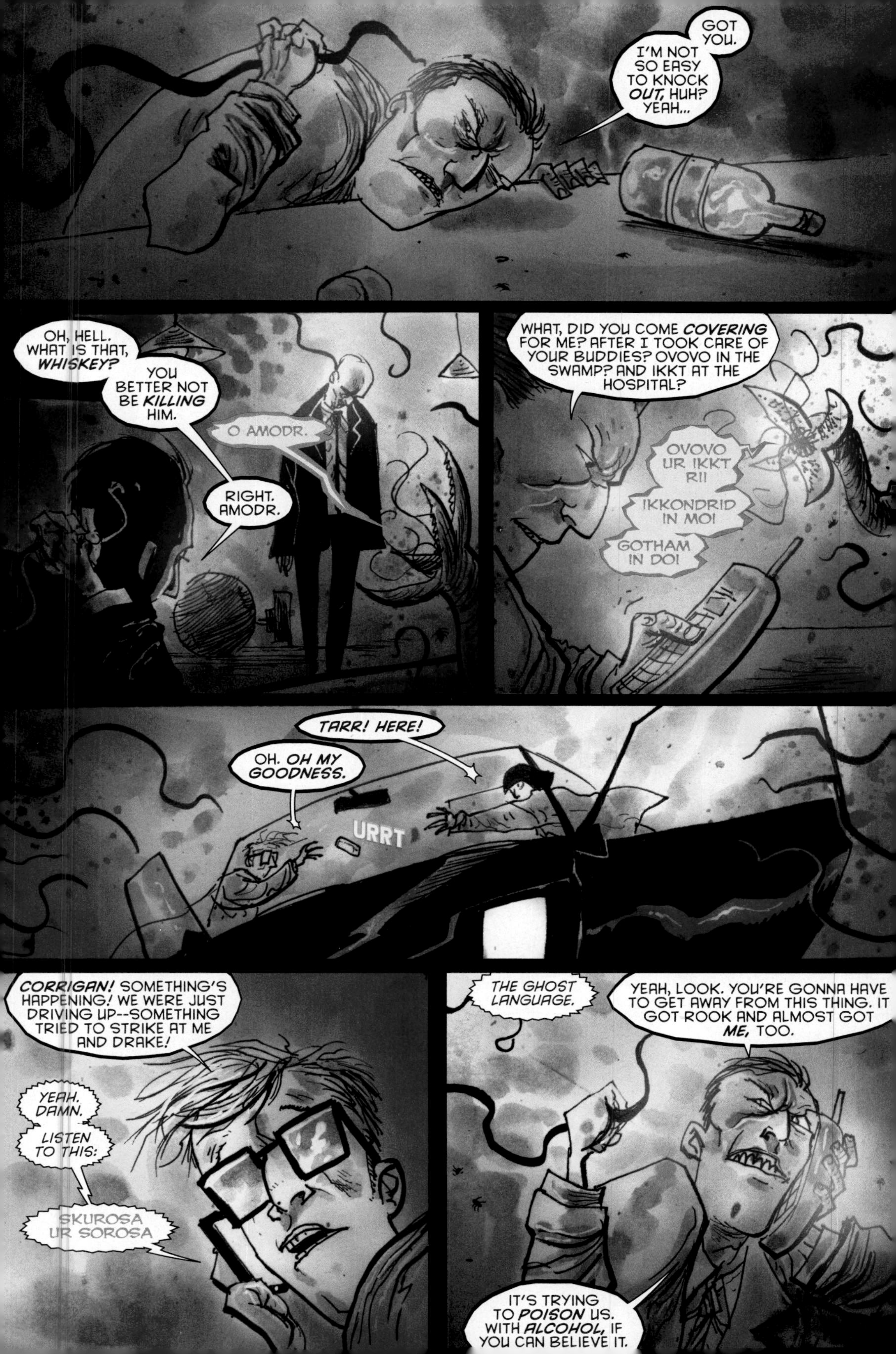

GOT YOU.
I'M NOT SO EASY TO KNOCK OUT, HUH? YEAH...
OH, HELL. WHAT IS THAT, WHISKEY?
YOU BETTER NOT BE KILLING HIM.
O AMODR.
RIGHT. AMODR.
WHAT, DID YOU COME COVERING FOR ME? AFTER I TOOK CARE OF YOUR BUDDIES? OVOVO IN THE SWAMP? AND IKKT AT THE HOSPITAL?
OVOVO UR IKKT RI!
IKKONDRID IN MO!
GOTHAM IN DO!
TARR! HERE!
OH. OH MY GOODNESS.
URRT
CORRIGAN! SOMETHING'S HAPPENING! WE WERE JUST DRIVING UP--SOMETHING TRIED TO STRIKE AT ME AND DRAKE!
YEAH. DAMN.
LISTEN TO THIS:
SKUROSA UR SOROSA
THE GHOST LANGUAGE.
YEAH, LOOK. YOU'RE GONNA HAVE TO GET AWAY FROM THIS THING. IT GOT ROOK AND ALMOST GOT ME, TOO.
IT'S TRYING TO POISON US. WITH ALCOHOL, IF YOU CAN BELIEVE IT.

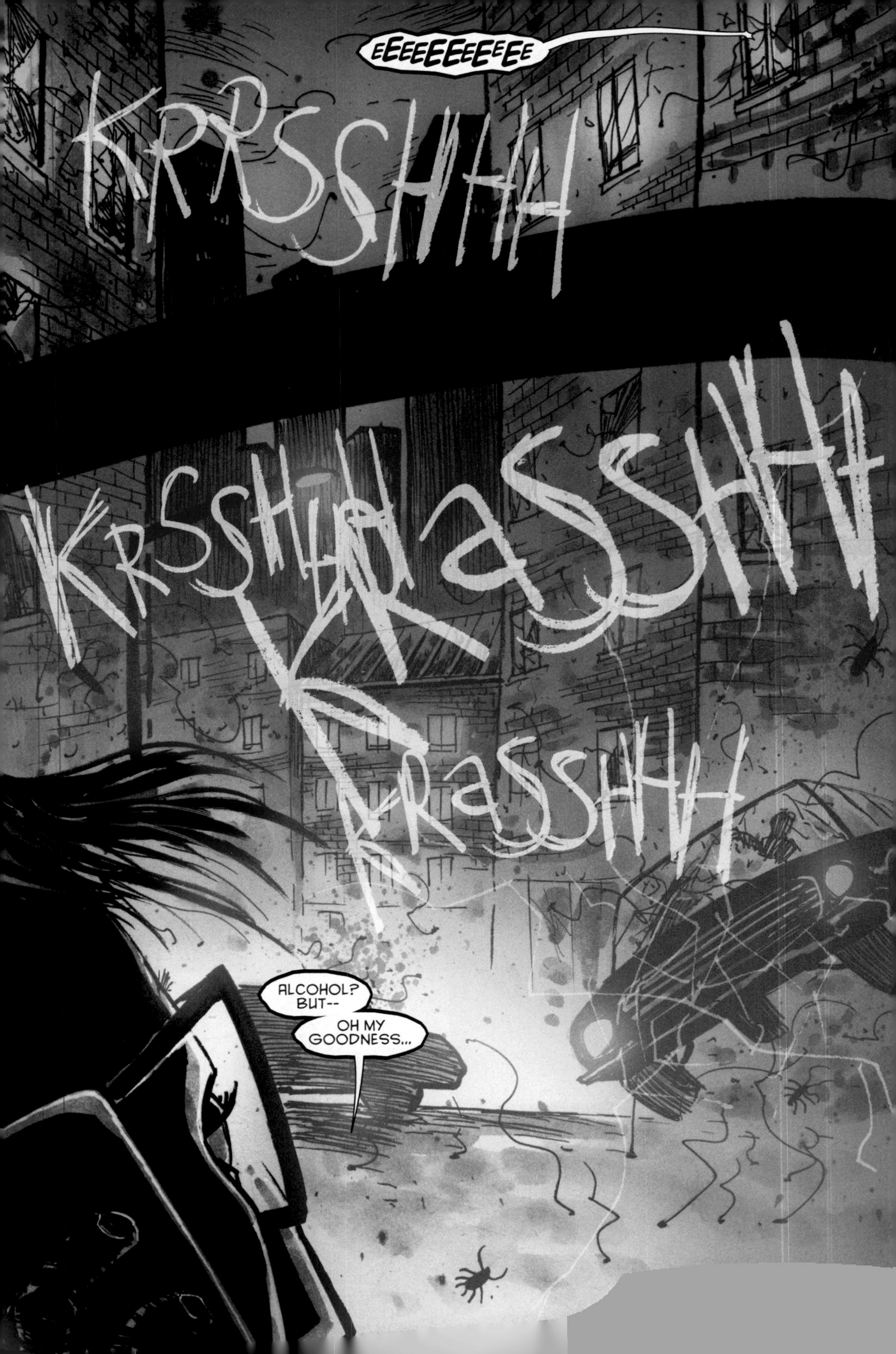
EEEEEEEEEEE
KRRSSHHH
KRSSHHH KRASSHH
KRASSHH
ALCOHOL? BUT--
OH MY GOODNESS...

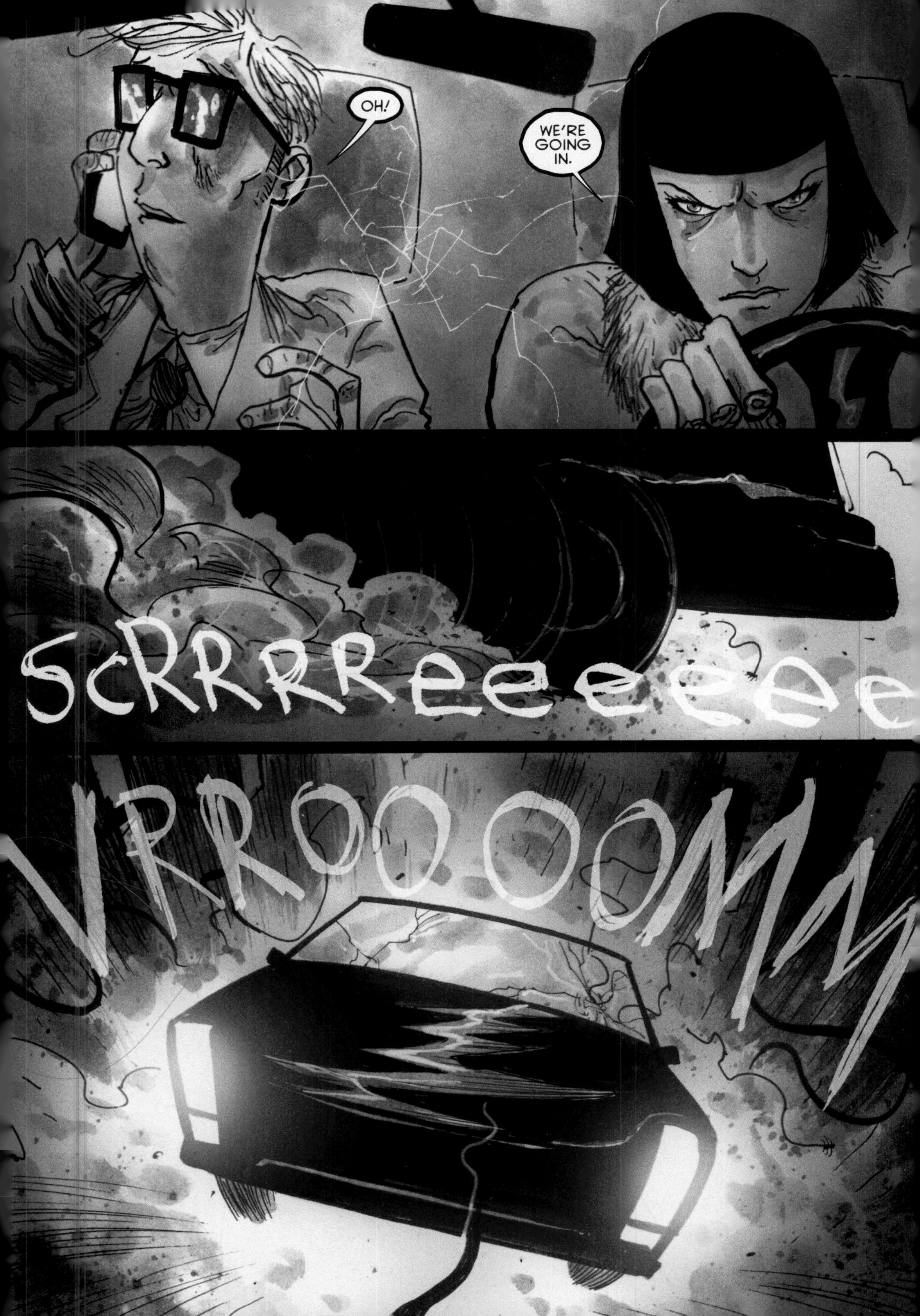
OH!
WE'RE GOING IN.
SCRRRREEEEEE
VRROOOOMM

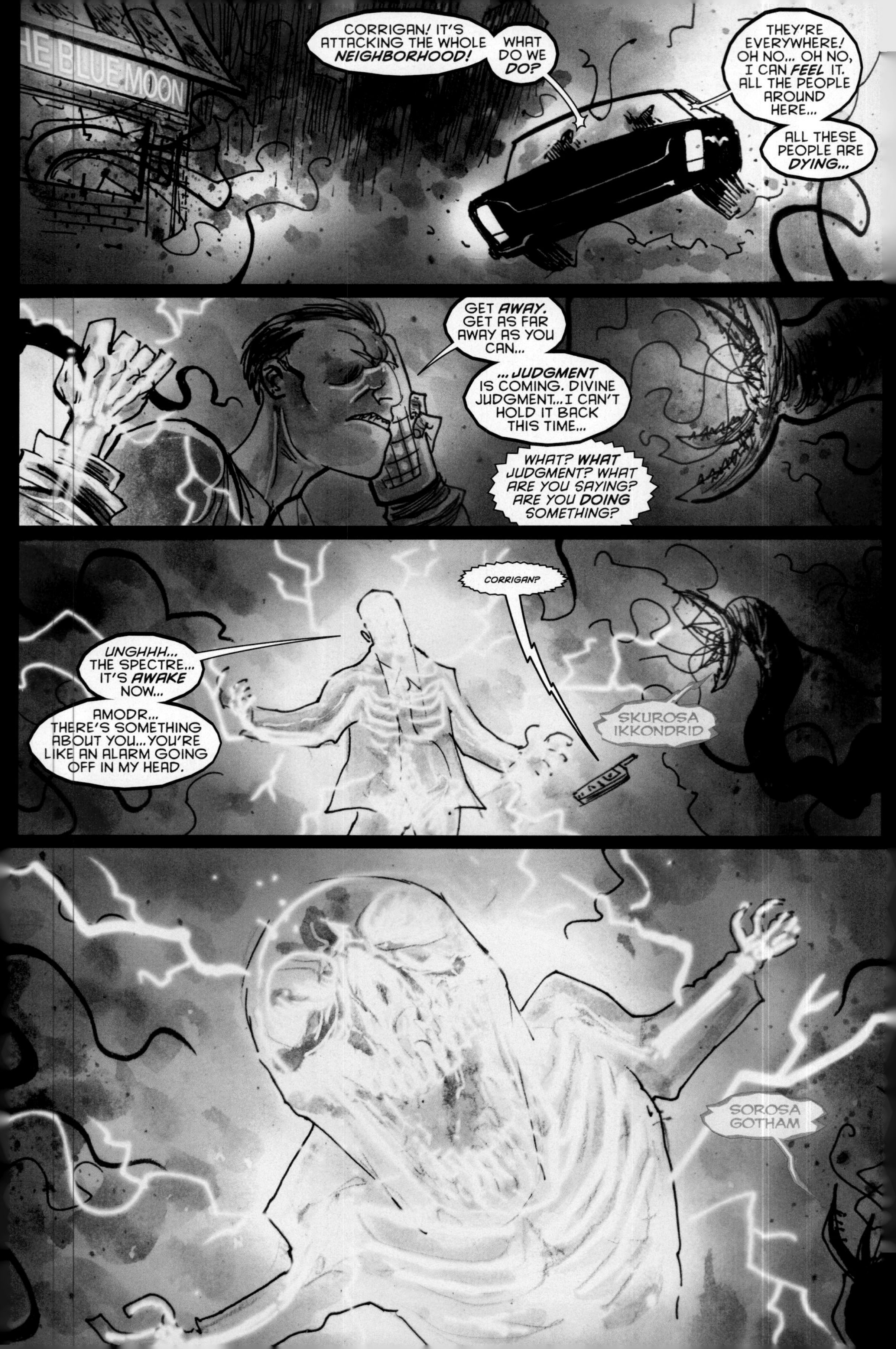
HE BLUE MOON
CORRIGAN! IT'S ATTACKING THE WHOLE NEIGHBORHOOD!
WHAT DO WE DO?
THEY'RE EVERYWHERE! OH NO... OH NO, I CAN FEEL IT. ALL THE PEOPLE AROUND HERE...
ALL THESE PEOPLE ARE DYING...
GET AWAY. GET AS FAR AWAY AS YOU CAN...
...JUDGMENT IS COMING. DIVINE JUDGMENT...I CAN'T HOLD IT BACK THIS TIME...
WHAT? WHAT JUDGMENT? WHAT ARE YOU SAYING? ARE YOU DOING SOMETHING?
CORRIGAN?
UNGHHH... THE SPECTRE... IT'S AWAKE NOW...
AMODR... THERE'S SOMETHING ABOUT YOU...YOU'RE LIKE AN ALARM GOING OFF IN MY HEAD.
SKUROSA IKKONDRID
SOROSA GOTHAM

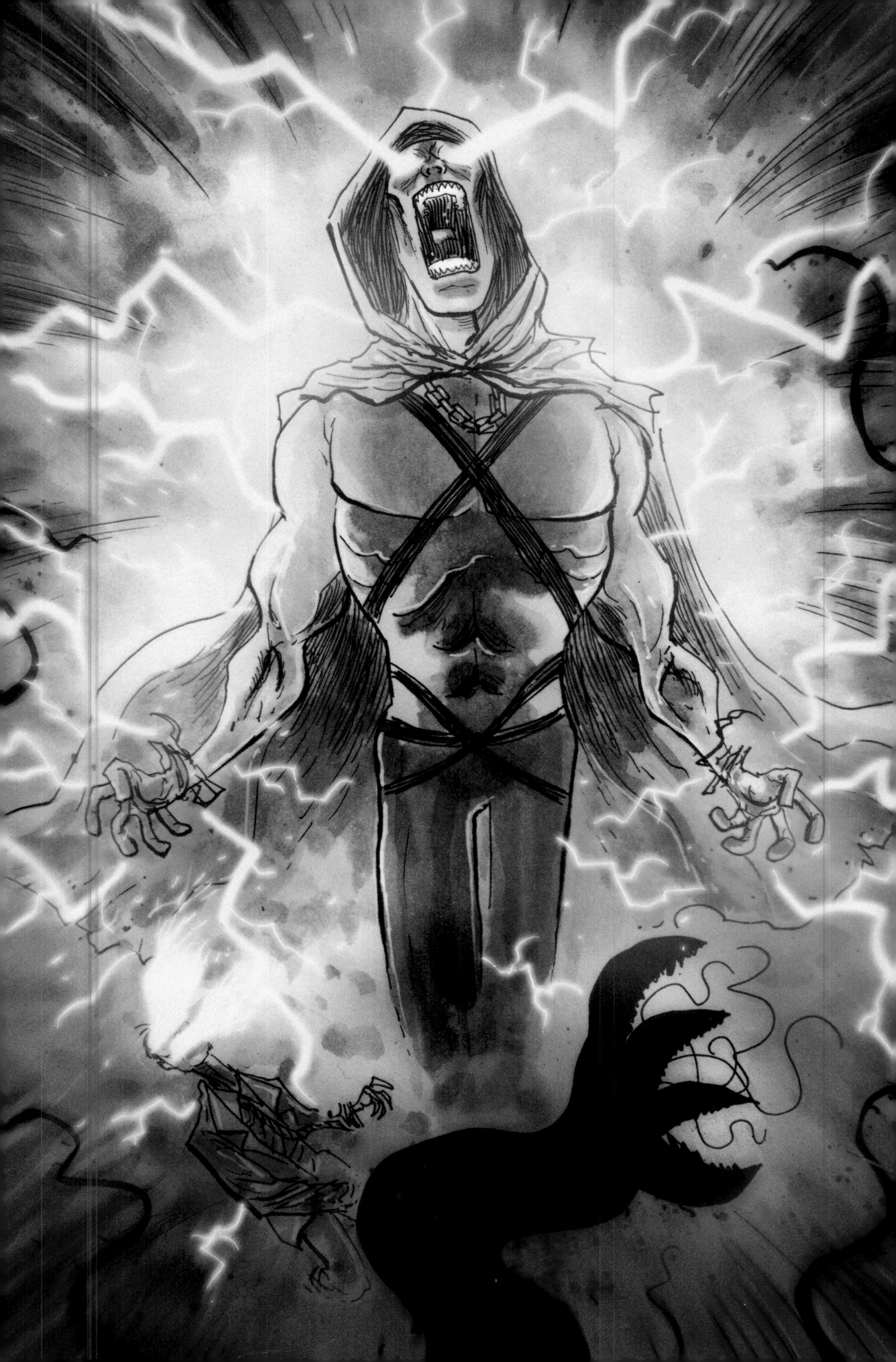

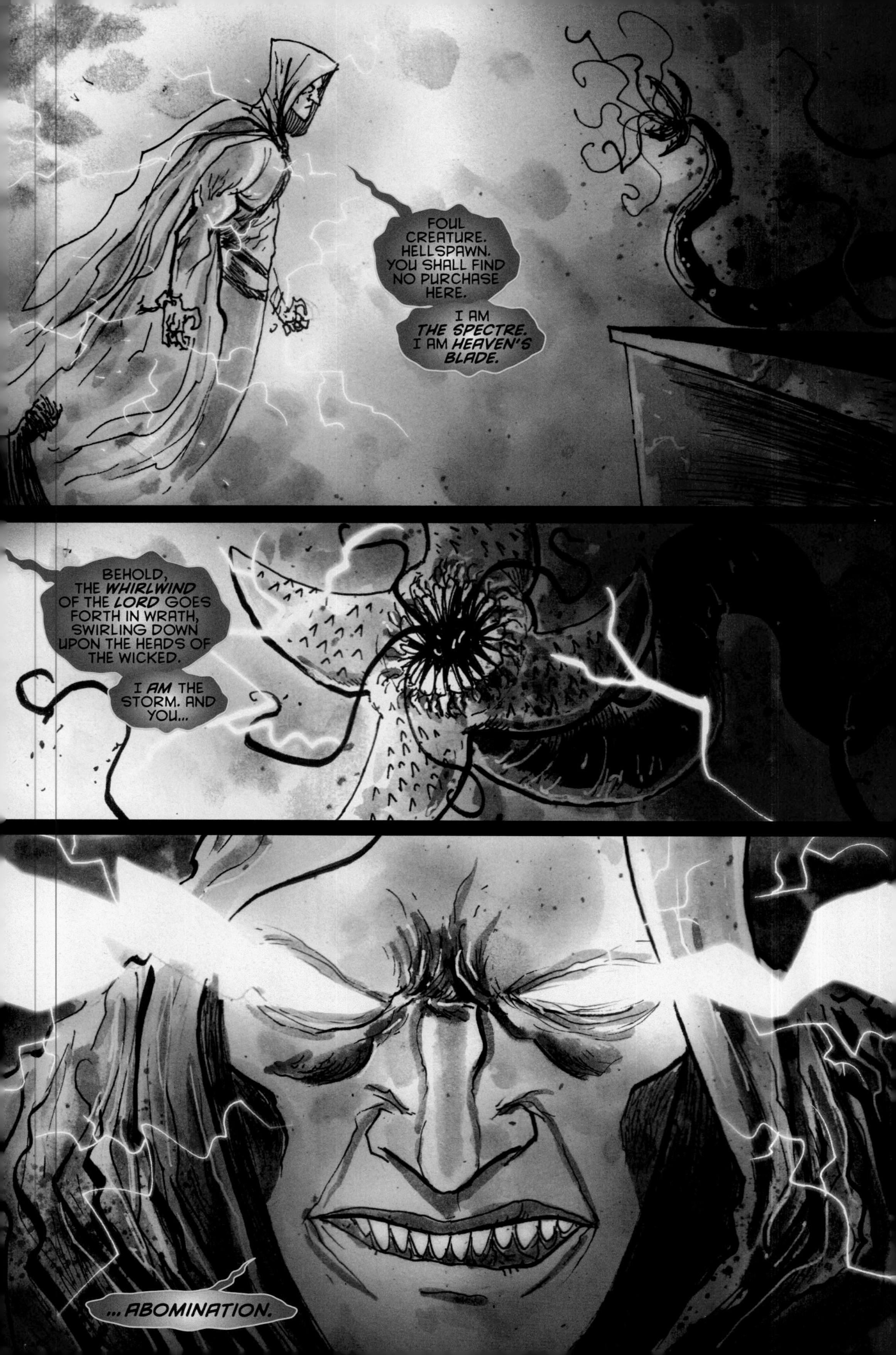
FOUL CREATURE. HELLSPAWN. YOU SHALL FIND NO PURCHASE HERE.
I AM THE SPECTRE. I AM HEAVEN'S BLADE.
BEHOLD, THE WHIRLWIND OF THE LORD GOES FORTH IN WRATH, SWIRLING DOWN UPON THE HEADS OF THE WICKED.
I AM THE STORM. AND YOU...
...ABOMINATION.

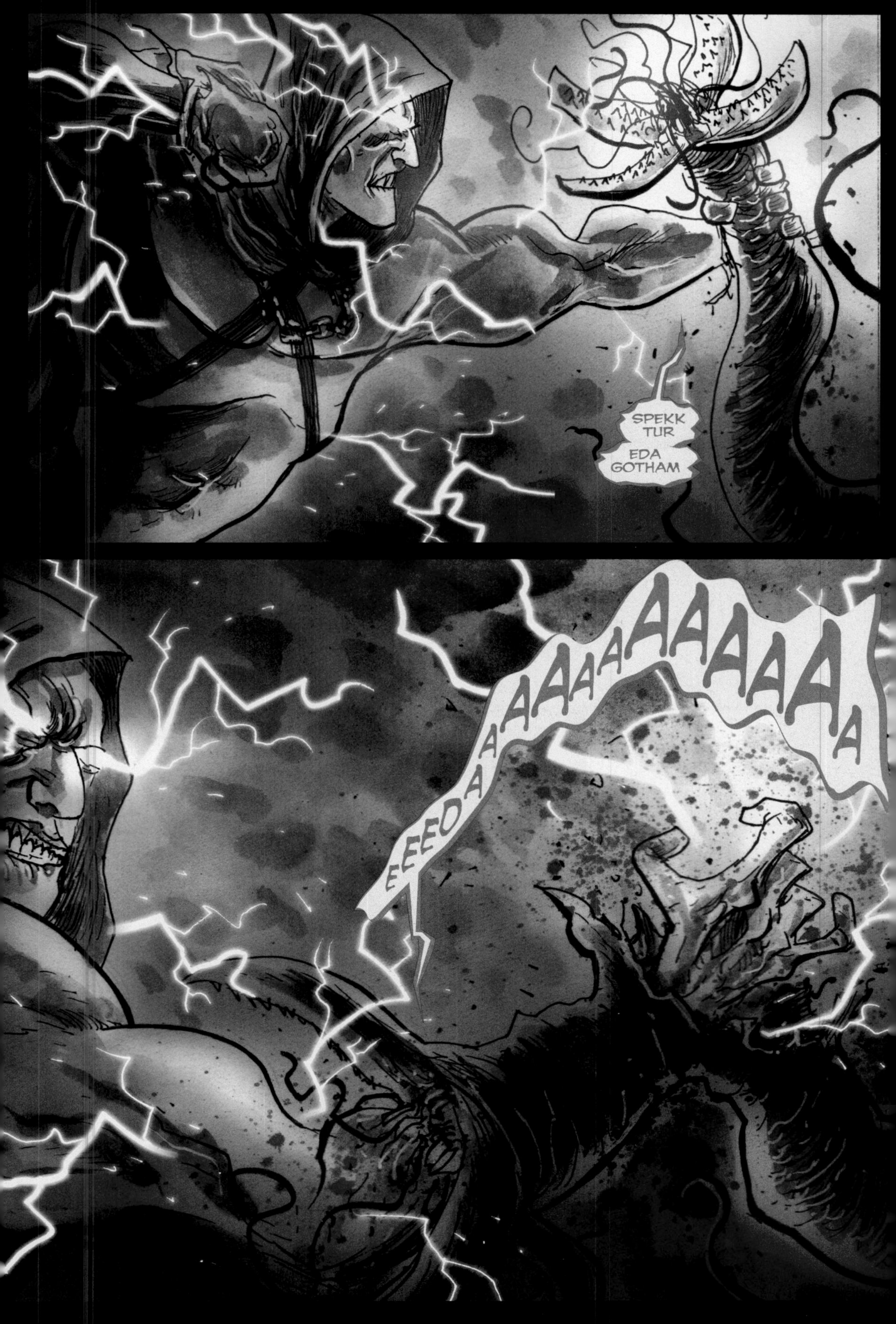
SPEKK TUR
EDA GOTHAM
EEEDAAAAAAAAAAAAAAA

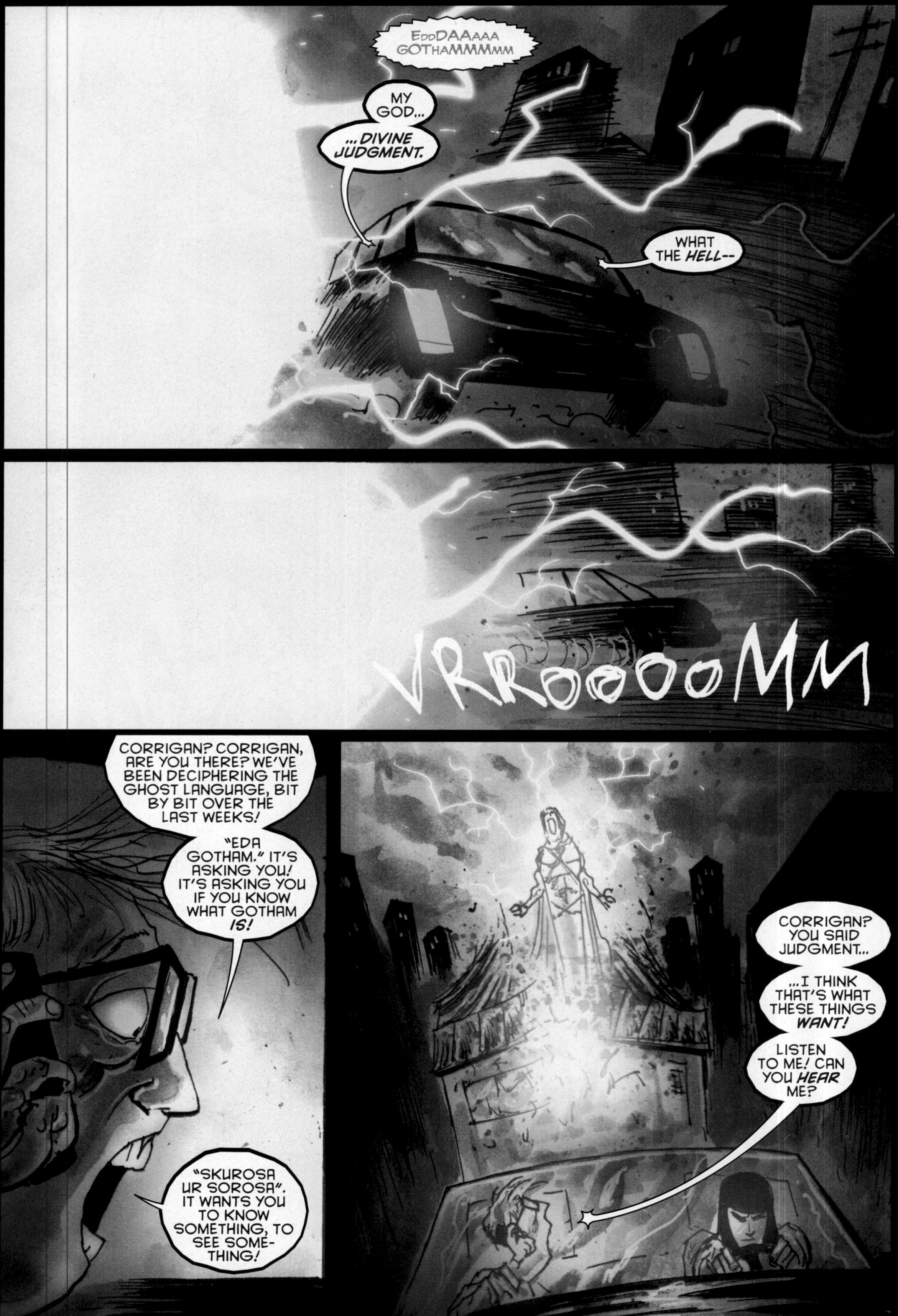
EddDAAaaa GOThaMMMmm
MY GOD...
...DIVINE JUDGMENT.
WHAT THE HELL--
VRROOOOMM
CORRIGAN? CORRIGAN, ARE YOU THERE? WE'VE BEEN DECIPHERING THE GHOST LANGUAGE, BIT BY BIT OVER THE LAST WEEKS!
"EDA GOTHAM." IT'S ASKING YOU! IT'S ASKING YOU IF YOU KNOW WHAT GOTHAM IS!
"SKUROSA UR SOROSA". IT WANTS YOU TO KNOW SOMETHING, TO SEE SOME-THING!
CORRIGAN? YOU SAID JUDGMENT...
...I THINK THAT'S WHAT THESE THINGS WANT!
LISTEN TO ME! CAN YOU HEAR ME?

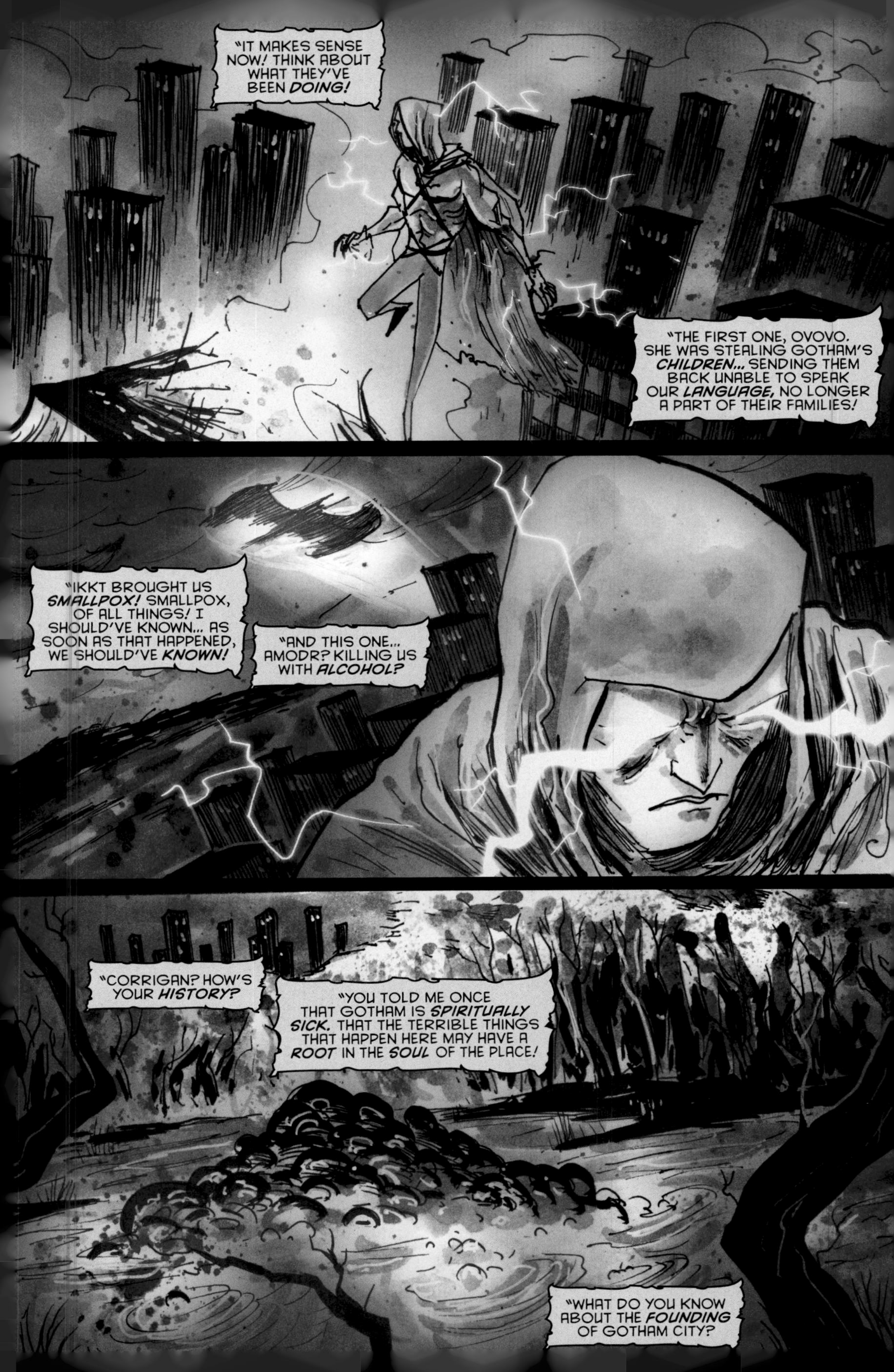
"IT MAKES SENSE NOW! THINK ABOUT WHAT THEY'VE BEEN DOING!
"THE FIRST ONE, OVOVO. SHE WAS STEALING GOTHAM'S CHILDREN... SENDING THEM BACK UNABLE TO SPEAK OUR LANGUAGE, NO LONGER A PART OF THEIR FAMILIES!
"IKKT BROUGHT US SMALLPOX! SMALLPOX, OF ALL THINGS! I SHOULD'VE KNOWN... AS SOON AS THAT HAPPENED, WE SHOULD'VE KNOWN!
"AND THIS ONE... AMODR? KILLING US WITH ALCOHOL?
"CORRIGAN? HOW'S YOUR HISTORY?
"YOU TOLD ME ONCE THAT GOTHAM IS SPIRITUALLY SICK. THAT THE TERRIBLE THINGS THAT HAPPEN HERE MAY HAVE A ROOT IN THE SOUL OF THE PLACE!
"WHAT DO YOU KNOW ABOUT THE FOUNDING OF GOTHAM CITY?

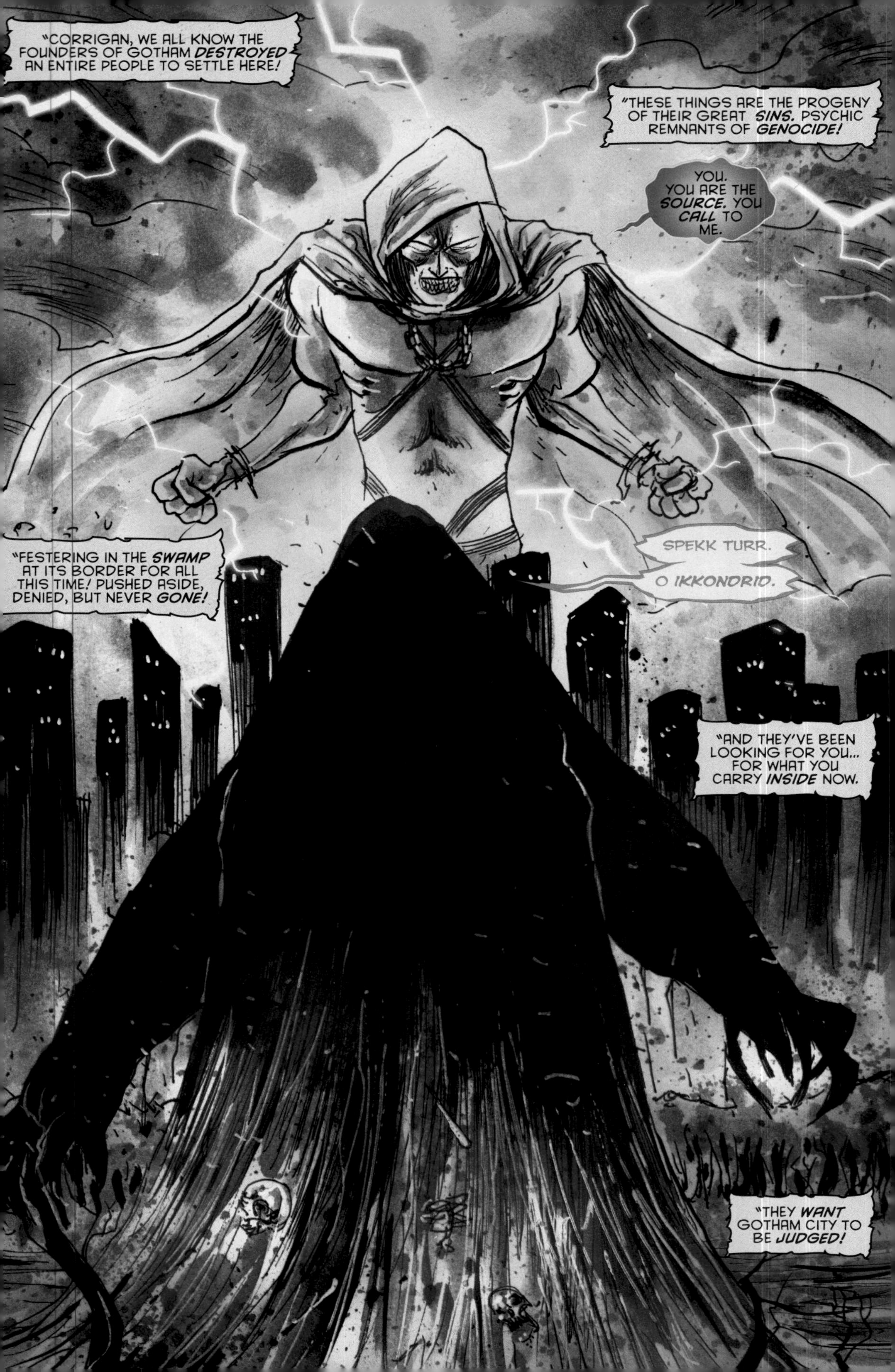
"CORRIGAN, WE ALL KNOW THE FOUNDERS OF GOTHAM DESTROYED AN ENTIRE PEOPLE TO SETTLE HERE!
"THESE THINGS ARE THE PROGENY OF THEIR GREAT SINS. PSYCHIC REMNANTS OF GENOCIDE!
YOU. YOU ARE THE SOURCE. YOU CALL TO ME.
"FESTERING IN THE SWAMP AT ITS BORDER FOR ALL THIS TIME! PUSHED ASIDE, DENIED, BUT NEVER GONE!
SPEKK TURR.
O IKKONORIO.
"AND THEY'VE BEEN LOOKING FOR YOU... FOR WHAT YOU CARRY INSIDE NOW.
"THEY WANT GOTHAM CITY TO BE JUDGED!

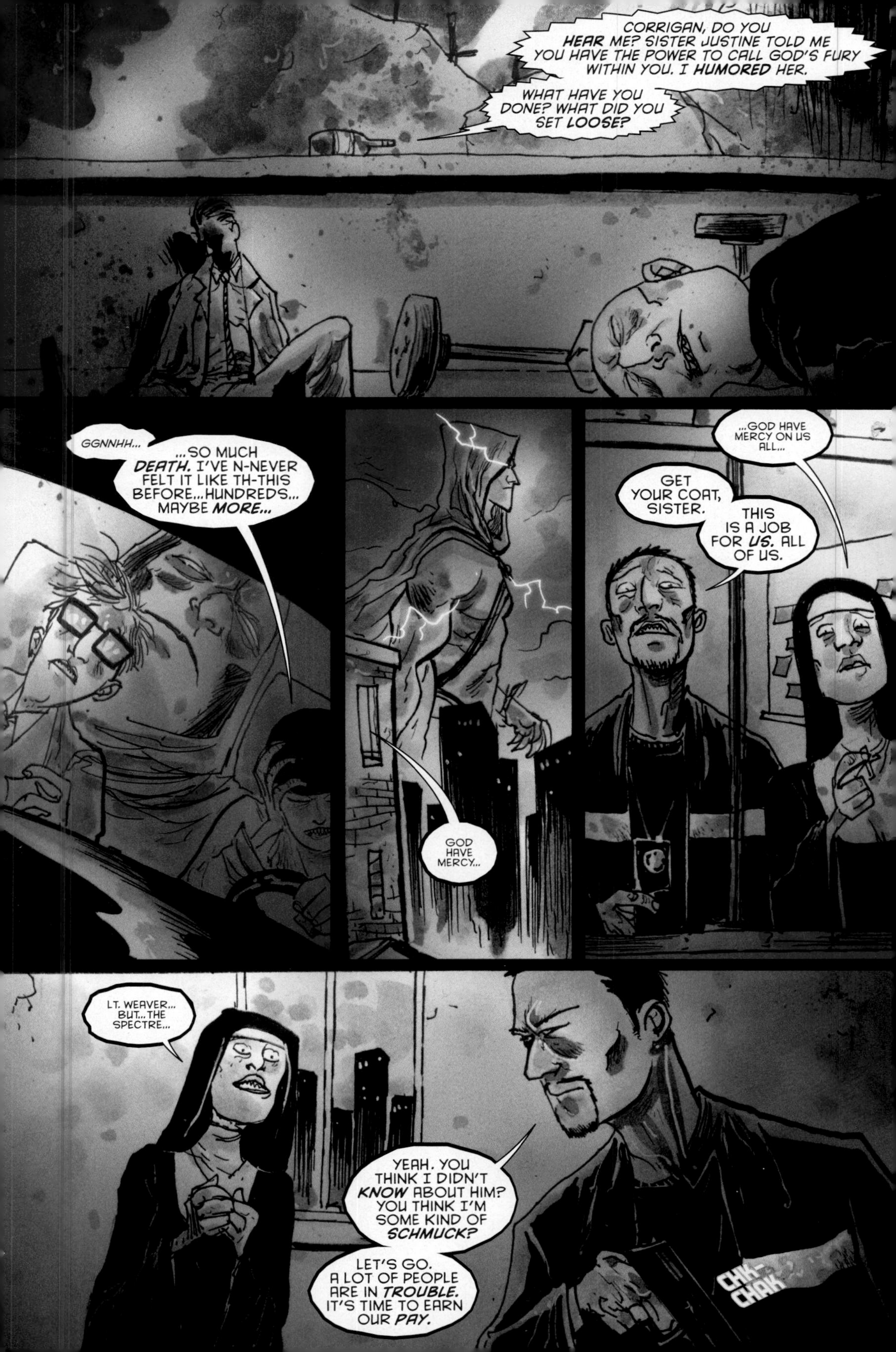

CORRIGAN, DO YOU HEAR ME? SISTER JUSTINE TOLD ME YOU HAVE THE POWER TO CALL GOD'S FURY WITHIN YOU. I HUMORED HER.
WHAT HAVE YOU DONE? WHAT DID YOU SET LOOSE?
GGNNHH...
...SO MUCH DEATH. I'VE N-NEVER FELT IT LIKE TH-THIS BEFORE...HUNDREDS... MAYBE MORE...
GOD HAVE MERCY...
...GOD HAVE MERCY ON US ALL...
GET YOUR COAT, SISTER.
THIS IS A JOB FOR US. ALL OF US.
LT. WEAVER... BUT... THE SPECTRE...
YEAH. YOU THINK I DIDN'T KNOW ABOUT HIM? YOU THINK I'M SOME KIND OF SCHMUCK?
LET'S GO. A LOT OF PEOPLE ARE IN TROUBLE. IT'S TIME TO EARN OUR PAY.
CHK-CHAK

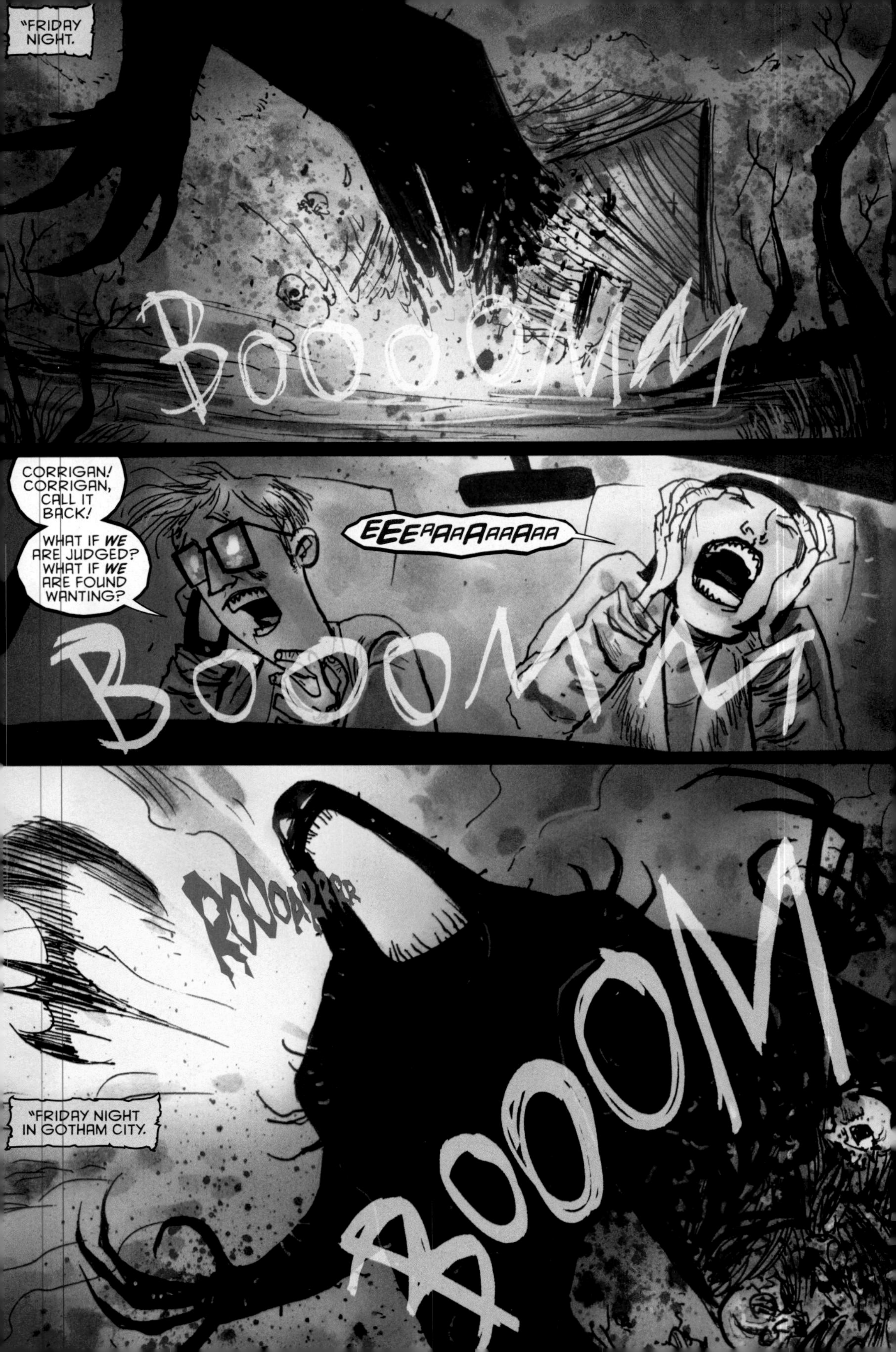
"FRIDAY NIGHT.
BOOOOMM
CORRIGAN! CORRIGAN, CALL IT BACK!
WHAT IF *WE* ARE JUDGED? WHAT IF *WE* ARE FOUND WANTING?
EEEAAAAAAAAA
BOOOMM
RROOARRRR
"FRIDAY NIGHT IN GOTHAM CITY.
BOOOM

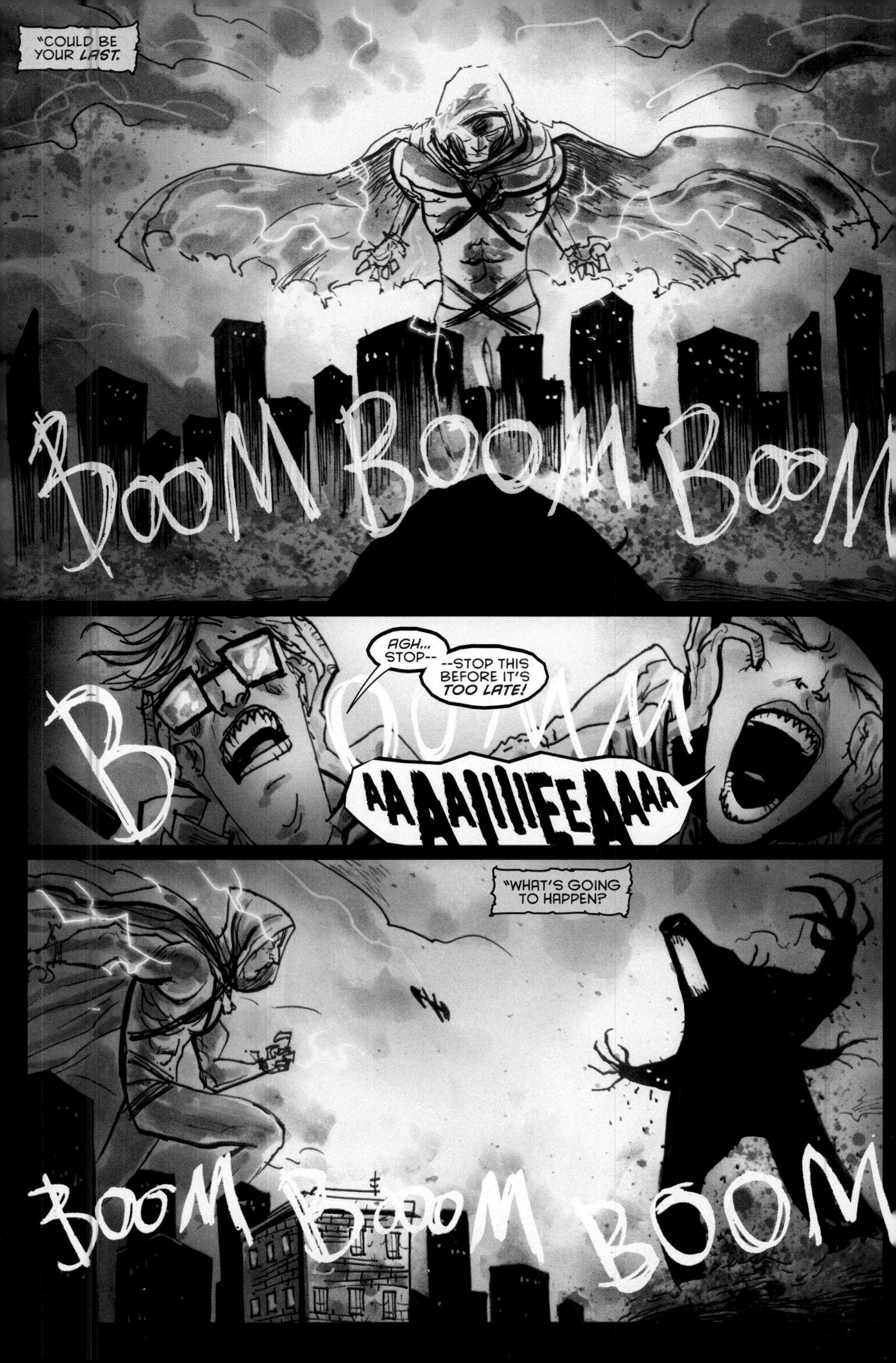
"COULD BE YOUR *LAST*.
BOOM BOOM BOOM
BOOM
AGH... STOP--
--STOP THIS BEFORE IT'S *TOO LATE!*
AAAIIIIEAAAA
"WHAT'S GOING TO HAPPEN?
BOOM BOOOM BOOM

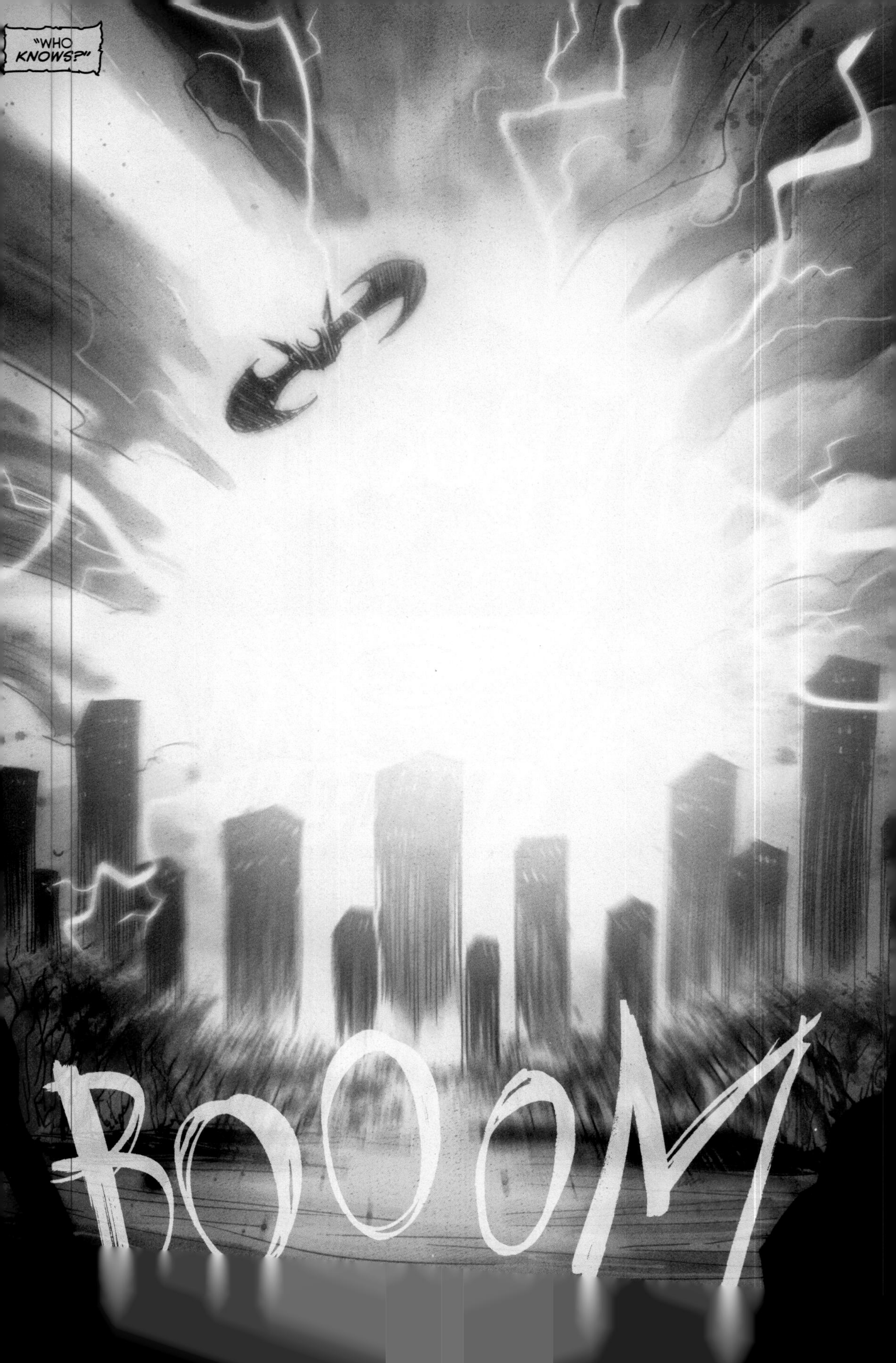
"WHO KNOWS?"
BOOOM

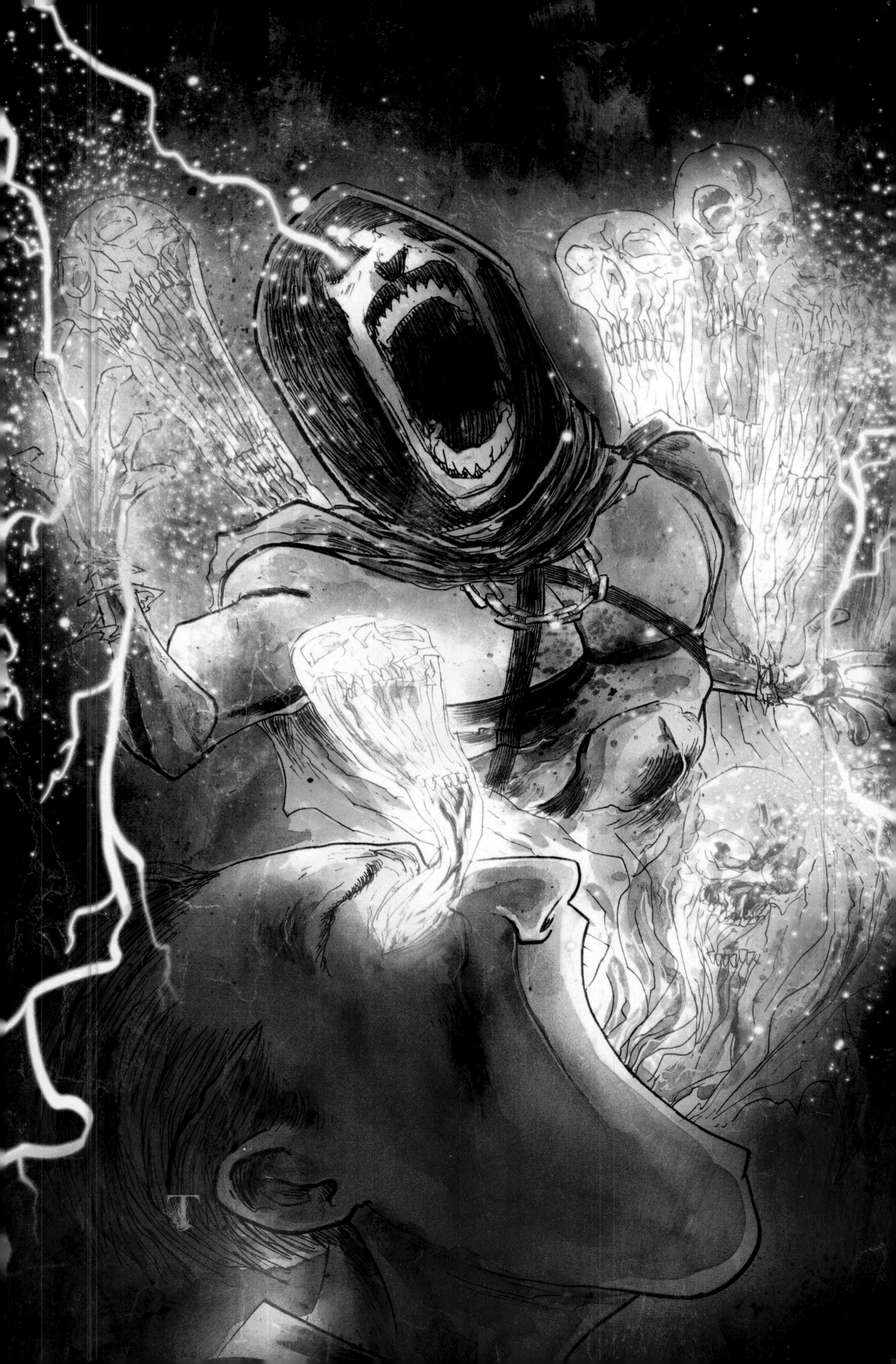

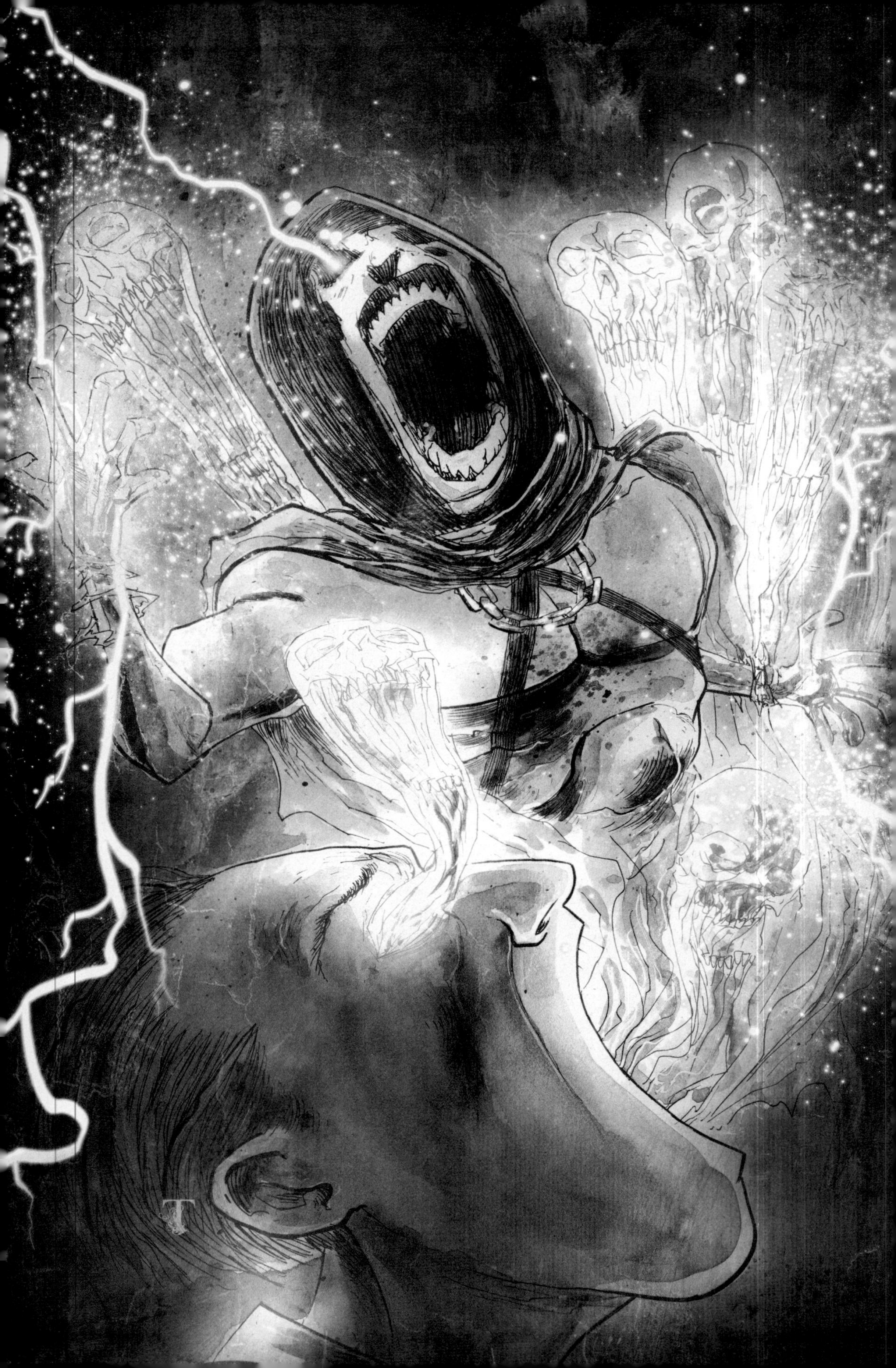

WE ARE PAST THE BREAKING POINT.

BATTLE HAS BROKEN LOOSE.

MILLIONS WILL DIE TONIGHT...

...IF WE ARE NOT STRONG.

CHAPTER FIVE:
JUDGMENT ON GOTHAM

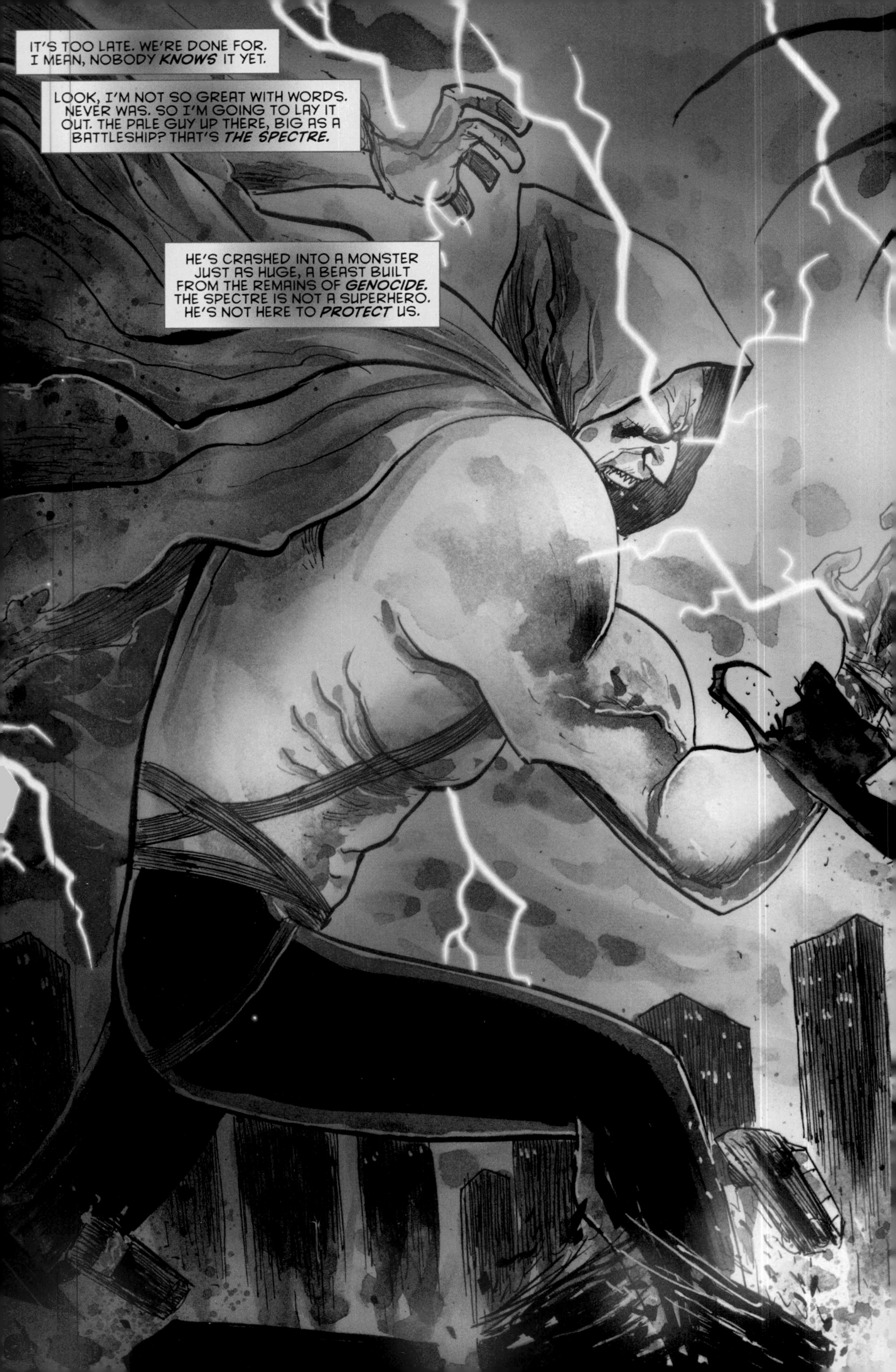
IT'S TOO LATE. WE'RE DONE FOR. I MEAN, NOBODY *KNOWS* IT YET.
LOOK, I'M NOT SO GREAT WITH WORDS. NEVER WAS. SO I'M GOING TO LAY IT OUT. THE PALE GUY UP THERE, BIG AS A BATTLESHIP? THAT'S *THE SPECTRE.*
HE'S CRASHED INTO A MONSTER JUST AS HUGE, A BEAST BUILT FROM THE REMAINS OF *GENOCIDE.* THE SPECTRE IS NOT A SUPERHERO. HE'S NOT HERE TO *PROTECT* US.

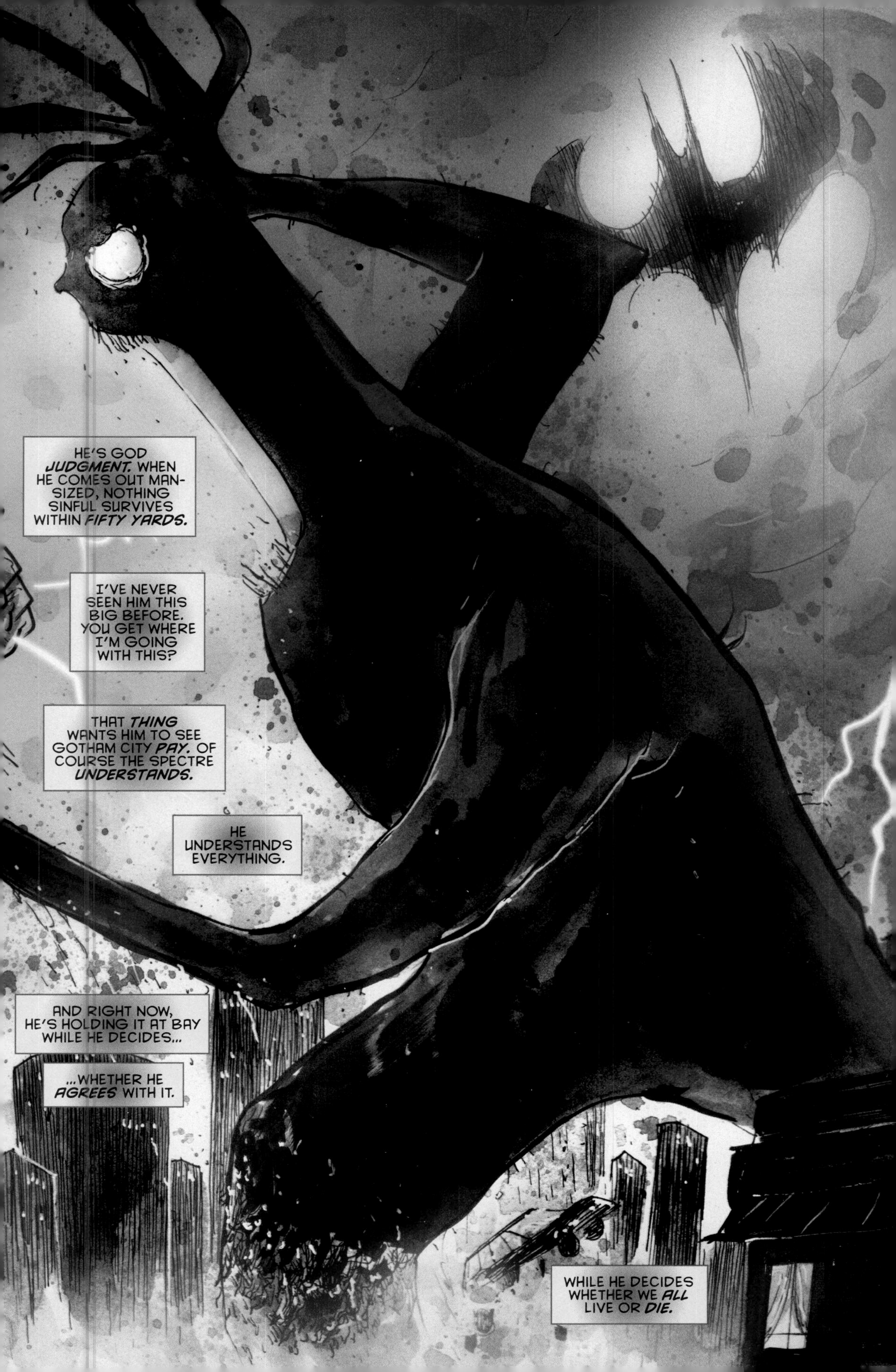
HE'S GOD JUDGMENT. WHEN HE COMES OUT MAN-SIZED, NOTHING SINFUL SURVIVES WITHIN FIFTY YARDS.
I'VE NEVER SEEN HIM THIS BIG BEFORE. YOU GET WHERE I'M GOING WITH THIS?
THAT THING WANTS HIM TO SEE GOTHAM CITY PAY. OF COURSE THE SPECTRE UNDERSTANDS.
HE UNDERSTANDS EVERYTHING.
AND RIGHT NOW, HE'S HOLDING IT AT BAY WHILE HE DECIDES...
...WHETHER HE AGREES WITH IT.
WHILE HE DECIDES WHETHER WE ALL LIVE OR DIE.

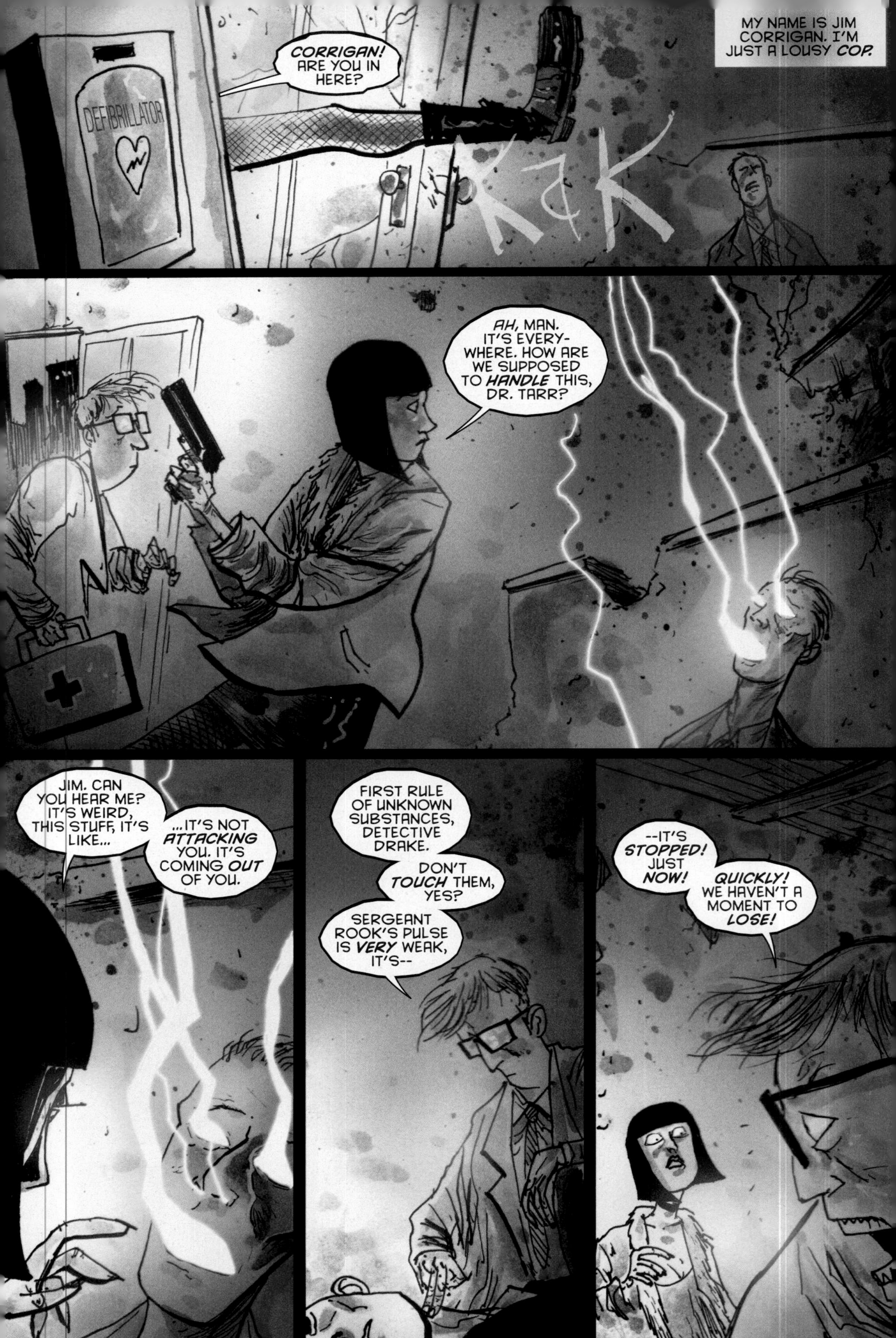

MY NAME IS JIM CORRIGAN. I'M JUST A LOUSY COP.
CORRIGAN! ARE YOU IN HERE?
DEFIBRILLATOR
KAK
AH, MAN. IT'S EVERY-WHERE. HOW ARE WE SUPPOSED TO HANDLE THIS, DR. TARR?
JIM. CAN YOU HEAR ME? IT'S WEIRD, THIS STUFF, IT'S LIKE...
...IT'S NOT ATTACKING YOU. IT'S COMING OUT OF YOU.
FIRST RULE OF UNKNOWN SUBSTANCES, DETECTIVE DRAKE.
DON'T TOUCH THEM, YES?
SERGEANT ROOK'S PULSE IS VERY WEAK, IT'S--
--IT'S STOPPED! JUST NOW!
QUICKLY! WE HAVEN'T A MOMENT TO LOSE!

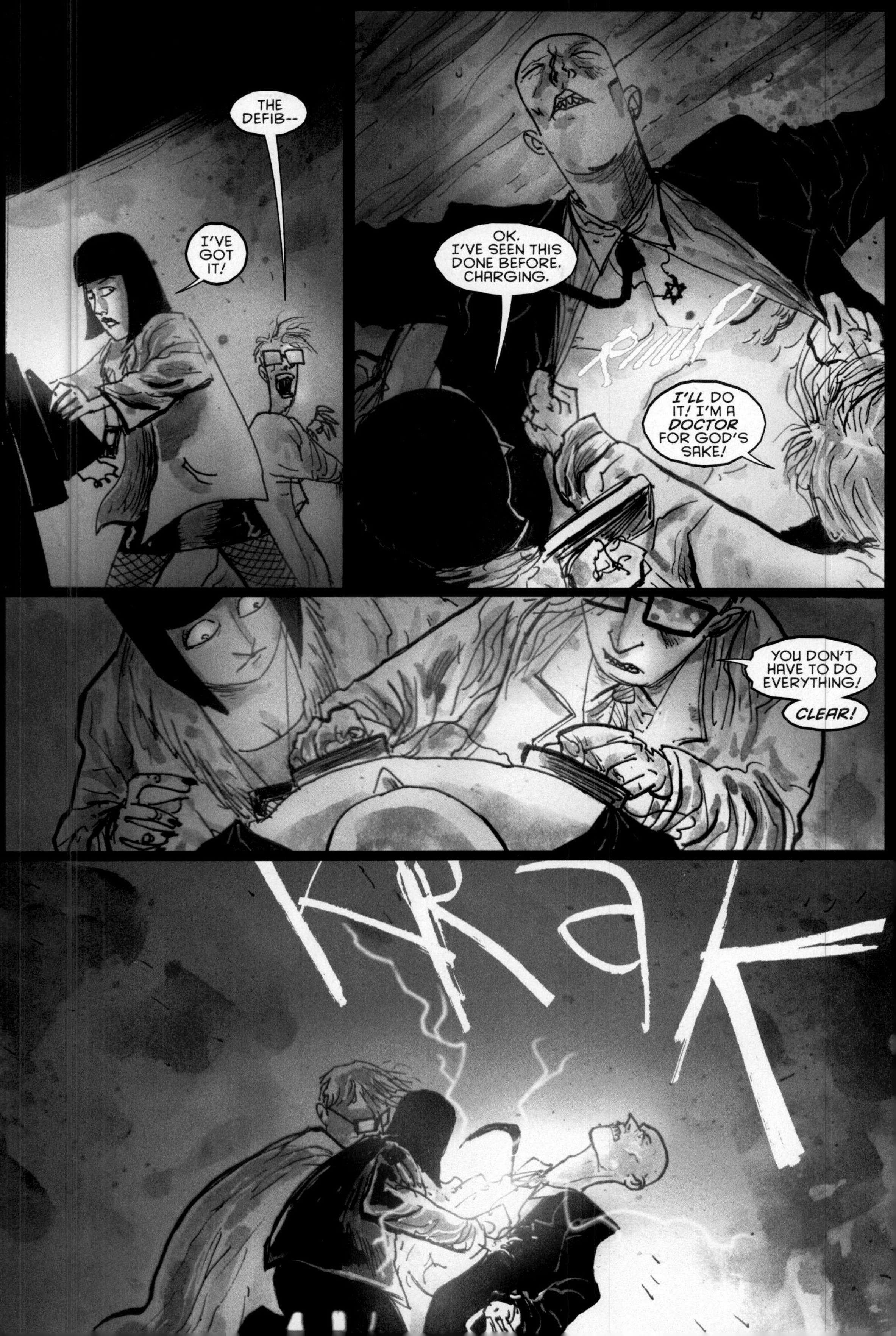
THE DEFIB--
I'VE GOT IT!
OK. I'VE SEEN THIS DONE BEFORE. CHARGING.
RIIIIP
I'LL DO IT! I'M A DOCTOR FOR GOD'S SAKE!
YOU DON'T HAVE TO DO EVERYTHING!
CLEAR!
KRAK

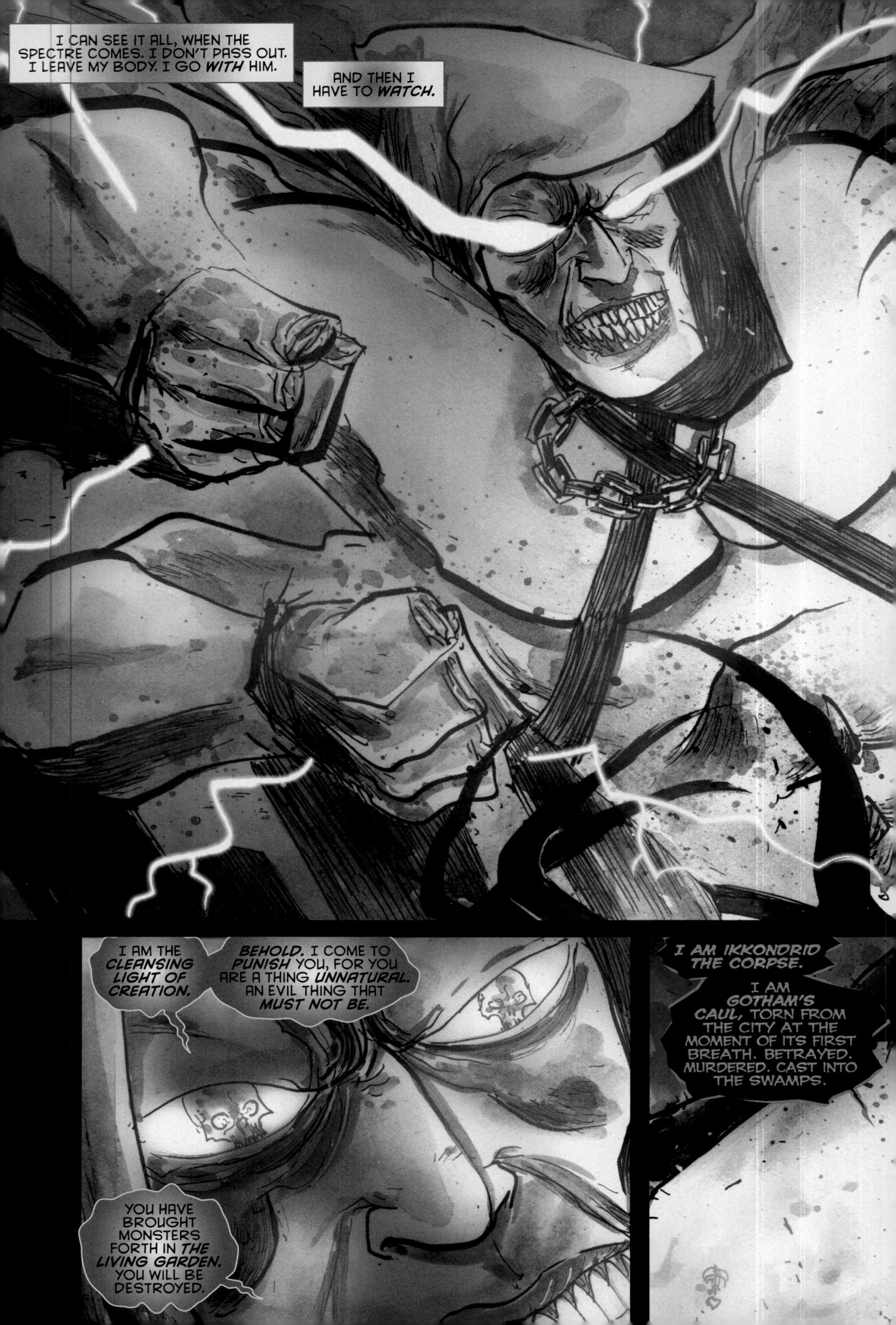
I CAN SEE IT ALL, WHEN THE SPECTRE COMES. I DON'T PASS OUT. I LEAVE MY BODY. I GO *WITH* HIM.
AND THEN I HAVE TO *WATCH.*
I AM THE *CLEANSING LIGHT OF CREATION.*
BEHOLD. I COME TO *PUNISH* YOU, FOR YOU ARE A THING *UNNATURAL.* AN EVIL THING THAT *MUST NOT BE.*
YOU HAVE BROUGHT MONSTERS FORTH IN *THE LIVING GARDEN.* YOU WILL BE DESTROYED.
I AM IKKONDRID THE CORPSE.
I AM *GOTHAM'S CAUL,* TORN FROM THE CITY AT THE MOMENT OF ITS FIRST BREATH. BETRAYED. MURDERED. CAST INTO THE SWAMPS.

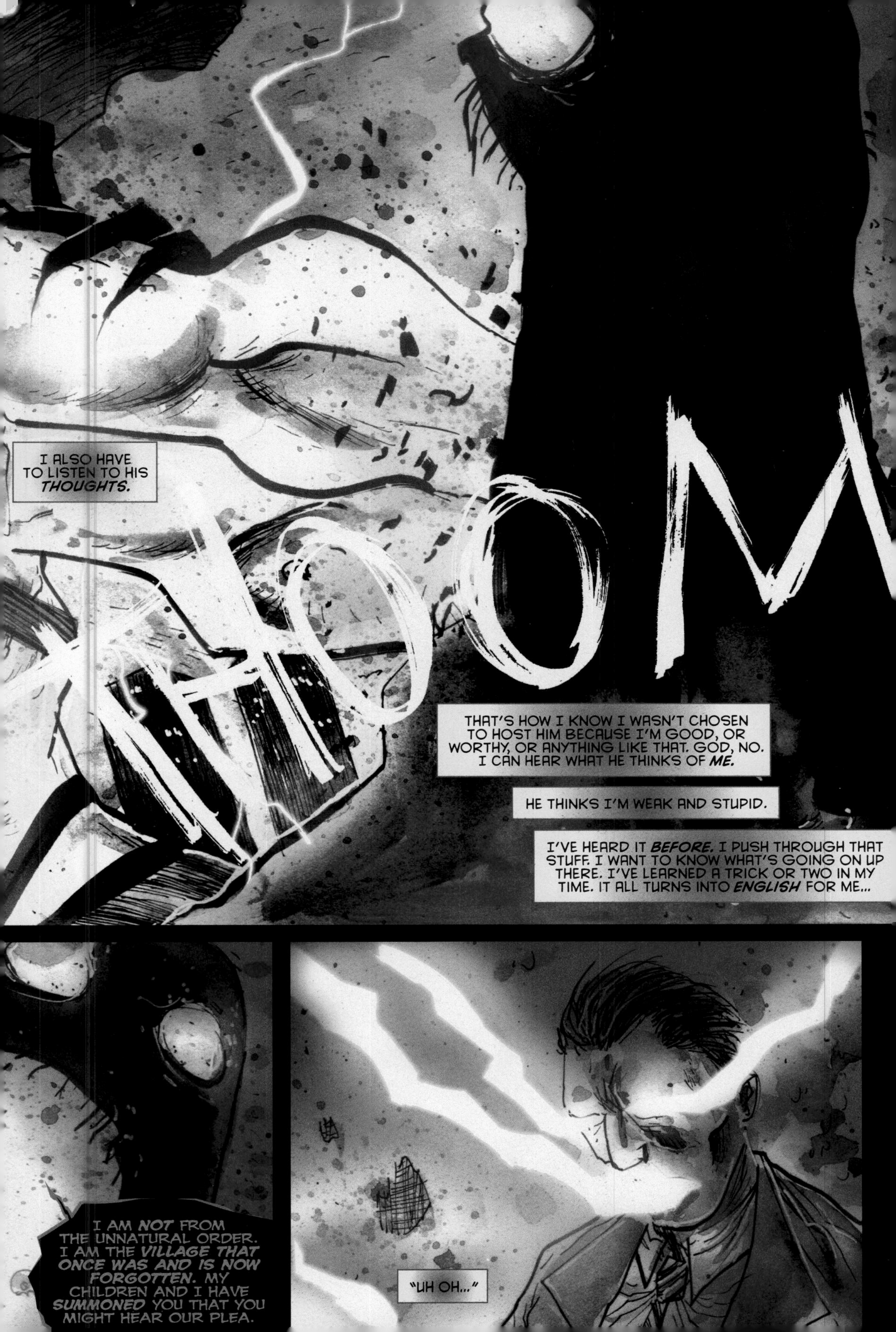
I ALSO HAVE TO LISTEN TO HIS *THOUGHTS.*
VHOOOM
THAT'S HOW I KNOW I WASN'T CHOSEN TO HOST HIM BECAUSE I'M GOOD, OR WORTHY, OR ANYTHING LIKE THAT. GOD, NO. I CAN HEAR WHAT HE THINKS OF *ME.*
HE THINKS I'M WEAK AND STUPID.
I'VE HEARD IT *BEFORE.* I PUSH THROUGH THAT STUFF. I WANT TO KNOW WHAT'S GOING ON UP THERE. I'VE LEARNED A TRICK OR TWO IN MY TIME. IT ALL TURNS INTO *ENGLISH* FOR ME...
I AM *NOT* FROM THE UNNATURAL ORDER. I AM THE *VILLAGE THAT ONCE WAS AND IS NOW FORGOTTEN.* MY CHILDREN AND I HAVE *SUMMONED* YOU THAT YOU MIGHT HEAR OUR PLEA.
"UH OH..."

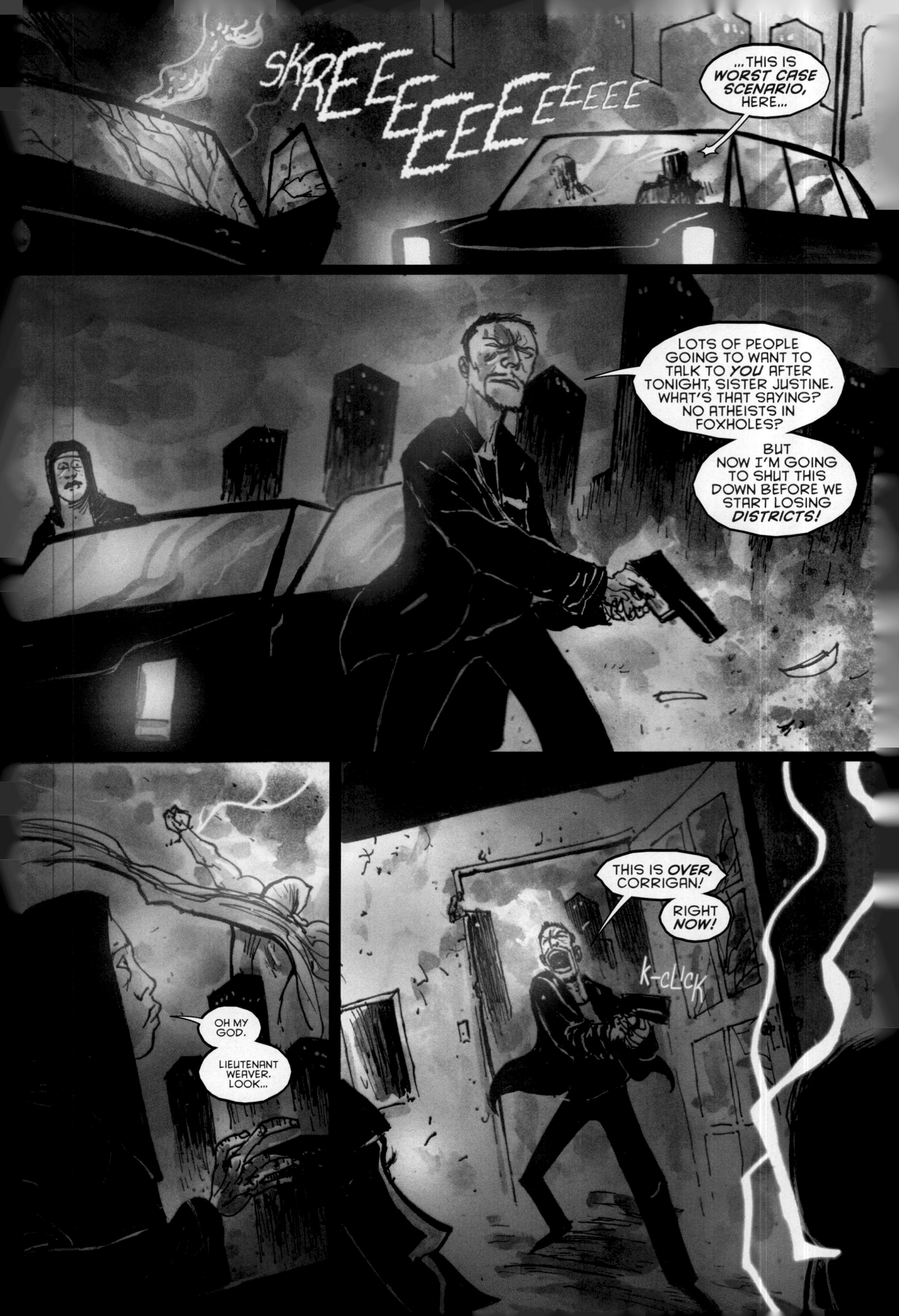
SKREEEEEEEEEEEE
...THIS IS WORST CASE SCENARIO, HERE...
LOTS OF PEOPLE GOING TO WANT TO TALK TO YOU AFTER TONIGHT, SISTER JUSTINE. WHAT'S THAT SAYING? NO ATHEISTS IN FOXHOLES?
BUT NOW I'M GOING TO SHUT THIS DOWN BEFORE WE START LOSING DISTRICTS!
OH MY GOD.
LIEUTENANT WEAVER. LOOK...
THIS IS OVER, CORRIGAN!
RIGHT NOW!
K-CLICK

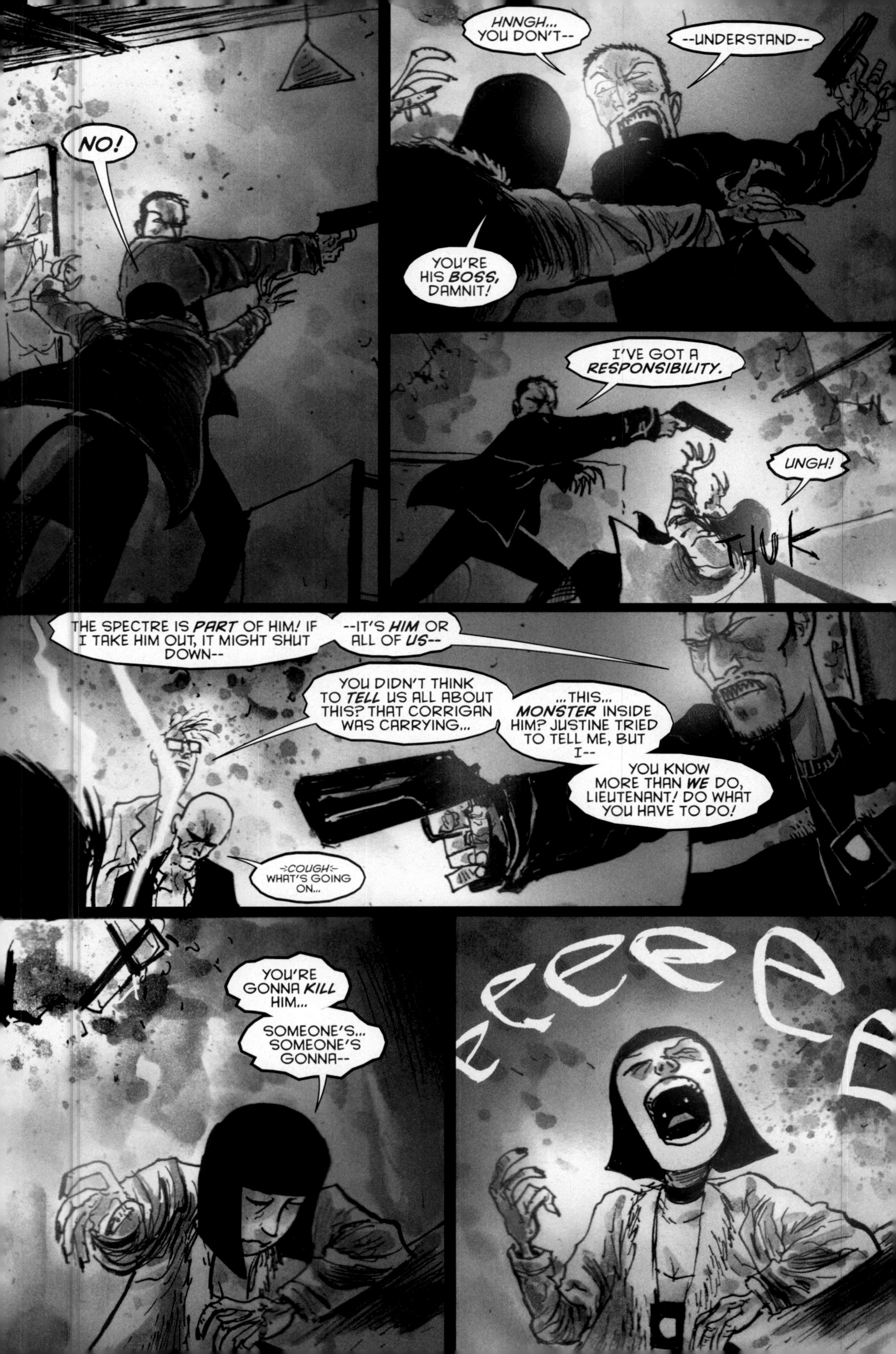
NO!
HNNGH... YOU DON'T--
--UNDERSTAND--
YOU'RE HIS BOSS, DAMNIT!
I'VE GOT A RESPONSIBILITY.
UNGH!
THUK
THE SPECTRE IS PART OF HIM! IF I TAKE HIM OUT, IT MIGHT SHUT DOWN--
--IT'S HIM OR ALL OF US--
YOU DIDN'T THINK TO TELL US ALL ABOUT THIS? THAT CORRIGAN WAS CARRYING...
...THIS... MONSTER INSIDE HIM? JUSTINE TRIED TO TELL ME, BUT I--
YOU KNOW MORE THAN WE DO, LIEUTENANT! DO WHAT YOU HAVE TO DO!
COUGH WHAT'S GOING ON...
YOU'RE GONNA KILL HIM...
SOMEONE'S... SOMEONE'S GONNA--
EEEEEE

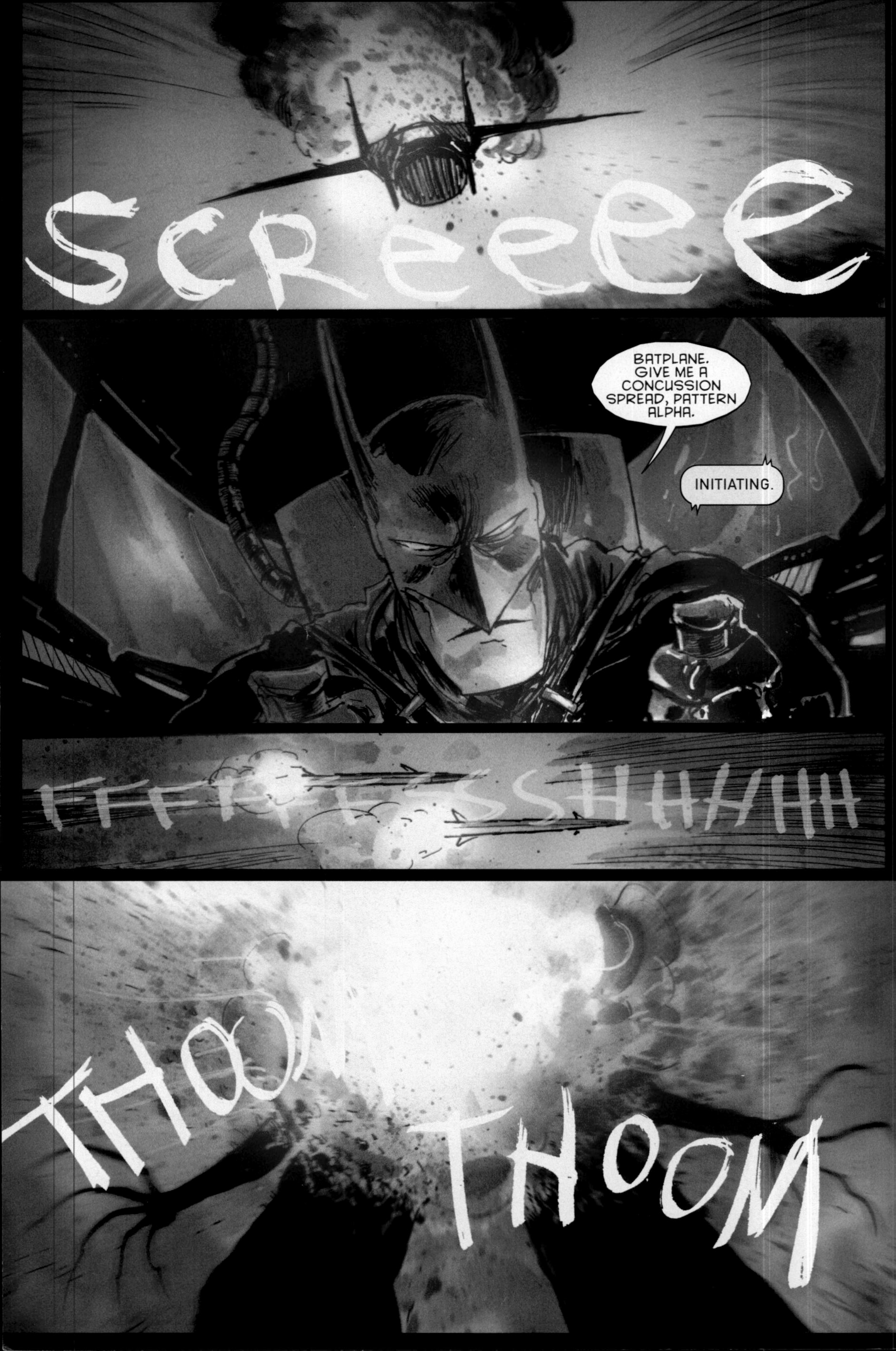
SCREEEE
BATPLANE. GIVE ME A CONCUSSION SPREAD, PATTERN ALPHA.
INITIATING.
FFFFFFFSSHHHHH
THOOM
THOOM

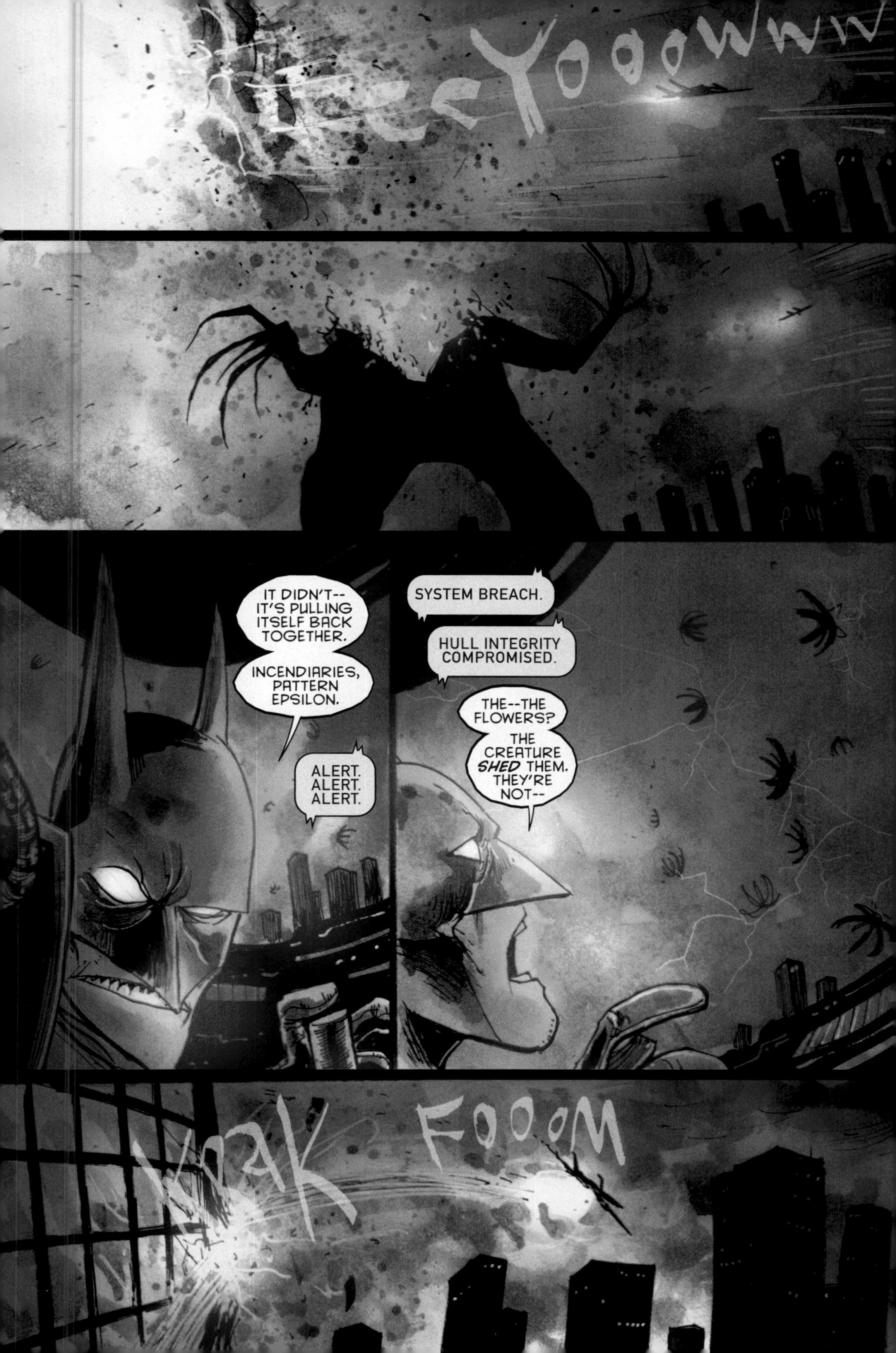
IT DIDN'T-- IT'S PULLING ITSELF BACK TOGETHER.
INCENDIARIES, PATTERN EPSILON.
ALERT. ALERT. ALERT.
SYSTEM BREACH.
HULL INTEGRITY COMPROMISED.
THE--THE FLOWERS?
THE CREATURE *SHED* THEM. THEY'RE NOT--
FOOOM

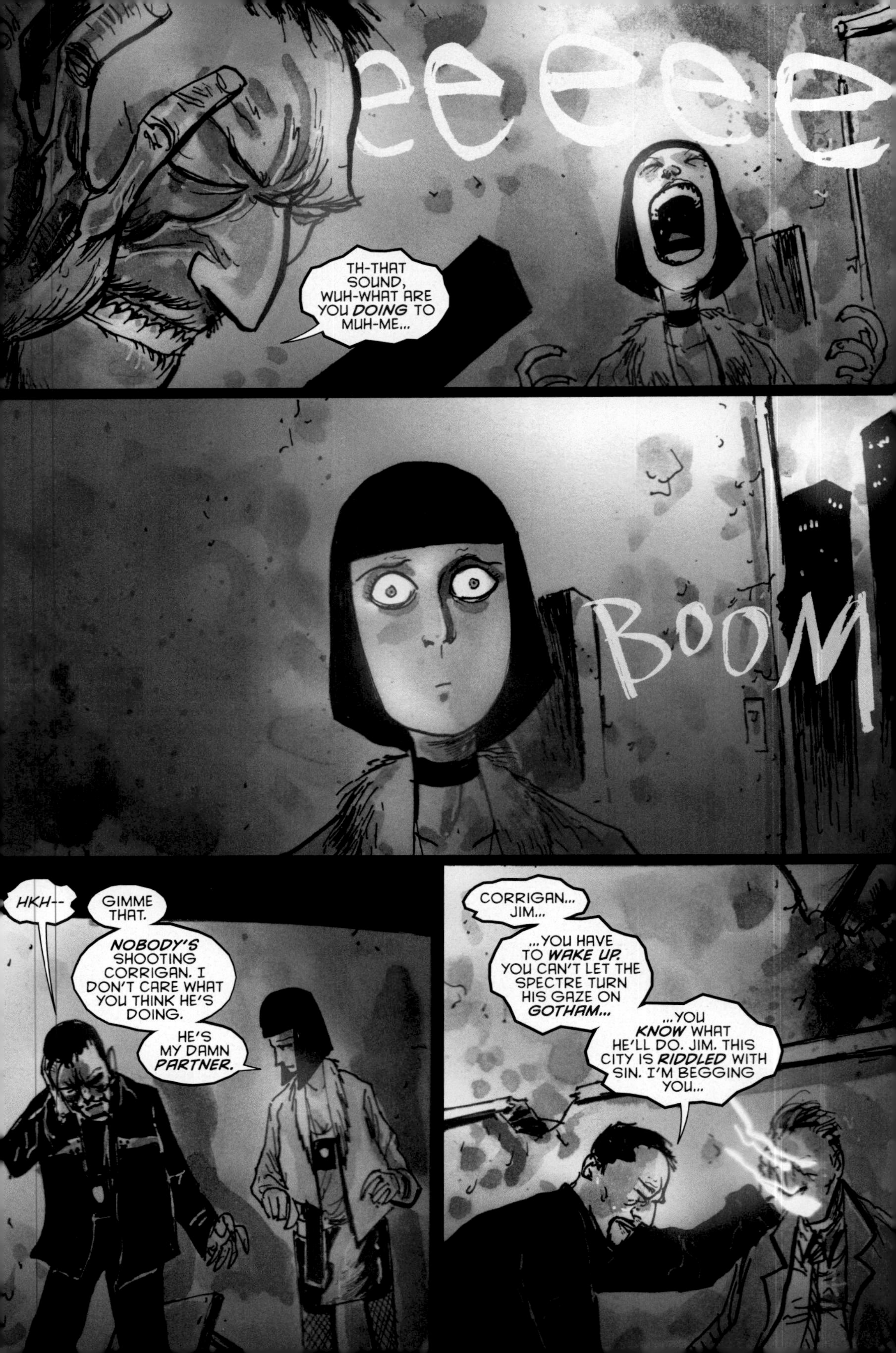
EEEEE
TH-THAT SOUND, WUH-WHAT ARE YOU DOING TO MUH-ME...
BOOM
HKH--
GIMME THAT.
NOBODY'S SHOOTING CORRIGAN. I DON'T CARE WHAT YOU THINK HE'S DOING.
HE'S MY DAMN PARTNER.
CORRIGAN... JIM...
...YOU HAVE TO WAKE UP. YOU CAN'T LET THE SPECTRE TURN HIS GAZE ON GOTHAM...
...YOU KNOW WHAT HE'LL DO. JIM. THIS CITY IS RIDDLED WITH SIN. I'M BEGGING YOU...

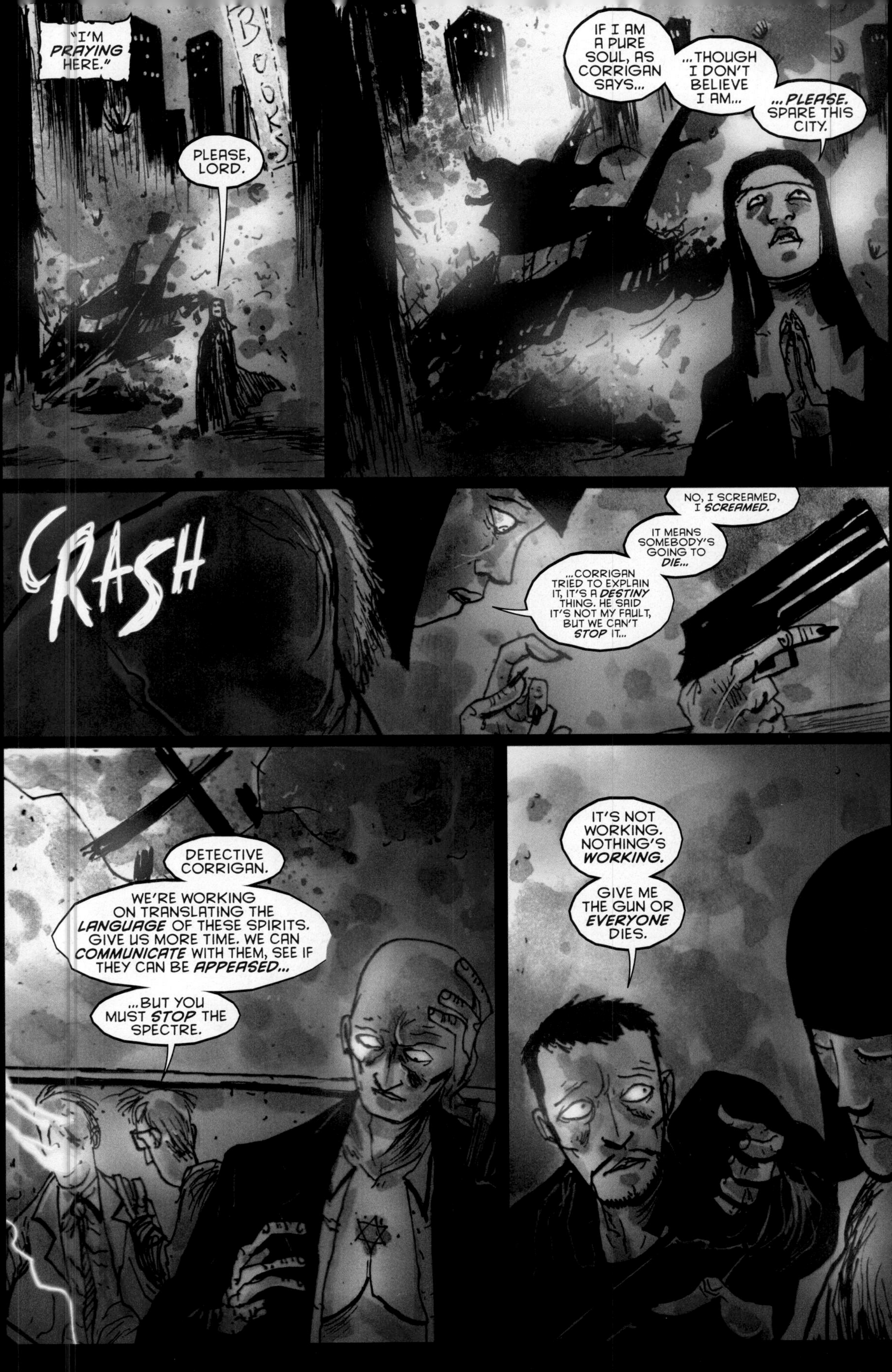

"I'M PRAYING HERE."
BOOKS
PLEASE, LORD.
IF I AM A PURE SOUL, AS CORRIGAN SAYS...
...THOUGH I DON'T BELIEVE I AM...
...PLEASE. SPARE THIS CITY.
CRASH
NO, I SCREAMED, I SCREAMED.
IT MEANS SOMEBODY'S GOING TO DIE...
...CORRIGAN TRIED TO EXPLAIN IT, IT'S A DESTINY THING. HE SAID IT'S NOT MY FAULT, BUT WE CAN'T STOP IT...
DETECTIVE CORRIGAN.
WE'RE WORKING ON TRANSLATING THE LANGUAGE OF THESE SPIRITS. GIVE US MORE TIME. WE CAN COMMUNICATE WITH THEM, SEE IF THEY CAN BE APPEASED...
...BUT YOU MUST STOP THE SPECTRE.
IT'S NOT WORKING. NOTHING'S WORKING.
GIVE ME THE GUN OR EVERYONE DIES.

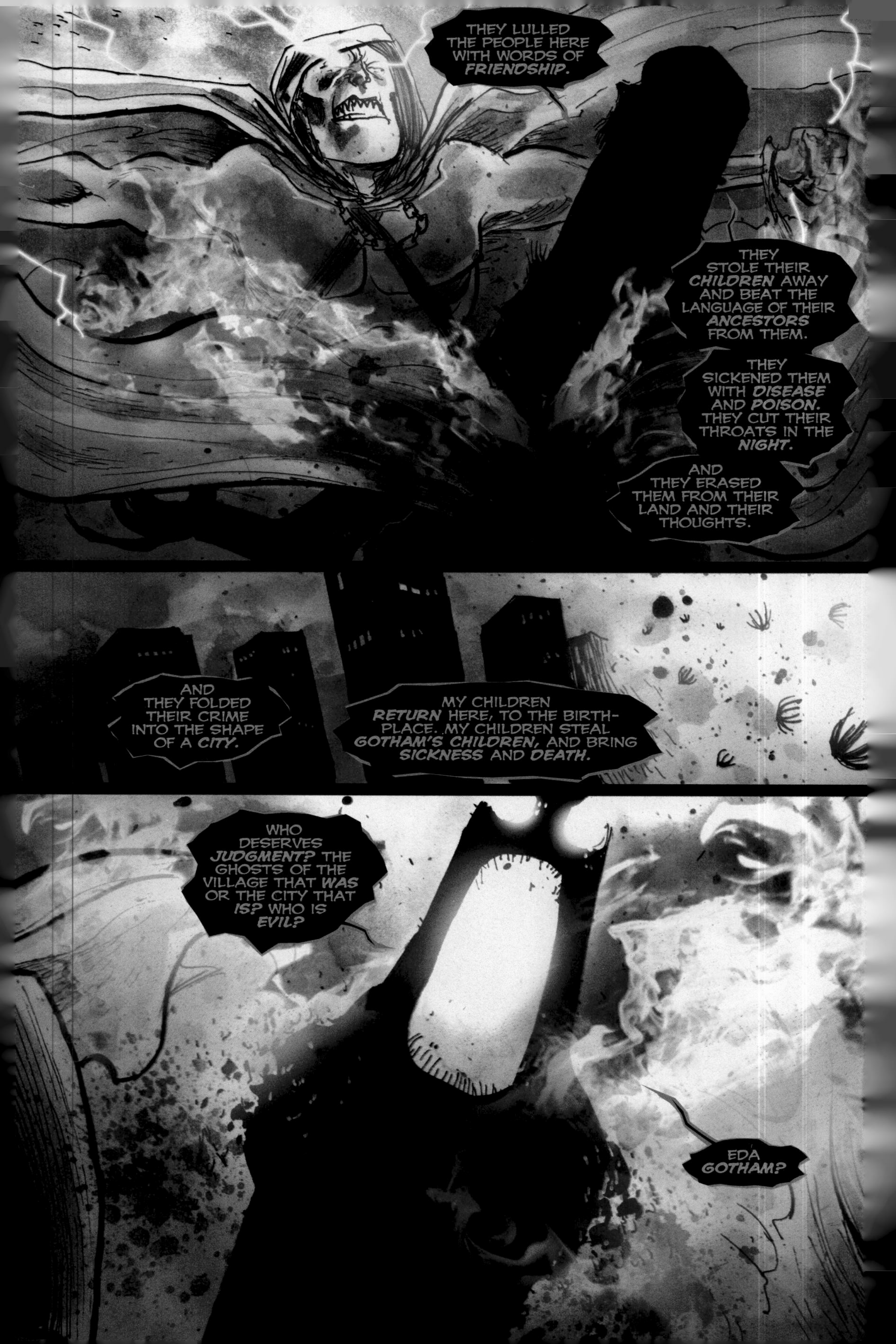
THEY LULLED THE PEOPLE HERE WITH WORDS OF FRIENDSHIP.
THEY STOLE THEIR CHILDREN AWAY AND BEAT THE LANGUAGE OF THEIR ANCESTORS FROM THEM.
THEY SICKENED THEM WITH DISEASE AND POISON. THEY CUT THEIR THROATS IN THE NIGHT.
AND THEY ERASED THEM FROM THEIR LAND AND THEIR THOUGHTS.
AND THEY FOLDED THEIR CRIME INTO THE SHAPE OF A CITY.
MY CHILDREN RETURN HERE, TO THE BIRTH-PLACE. MY CHILDREN STEAL GOTHAM'S CHILDREN, AND BRING SICKNESS AND DEATH.
WHO DESERVES JUDGMENT? THE GHOSTS OF THE VILLAGE THAT WAS OR THE CITY THAT IS? WHO IS EVIL?
EDA GOTHAM?

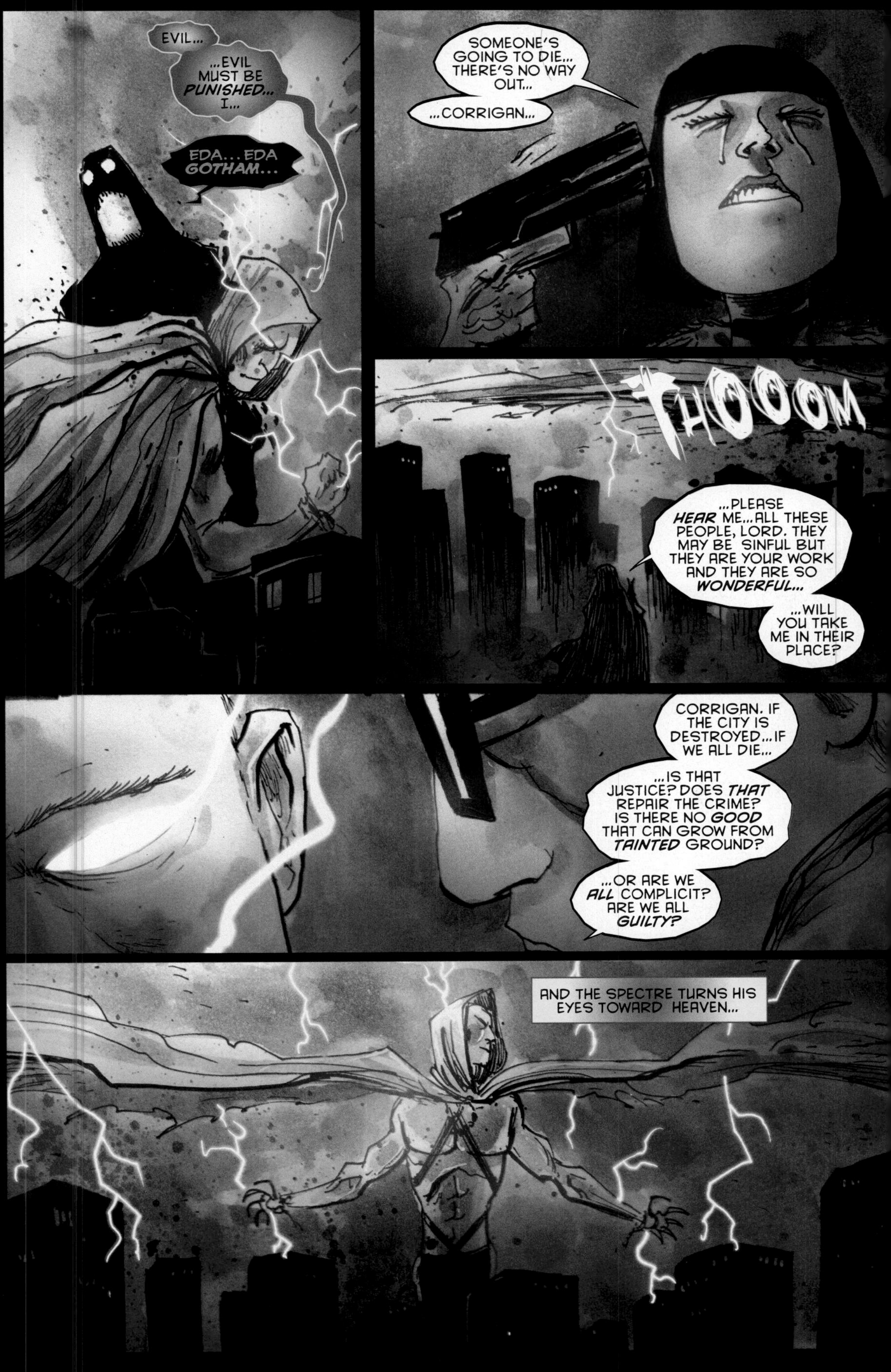
EVIL...
...EVIL MUST BE PUNISHED... I...
EDA... EDA GOTHAM...
SOMEONE'S GOING TO DIE... THERE'S NO WAY OUT...
...CORRIGAN...
THOOOM
...PLEASE HEAR ME...ALL THESE PEOPLE, LORD. THEY MAY BE SINFUL BUT THEY ARE YOUR WORK AND THEY ARE SO WONDERFUL...
...WILL YOU TAKE ME IN THEIR PLACE?
CORRIGAN. IF THE CITY IS DESTROYED...IF WE ALL DIE...
...IS THAT JUSTICE? DOES THAT REPAIR THE CRIME? IS THERE NO GOOD THAT CAN GROW FROM TAINTED GROUND?
...OR ARE WE ALL COMPLICIT? ARE WE ALL GUILTY?
AND THE SPECTRE TURNS HIS EYES TOWARD HEAVEN...

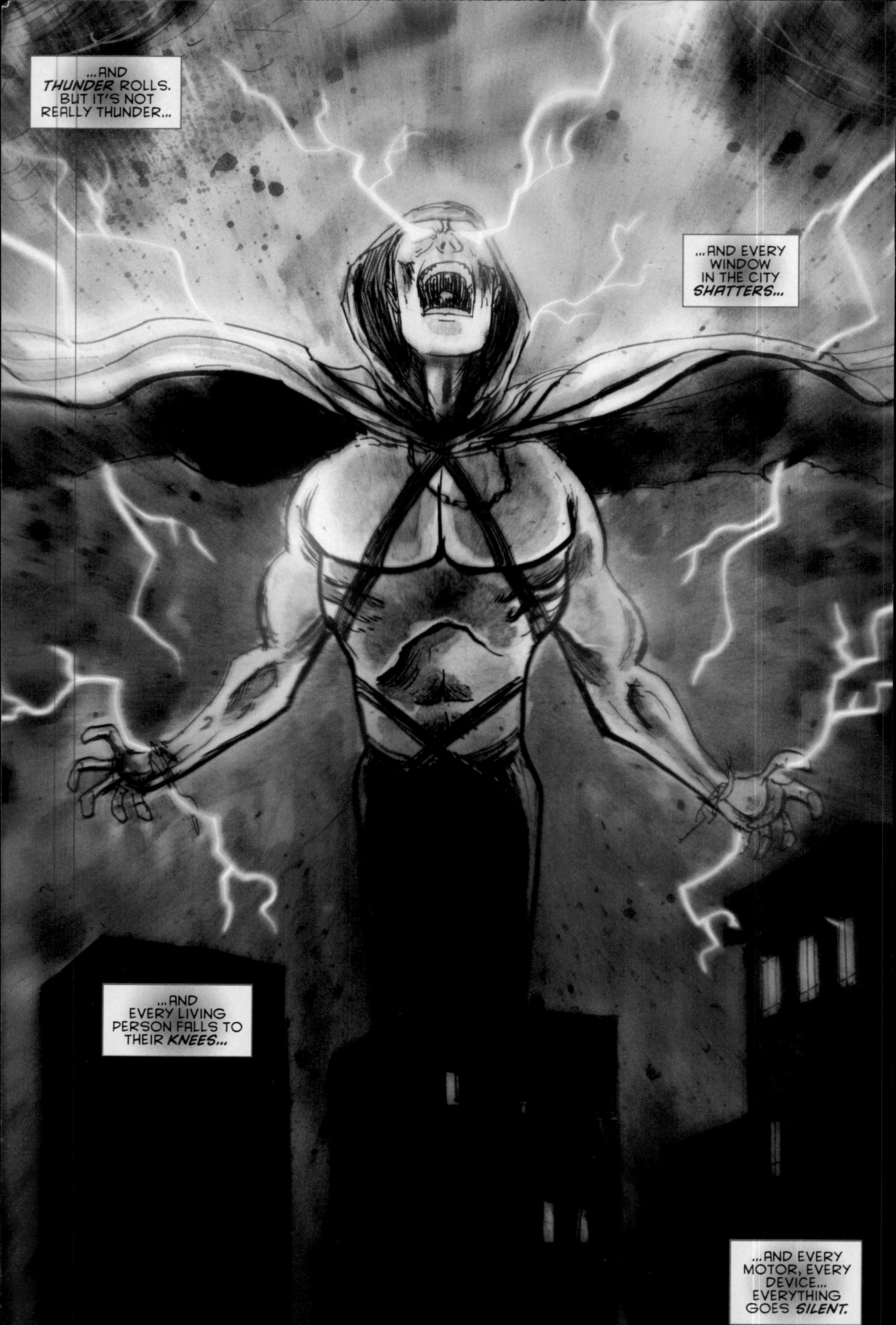
...AND THUNDER ROLLS. BUT IT'S NOT REALLY THUNDER...
...AND EVERY WINDOW IN THE CITY SHATTERS...
...AND EVERY LIVING PERSON FALLS TO THEIR KNEES...
...AND EVERY MOTOR, EVERY DEVICE... EVERYTHING GOES SILENT.

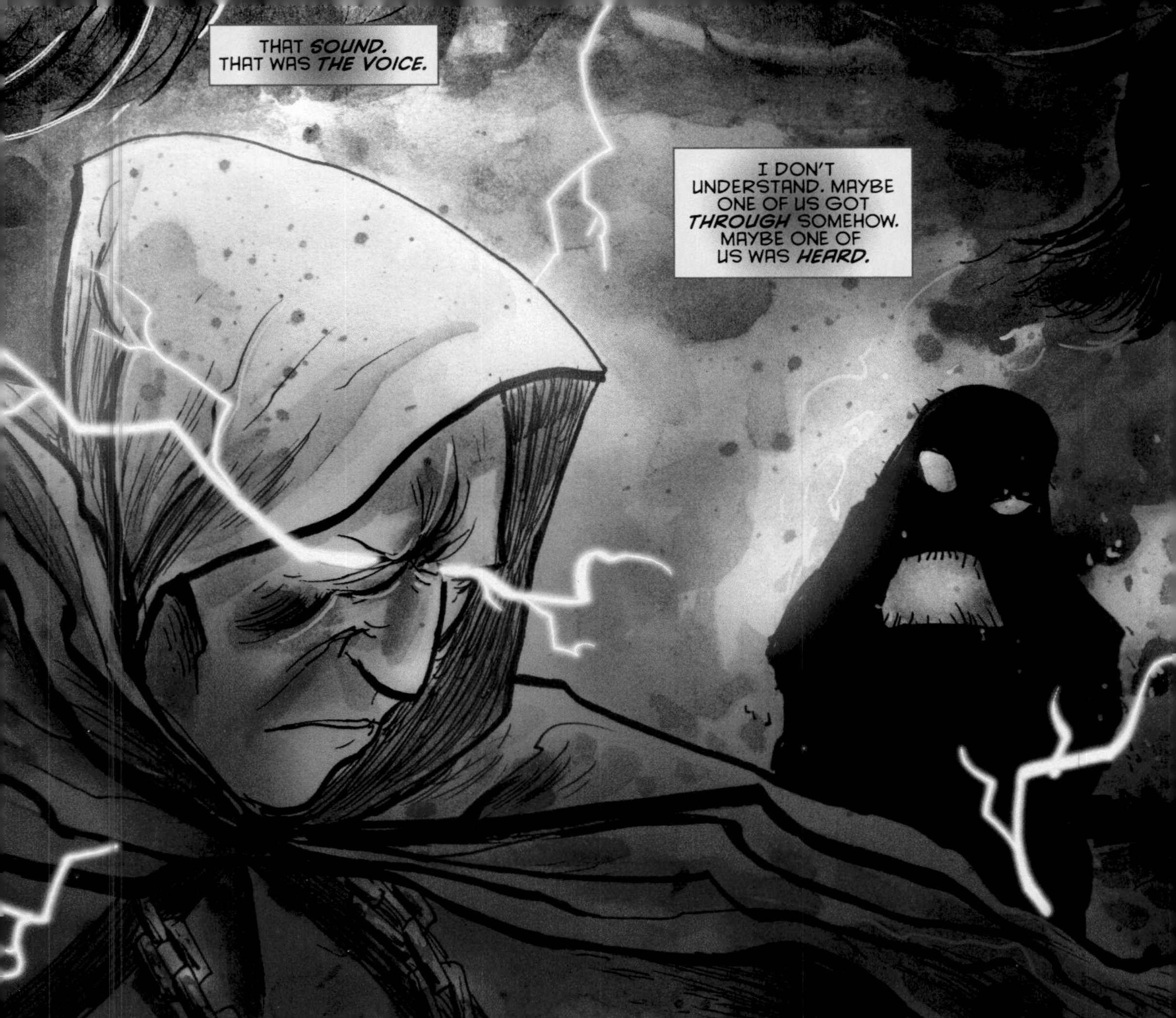
THAT *SOUND.* THAT WAS *THE VOICE.*
I DON'T UNDERSTAND. MAYBE ONE OF US GOT *THROUGH* SOMEHOW. MAYBE ONE OF US WAS *HEARD.*

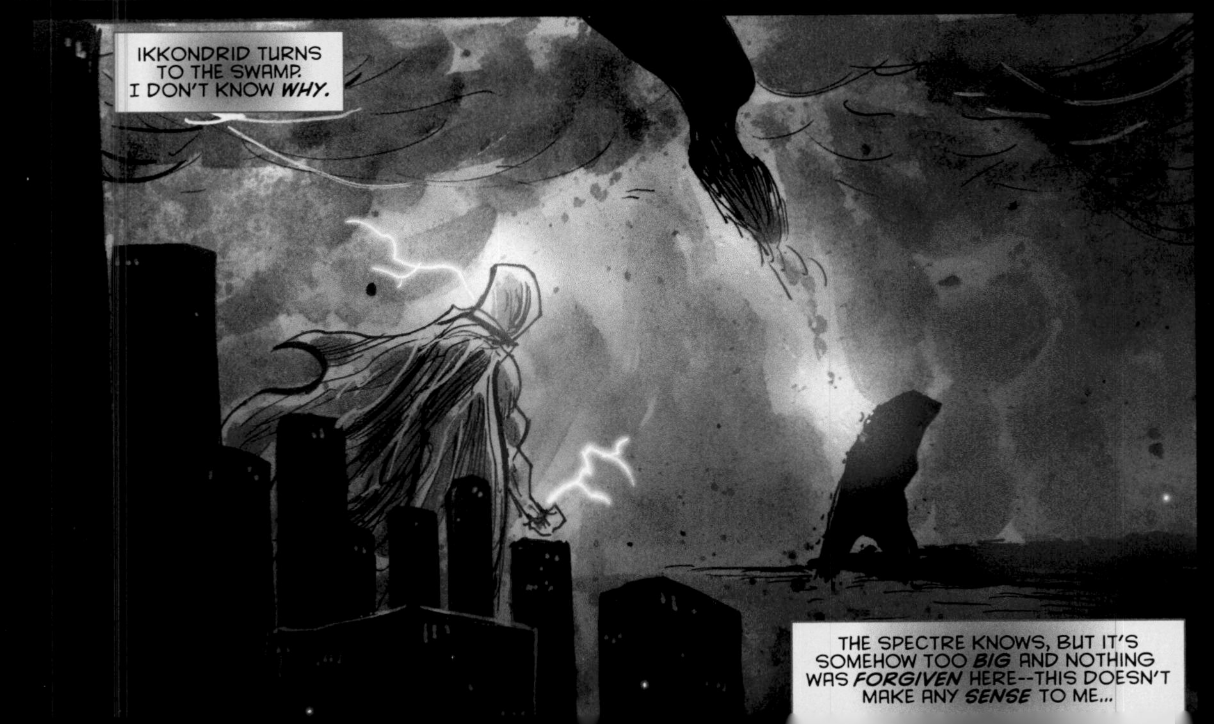
IKKONDRID TURNS TO THE SWAMP. I DON'T KNOW *WHY.*
THE SPECTRE KNOWS, BUT IT'S SOMEHOW TOO *BIG* AND NOTHING WAS *FORGIVEN* HERE--THIS DOESN'T MAKE ANY *SENSE* TO ME...

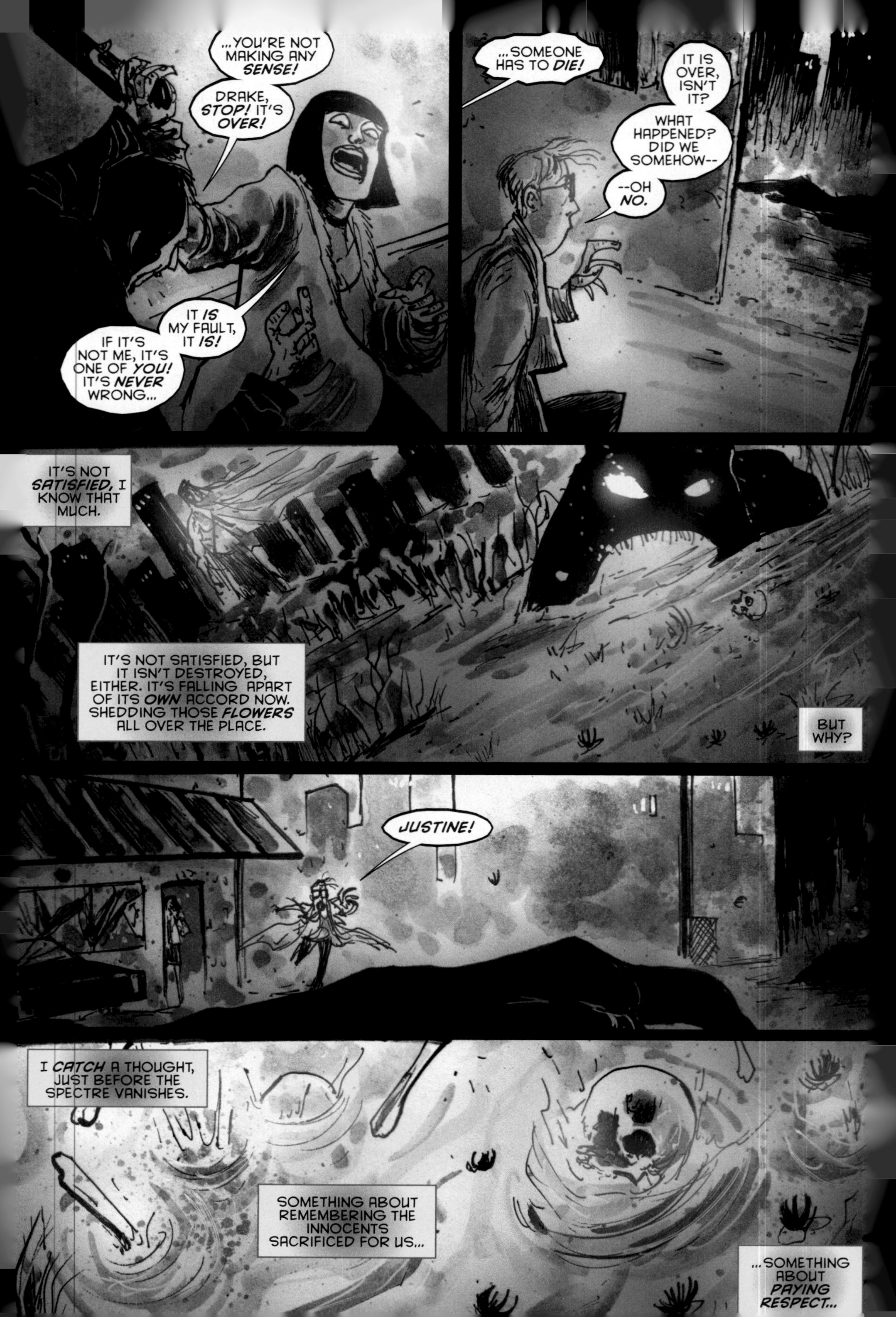

...YOU'RE NOT MAKING ANY SENSE!
DRAKE, STOP! IT'S OVER!
IT IS MY FAULT, IT IS!
IF IT'S NOT ME, IT'S ONE OF YOU! IT'S NEVER WRONG...
...SOMEONE HAS TO DIE!
IT IS OVER, ISN'T IT?
WHAT HAPPENED? DID WE SOMEHOW--
--OH NO.
IT'S NOT SATISFIED, I KNOW THAT MUCH.
IT'S NOT SATISFIED, BUT IT ISN'T DESTROYED, EITHER. IT'S FALLING APART OF ITS OWN ACCORD NOW. SHEDDING THOSE FLOWERS ALL OVER THE PLACE.
BUT WHY?
JUSTINE!
I CATCH A THOUGHT, JUST BEFORE THE SPECTRE VANISHES.
SOMETHING ABOUT REMEMBERING THE INNOCENTS SACRIFICED FOR US...
...SOMETHING ABOUT PAYING RESPECT...

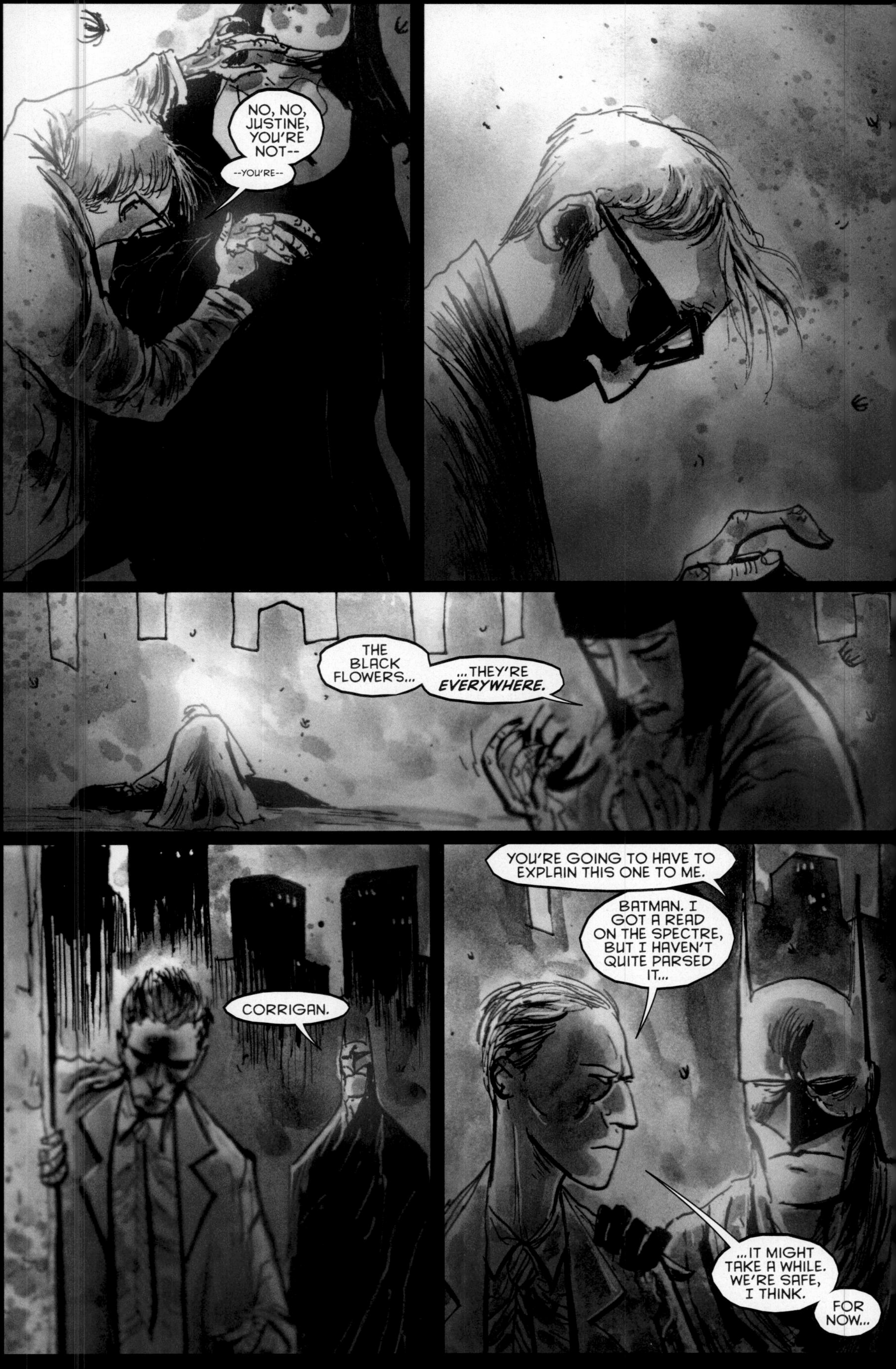
NO, NO, JUSTINE, YOU'RE NOT--
--YOU'RE--
THE BLACK FLOWERS...
...THEY'RE *EVERYWHERE.*
CORRIGAN.
YOU'RE GOING TO HAVE TO EXPLAIN THIS ONE TO ME.
BATMAN. I GOT A READ ON THE SPECTRE, BUT I HAVEN'T QUITE PARSED IT...
...IT MIGHT TAKE A WHILE. WE'RE SAFE, I THINK.
FOR NOW...

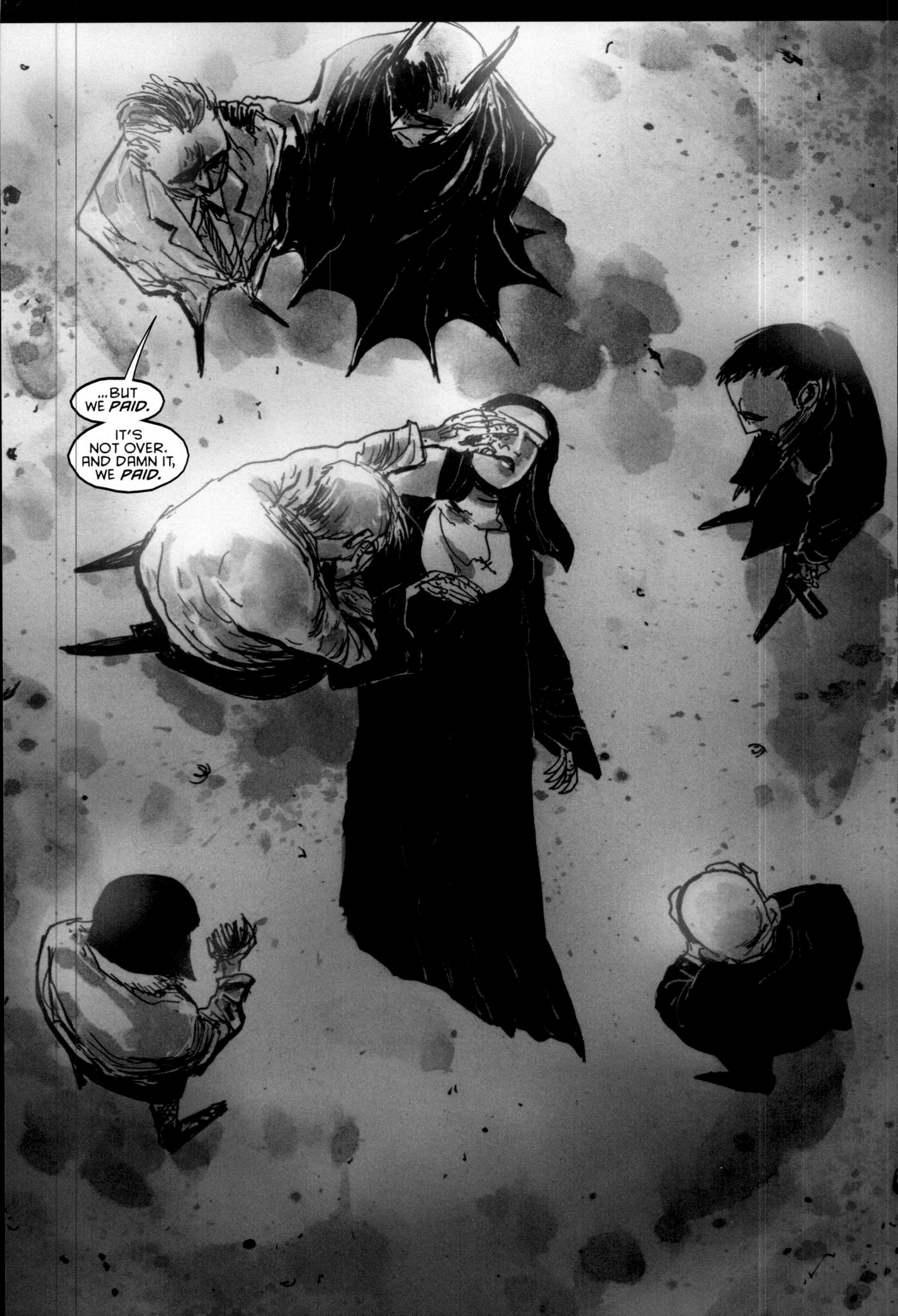
...BUT WE *PAID.*
IT'S NOT OVER. AND DAMN IT, WE *PAID.*

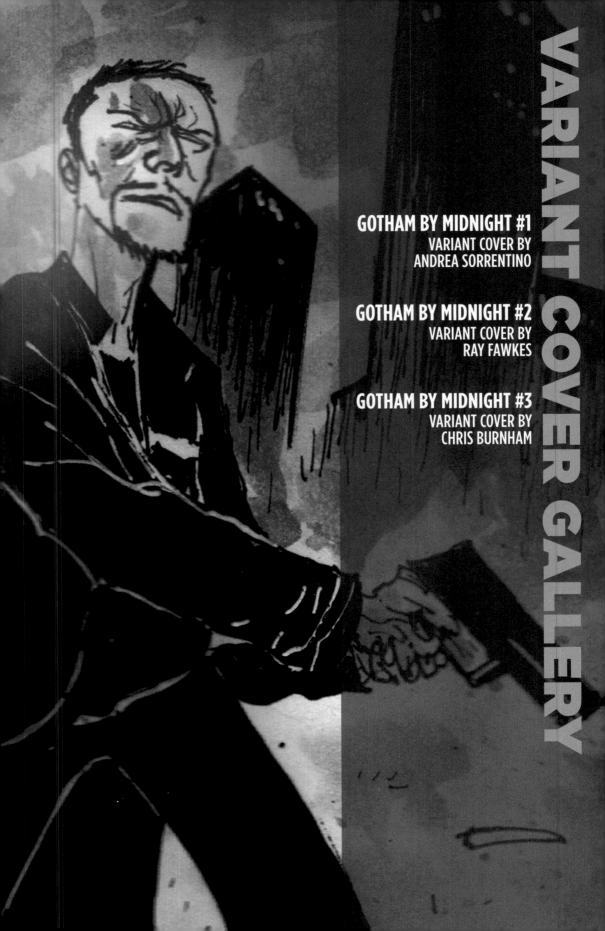

GOTHAM BY MIDNIGHT #1
VARIANT COVER BY
ANDREA SORRENTINO

GOTHAM BY MIDNIGHT #2
VARIANT COVER BY
RAY FAWKES

GOTHAM BY MIDNIGHT #3
VARIANT COVER BY
CHRIS BURNHAM

VARIANT COVER GALLERY

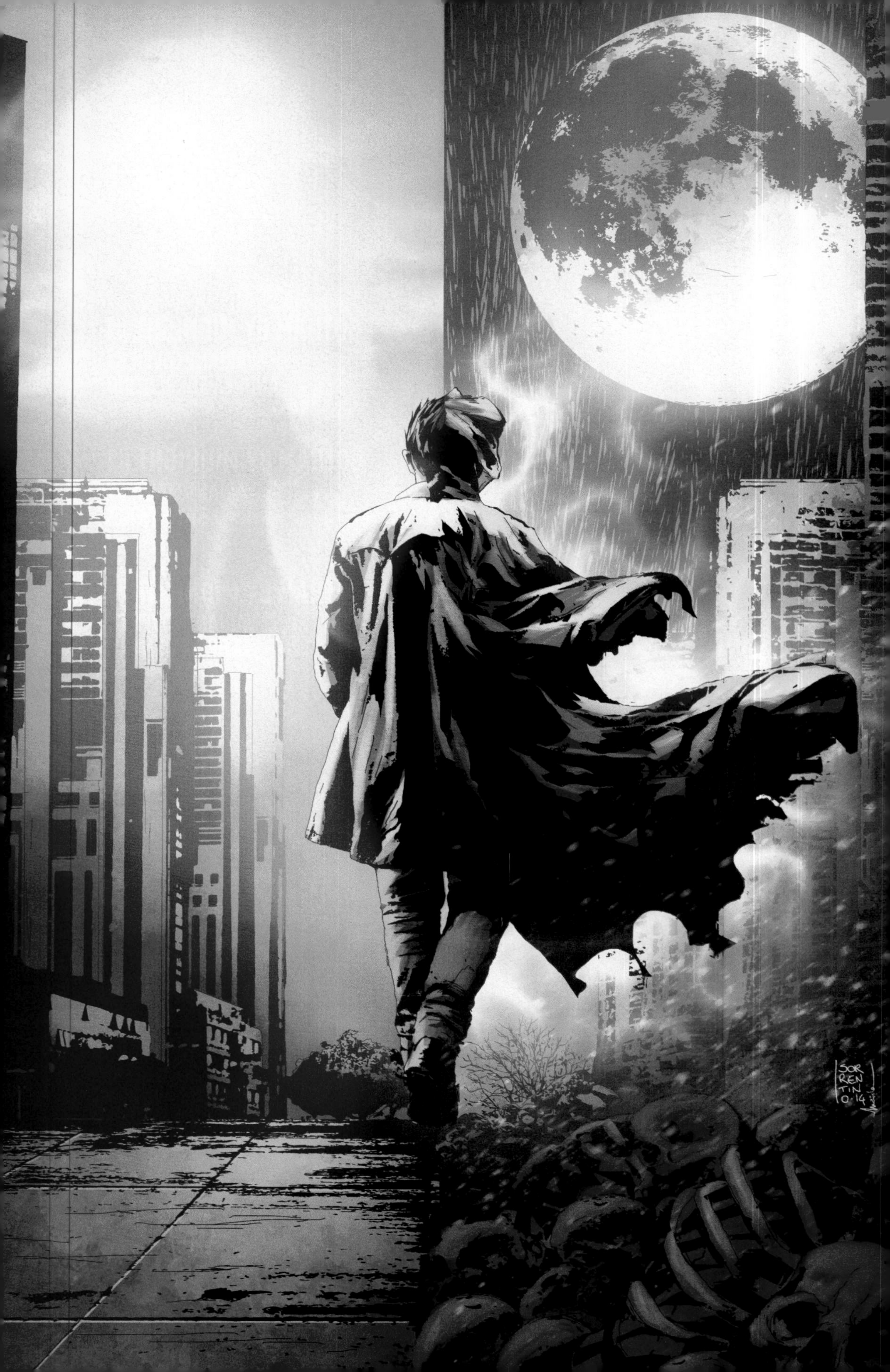

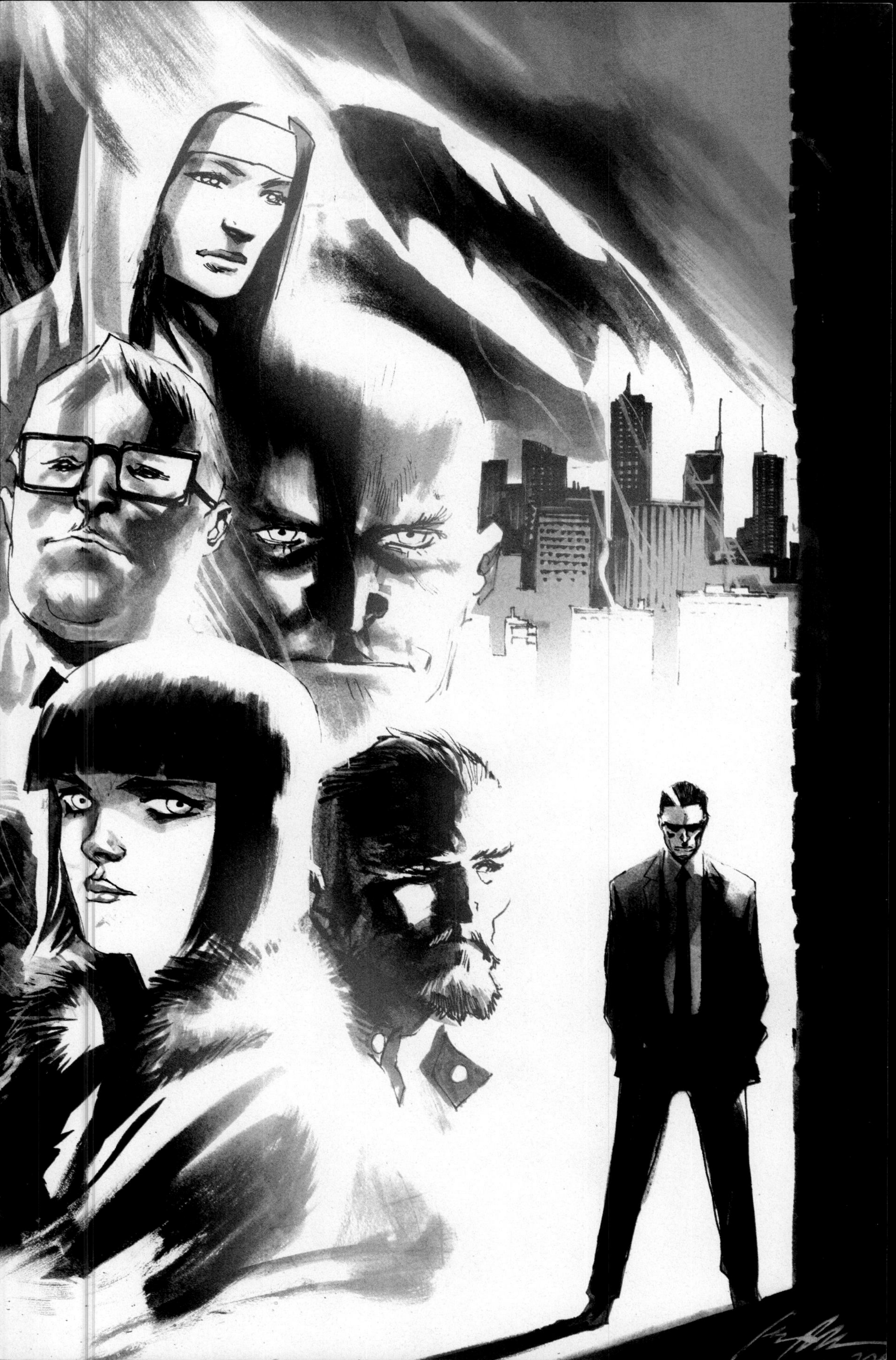

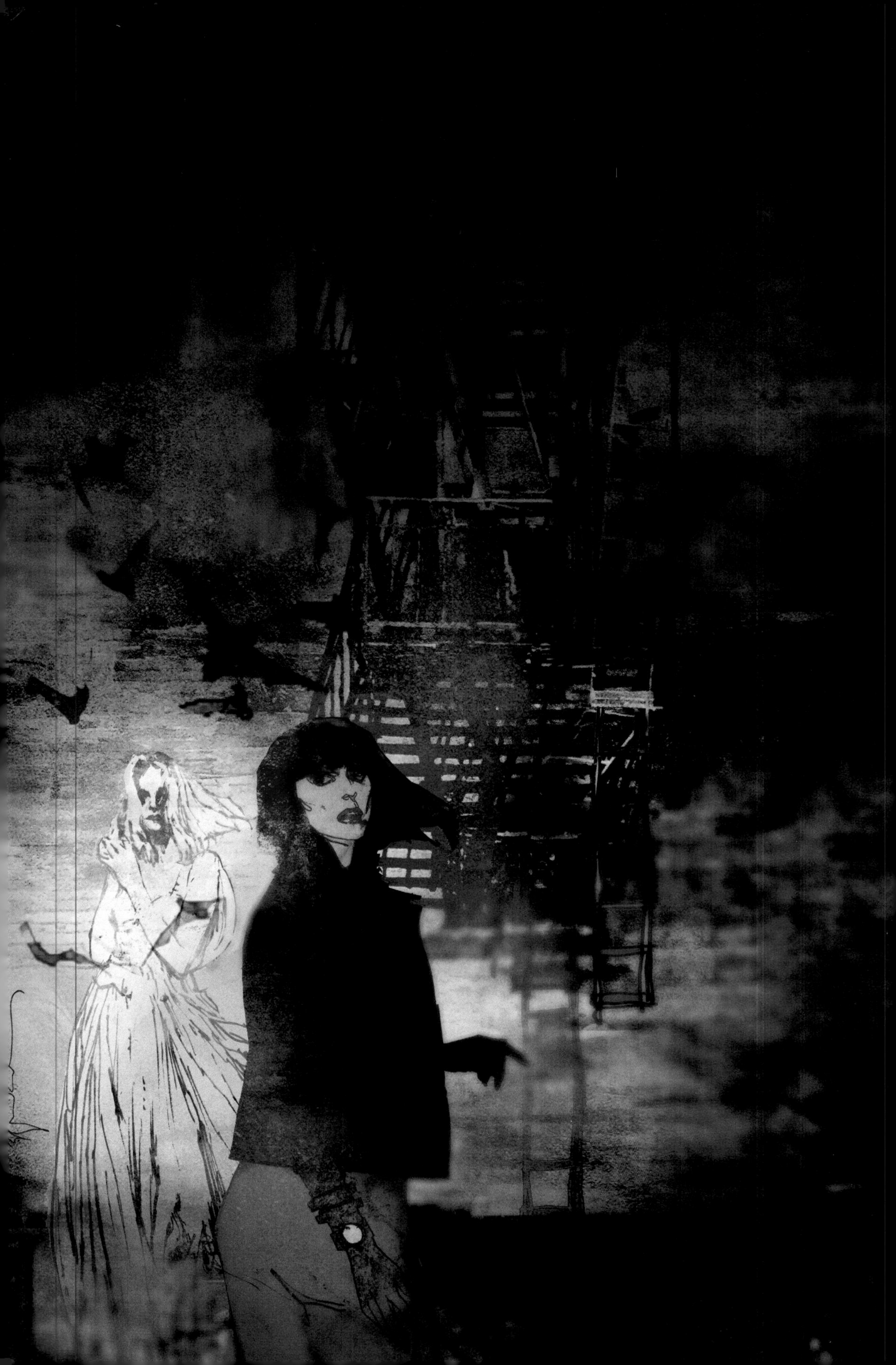

BATMAN

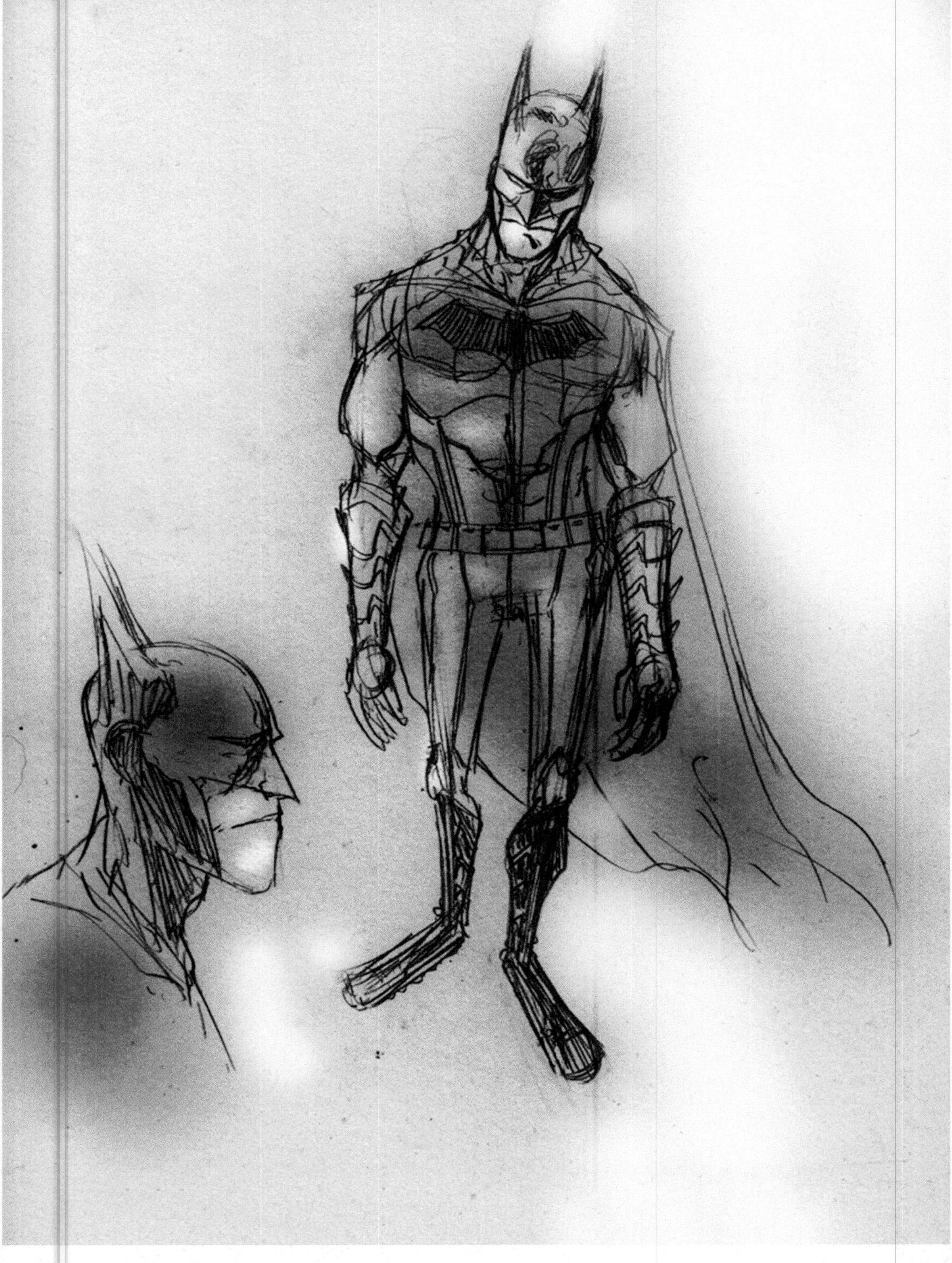

DOCTOR SZANDOR TARR

JIM CORRIGAN

DETECTIVE LISA DRAKE

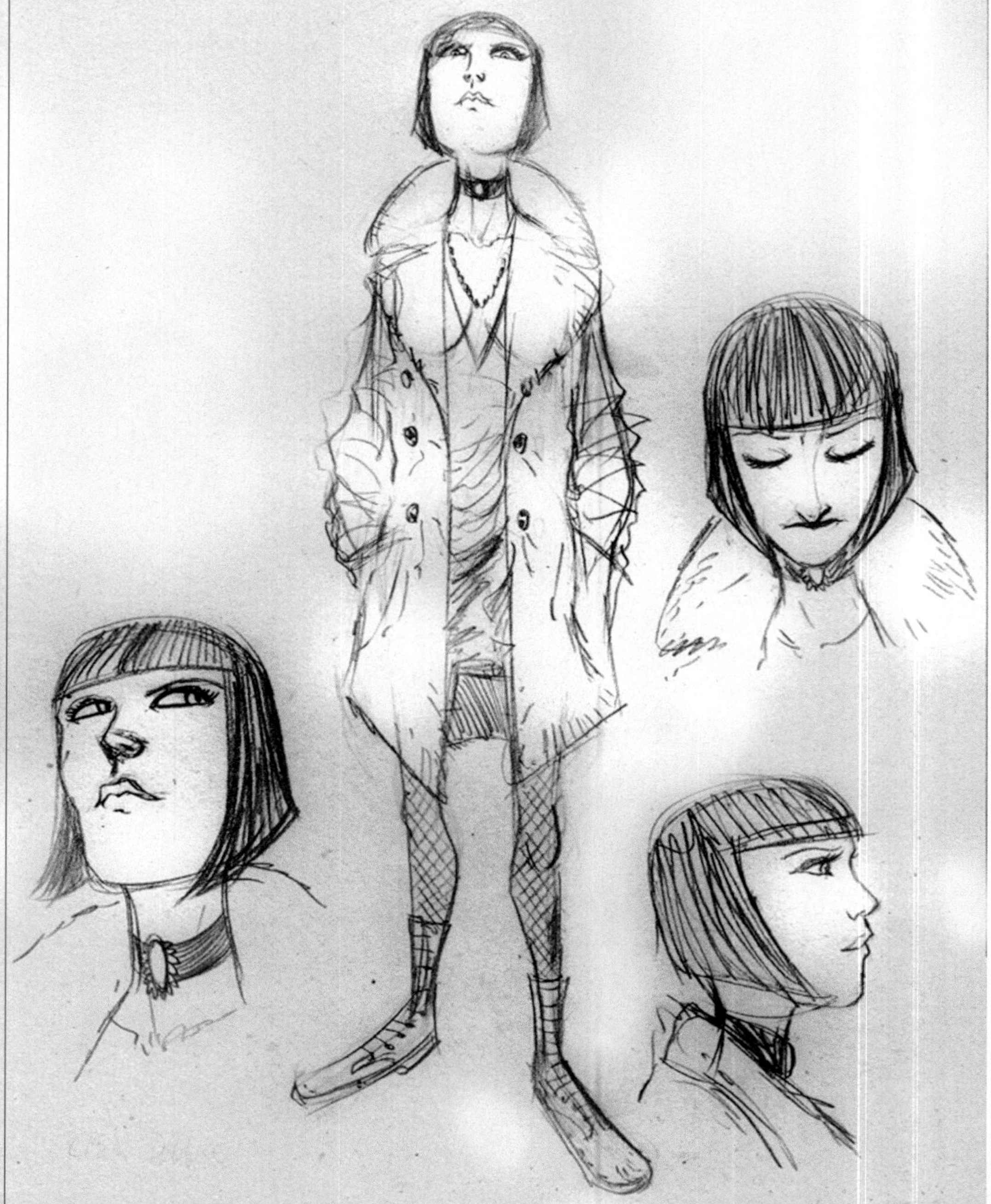

SERGEANT PEYTON ROOK

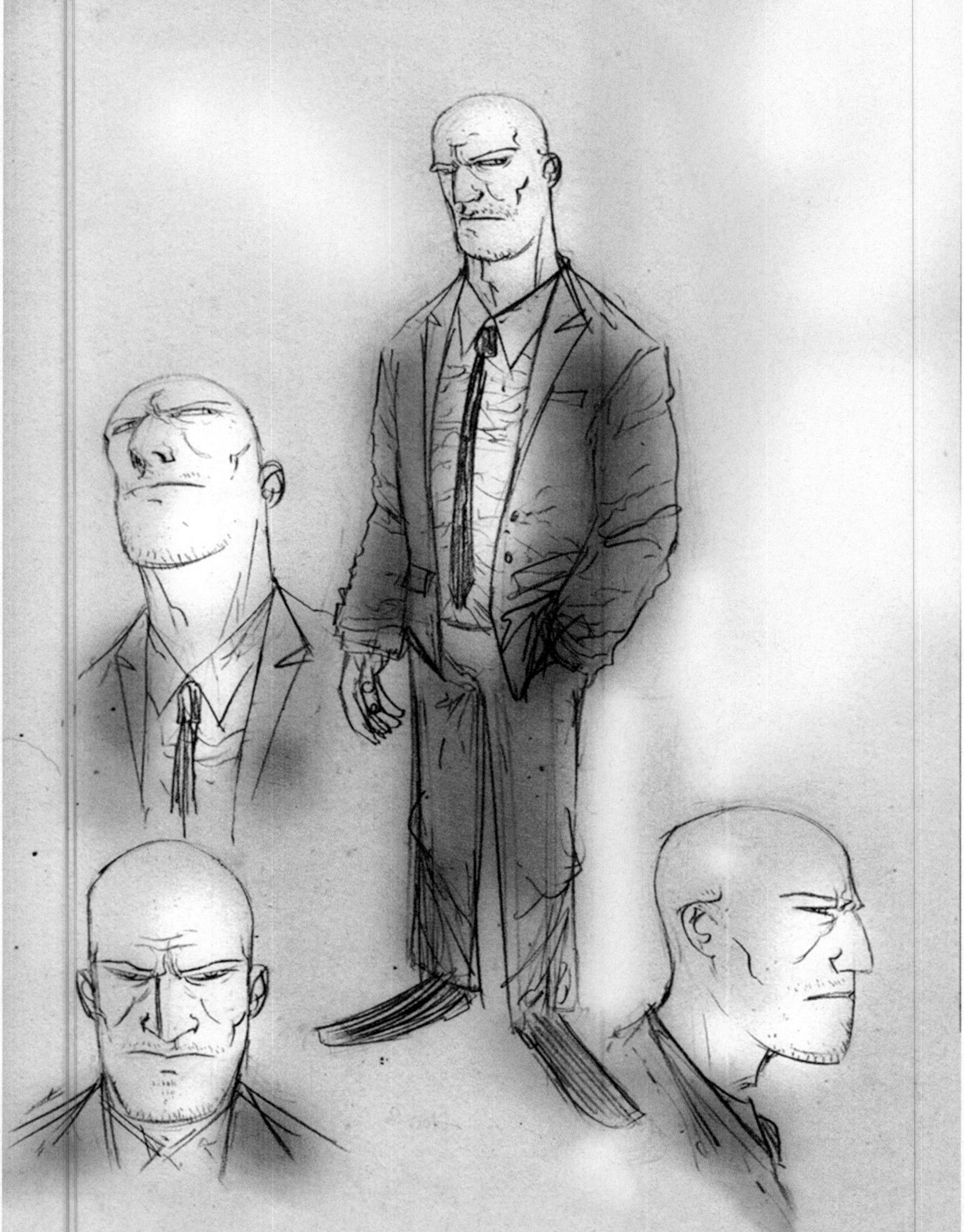

LIEUTENANT SAM WEAVER

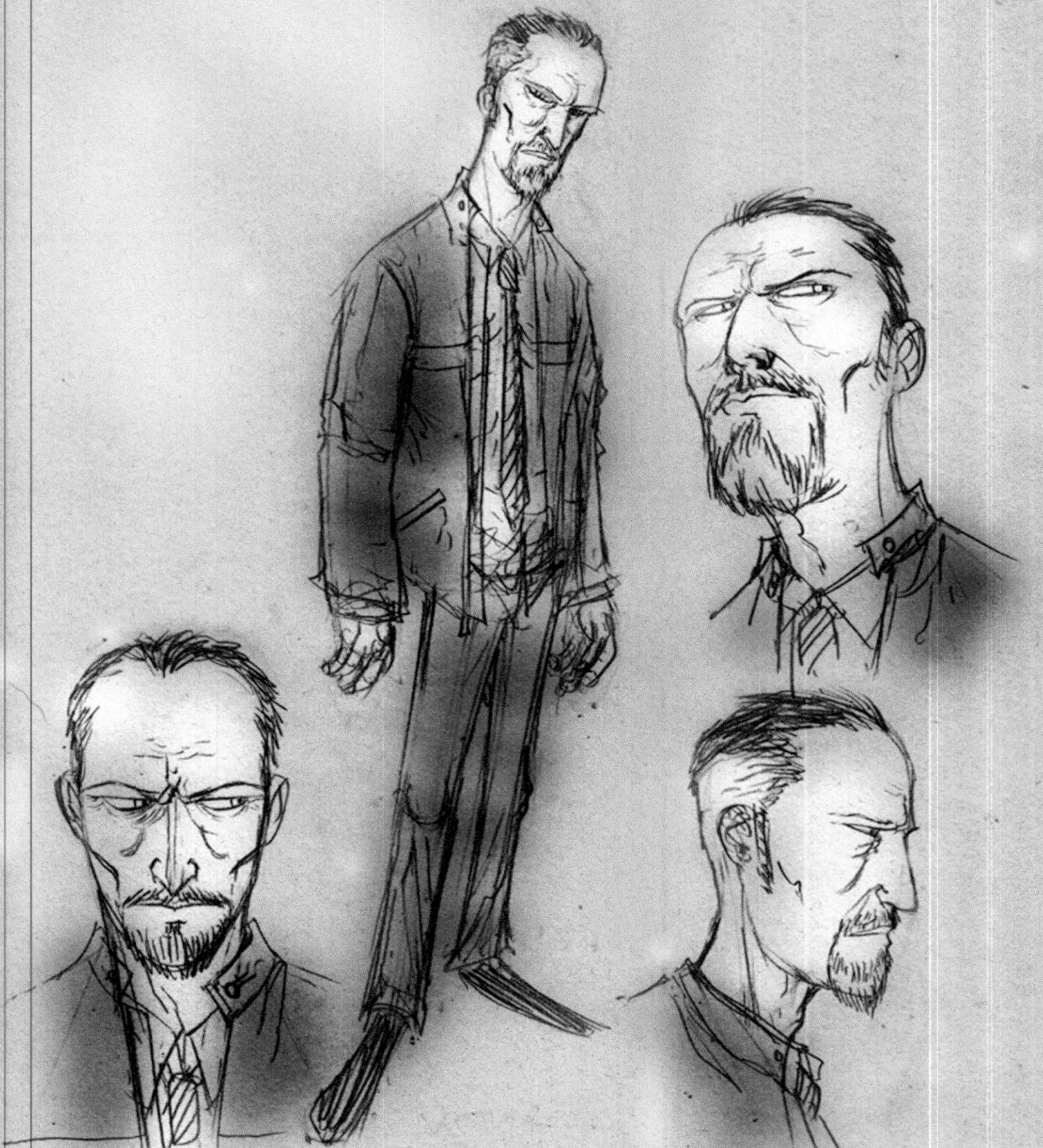

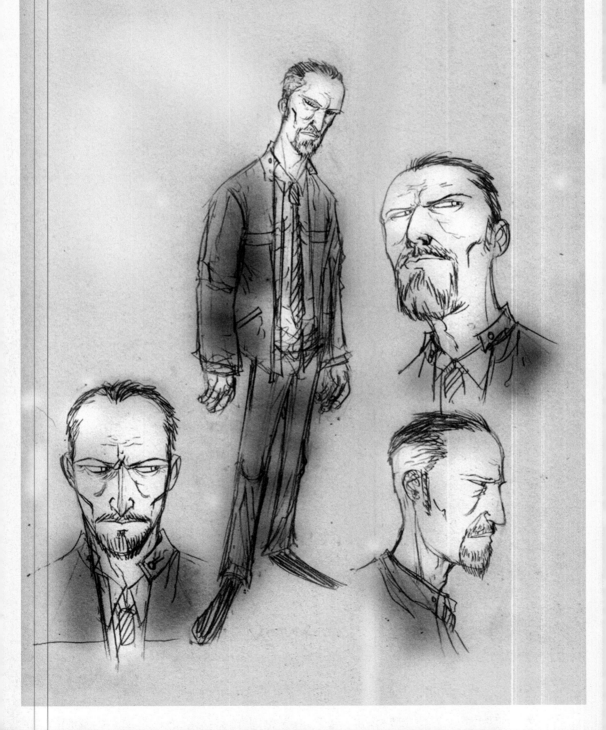

"Compelling drama. A great example of the literary and artistic maturity of the graphic novel format."
—SCHOOL LIBRARY JOURNAL

FROM THE *NEW YORK TIMES* BEST-SELLING WRITERS

ED BRUBAKER & GREG RUCKA

with MICHAEL LARK

GOTHAM CENTRAL BOOK TWO: JOKERS AND MADMEN

GOTHAM CENTRAL BOOK THREE: ON THE FREAK BEAT

GOTHAM CENTRAL BOOK FOUR: CORRIGAN

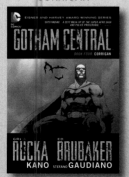

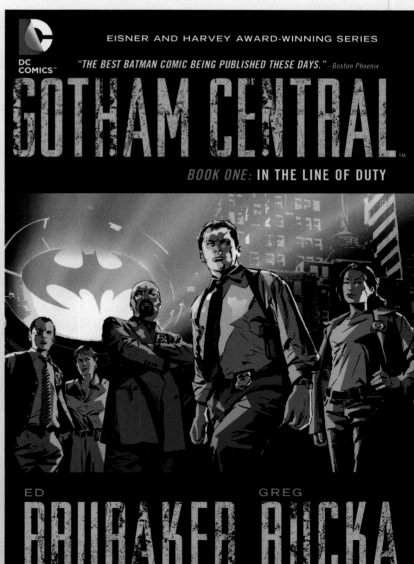

DC COMICS™

"[Writer Scott Snyder] pulls from the oldest aspects of the Batman myth, combines it with sinister-comic elements from the series' best period, and gives the whole thing terrific forward-spin."—ENTERTAINMENT WEEKLY

START AT THE BEGINNING!

BATMAN VOLUME 1: THE COURT OF OWLS

BATMAN VOL. 2: THE CITY OF OWLS

with SCOTT SNYDER and GREG CAPULLO

BATMAN VOL. 3: DEATH OF THE FAMILY

with SCOTT SNYDER and GREG CAPULLO

BATMAN: NIGHT OF THE OWLS

with SCOTT SNYDER and GREG CAPULLO

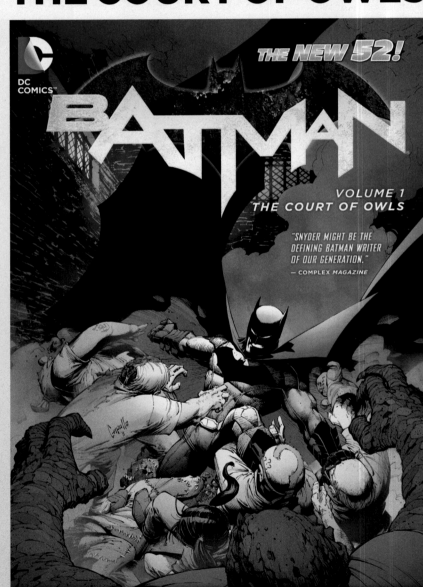

THE NEW 52!

DC COMICS™

BATMAN

VOLUME 1 THE COURT OF OWLS

"SNYDER MIGHT BE THE DEFINING BATMAN WRITER OF OUR GENERATION."
— COMPLEX MAGAZINE

SCOTT SNYDER   GREG CAPULLO   JONATHAN GLAPION

"Worthy of the adjective, but in a good way."
—THE NEW YORK TIMES

"There are some threats that are too much for
even Superman, Batman and Wonder Woman
to handle. That's when you call the people
who make magic their method."—CRAVE ONLINE

START AT THE BEGINNING!

JUSTICE LEAGUE DARK
VOLUME 1: IN THE DARK

JUSTICE LEAGUE
DARK VOL. 2: THE
BOOKS OF MAGIC

with JEFF LEMIRE

JUSTICE LEAGUE
DARK VOL. 3:
THE DEATH OF MAGIC

with JEFF LEMIRE

CONSTANTINE
VOL. 1: THE SPARKLE
AND THE FLAME

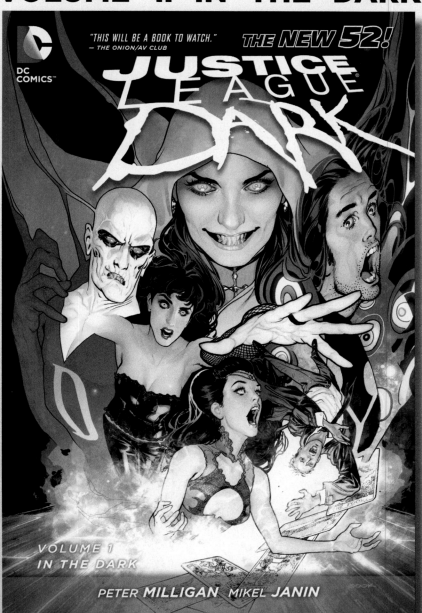

PETER MILLIGAN   Mikel JANIN

START AT THE BEGINNING!

NIGHTWING
VOLUME 1: TRAPS AND TRAPEZES

**NIGHTWING VOL. 2:
NIGHT OF THE OWLS**

**NIGHTWING VOL. 3:
DEATH OF THE FAMILY**

**BATMAN:
NIGHT OF THE OWLS**

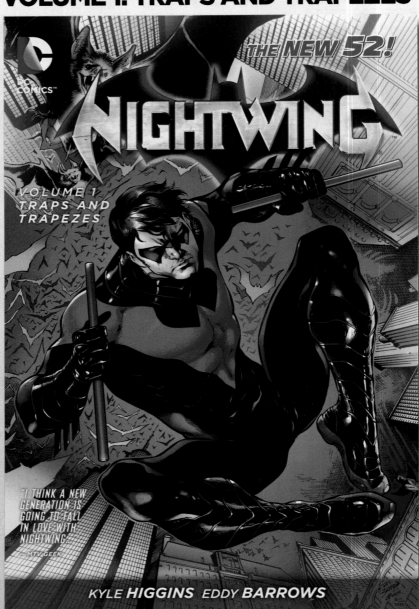